D0922836

THE
LIVING SEA

Books by Captain J. Y. Cousteau

CAPTAIN COUSTEAU'S UNDERWATER TREASURY
(edited with James Dugan)
THE SILENT WORLD (with Frédéric Dumas)

Books by James Dugan

AMERICAN VIKING
PLOESTI (with Carroll Stewart)
MAN UNDER THE SEA
THE GREAT IRON SHIP

by JACQUES-YVES COUSTEAU

with JAMES DUGAN

HARPER & ROW, PUBLISHERS, NEW YORK AND EVANSTON

THE

CALYPSO

LIVING SEA

The publishers and authors wish to express their gratitude to the National Geographic Society for making possible the inclusion of twenty-four pages of color photographs in this volume which originally appeared in the *National Geographic* Magazine.

THE LIVING SEA. Copyright © 1963 by Harper & Row, Publishers, Incorporated. Printed in the United States of America. All rights reserved. No part of this book may be used or reproduced in any manner whatsoever without written permission except in the case of brief quotations embodied in critical articles and reviews. For information address Harper & Row, Publishers, Incorporated, 49 East 33rd Street, New York 16, N. Y.

FIRST EDITION

C-N

LIBRARY OF CONGRESS CATALOG CARD NUMBER: 62-14525

To *my revered master*,

PROFESSOR LOUIS FAGE

contents

Twenty-four pages of photographs in full color follow page 64. Sixty-four pages of black-and-white photographs appear after page 184. A map will be found facing page 15.

Acknowledgments for Illustrations

The photographs and drawings in this book were made by staff members of Calypso Oceanographic Expeditions, l'Office Français de Recherches Sous-Marines, the National Geographic Society, the Oceanographic Museum at Monaco, and Les Requins Associés: Thomas Abercrombie, Jacques-Yves Cousteau, Armand Davso, James Dugan, Frédéric Dumas, Harold E. Edgerton, Jacques Ertaud, Albert Falco, Pierre Goupil, André Laban, Jean Lattès, Octave Léandri, Bates Littlehales, Louis Malle, Luis Marden, Jean-Loup Nivelleau de la Brunière, W. Edward Roscher, and Edmond Sechan.

The line drawing of Grand Congloué is by Jean-Charles Roux; the cartoon of shipboard life aboard *Calypso* is from James Dugan's *Calypso* journals. Lise Haas-Coenca researched the pictures.

Plates for the color section were generously afforded the publisher by the National Geographic Society, which we further thank for many copyright permissions. Several permissions were also given by *France-Soir*.

The map was drawn by Joan Emerson.

The *Calypso* insigne on the title page was designed by Luc-Marie Bayle.

THE AUTHORS

THE
LIVING SEA

chapter
one   DROP-OFF

It was a hushed hour before sunrise in December 1951 in the Red Sea. Frédéric Dumas and I were about to start work on our own first full-scale underwater scientific expedition. We were inside the dangerous Far-San reefs of Saudi Arabia, aboard my new civilian research ship, *Calypso*. Off in the gloom on the desert island of Abu Latt were the green tents of our field party.

The capstan swallowed the anchor chain with a cheerful rattle. From the forepeak the boatswain Jean Beltran sang out, *"L'ancre est haute et claire!"*

On the bridge my old French Navy comrade, skipper François Saôut, grumbled, "The weather is too good. It can only get worse."

I said, "This is not like your old Cape Horn!" However, I liked Saôut to feel that our precious new vessel was surrounded by evil—especially now that she really was. Between us and the day's diving grounds on the outer Far-San bank were ten miles of poorly charted, shallow coral heads and reefs.

I pushed both motors forward and climbed above the wheelhouse to the high observation bridge. From there *Calypso* looked small enough to snake her way through the half-concealed obstacles. In the faint light I took bearings from island features we had named Aircraft Carrier, Petite Termitière, and Scotch Cairn. Saôut swerved to avoid reefs and headed due west.

Below me in the chartroom my wife, Simone, manned the echo sounder, interpreting its pings through a headset and calling off soundings to a bearded, turbaned "Arab" on the bridge wing who relayed them to Saôut and me. The "native" was an Arabic-speaking French parachute lieutenant, Jean Dupas, detached to us for the cruise.

Under my lofty perch *Calypso* was awakening. I looked down on the white bonnet of Fernand Hanen, the cook, as he brought a pot of coffee to the bridge. Below decks René Montupet, the chief engineer, started our clattering compressors, which supply air for the day's dives, with a noise that finished sleep for all. On the diving deck aft, Dumas, Beltran, and Jacques Ertaud, our amphibious cameraman, charged the triple-tank Aqua-Lungs and protected them from the impending heat with water-soaked mats.

The sun came up like a blow, implacable to the skin. I inflated my lungs in eager anticipation of the big day. The program was deep exploration of the virgin reefs of Shab Suleim on the seaward fringe of the Far-Sans. We were going to investigate to a depth of two hundred feet, take specimens of fixed animal life in various environmental layers, and document the reef with artificial-light color photography. We also hoped to determine the thickness of living coral and to outline the general topography. For years I had looked forward to helping marine science with free-diving and hand-held submarine photography.

Shab Suleim is a long narrow chain of reefs oriented northwest-southeast, with a coral rim *à fleur d'eau,* or so near the surface that the prevailing wind sweeps the sea across in a white flowering. On the northwest cape I found a blue creek wide enough to anchor *Calypso.*

We swung our flat-bottomed aluminum work launch overboard. Five of us dropped in and moved to the reef. Wearing our masks, Dumas and I stepped into knee-deep water and waddled across the coral fringe, which was gnarled and trenched and bursting with life. We swam to the drop-off line. In the blue crystal below were tier upon tier of majestic gray-and-brown sharks interweaving lazily in a slow-motion ballet.

We returned to the launch and conferred with Ertaud and Professor Pierre Drach, a stocky, rosy-cheeked specialist in fixed marine fauna and the first oceanographer to seek out the Aqua-Lung as a working tool. Dumas said, "The shark problem can be handled by diving along the wall with our backs to it, so we have to watch only half the space around us."

Professor Drach said, "I'm here to collect specimens, not to turn round and watch sharks." He delivered a lecture on *"travaux pratiques sous-marine"* as though he were in his classroom at the Sorbonne instead of in a broiling pan on a desolate reef with a sea full of sharks below. He reviewed for us the main categories of madrepores, alcyonarians, ascidians and calcareous algae. I could not help thinking that his diving experience was a bit thin. Drach had been the first academician to pass our tough professional diving course at the Toulon Navy Undersea Research Group, but since then he had made few difficult descents—and only one to the two-hundred-foot level we faced today.

As the professor concluded his briefing, I said, "I believe the best technique for the dive will be for Dumas and me to act as bodyguards for Drach, to permit him maximum collecting time. Ertaud can go on his own to take pictures, and Beltran will stay in the boat, tracking our bubbles, ready for any emergency." They submerged—but I did not join them immediately. I found myself checking my equipment with a priestly solemnity. I was not exactly afraid of this dive, but I had a strong intuition that it was going to be meaningful for me. I was in an unaccustomed individualistic mood.

I went in, scarcely feeling the blood-warm water on my skin. The rest of the world passed. Down along the riotous plumage of the shelf my companions hung like marionettes, waiting for me. I joined them and we crossed the brink. Half the space below was a vertical living wall; the other half, infinity. Dumas scouted a protective rock fissure leading down, and we followed him to it. As we sank along the crack, out of nothingness appeared the nomads—powerful jacks, bonitos with intense blue scales, and silver sardinellas. They came to the wall, flirted about, and receded into the outer waters where they belonged. Big transparent jellyfish dragged along, pulsating drowsily. Those that came too near the reef were torn to pieces by fish as black as soot.

Ertaud began popping flash bulbs. Professor Drach halted to pry off animal colonies with his burglar's jimmy, made notes on a plastic tablet, and plumped his samples into the string shopping bag on his belt. He dribbled his way downward, his nose to the reef, seeing alive for the first time creatures he had known only from books or as specimens disfigured and bleached in jars of formaldehyde. He was in a biotope both familiar and new to him. He was no longer with us. I felt uneasy about it and pointed him out to Dumas. We exchanged glances, confirming that we must watch him diligently.

But when I stood off from that dainty and yet majestic cliff, it was hard to be a mere bodyguard. The coral took unexpected shapes and hues. There were skulls of dwarfs and giants; tufts of ocher and magenta mingled with petrified mauve bushes and red tubiporae fabricated like honeycombs. Superb parasols of acropora spread over idling fish that were painted with electric pigments of red and gold. Through this splendid tilted forest humpbacked sea snails traveled their winding ways. In reef recesses there were enough tridacna clams to furnish fonts for the churches of Christendom. Their shells were ajar, displaying swollen mantles painted like the lips of harlots.

The reef of Shab Suleim was an intaglio structure with porches of coral, winding *couloirs,* and countless narrow cracks aswarm with beings waiting in the wings like walk-on players at the opera. When I poked my head into one of these little grottoes, anxious fish huddled together snout to snout, or molded themselves to the walls, while the spiny-rayed animals erected their dorsals in fear. The little caves were plastered with gaudy patches of ascidians, hydrozoans, and calcareous algae.

As I wandered along the reef, mixed hordes of fish vanished ahead of me, as if retreating into the reef, then reassembled behind. There were yellow-spotted groupers, gold- and blue-striped butterfly fish, and a gay unicorn fish with a long horizontal horn protruding from its otherwise unprepossessing head. There were fish as flat as pancakes that flourished whip antennas, and mottled triggerfish with Fernandel profiles. The natives were out in their Sunday dress.

Moray eels glowered from crevices and bared their teeth to impress us. They were the concierges of the reef city, and the promenading tenants were not scared of them. My eye fell on an odd object hanging motionless in the water. It looked like a crumpled feather bonnet from the attic trunk of the Madwoman of Chaillot. The feathers were barred black-and-white. All at once the hat exploded into bristles—the stinging spines of a lion fish. I poked a finger at the venomous quills, taking care not to touch them. The fish did not flinch; it had confidence in its defenses.

I trudged on, occasionally stopping to press my mask close to the reef like a child at a candy-store window. Each square foot was a microcosm of worms, tiny hairy crabs, flowering slugs, and carousing vermin. Sixty feet down, I entered the alcyonarian kingdom—a vertical field of pliant growths shaped like celery plants, each stalk a different hue. Here and there in the hanging garden were tall coral umbrellas, funnel-shaped sponges, and gorgonian screens. Beneath the rainbow celery patch a tangle of white lines trailed ten feet out of the cliff. They were rigid and horny virgularians that looked like a slack lamp cord on a blue rug.

After all this novelty, at a depth of 130 feet came a shock of recognition—a landscape almost exactly like our customary cliffs at Cassis or Riou in the Mediterranean—the same small loggias in the dead walls, the same random splatter of ascidians and algae, and the same dusty appearance. The only things missing were the lobsters that lounge on such balconies at home and the red jeweler's coral, which oddly enough is not found in "coral seas."

Sharks had been in sight throughout the dive. As I progressed deeper, they turned faster, making me dizzy as I tried to keep them under scrutiny. There were one or two in every direction, and now they were closing in. Some swam straight toward me with vacant eyes and then withdrew. When I reached 150 feet, I glanced up. A dozen torpedo-shaped shadows were outlined against the viridescent ceiling. I looked down. Fifty feet below, pale sharks were strolling on a sand slope. I sighted my forgotten companions, naked and far from our boat, surrounded by Red Sea sharks of whose traits we knew nothing. It struck me that our situation was simply untenable.

Out of the roving pack, the biggest shark, an animal about twelve feet long, advanced with seeming deliberation toward the professor. I was thirty feet from Drach, and the shark was approaching him at ankle level. The sight of a man ogling a reef while *Carcharhinus* sniffed his legs was utterly revolting. I rushed toward them, grunting as loudly as I could through the mouthpiece but despairing of the outcome. Drach heard nothing. When I was ten feet from them, the big shark wheeled ponderously and swam away. I patted Drach's shoulder and tried to explain by signs what had happened. He looked at me severely and turned back to the reef. He did not wish to be disturbed again.

The scholar's *sang-froid* was contagious. I felt strangely reassured about everything. I sank lower, relaxed and receptive. At a depth of two hundred feet the cliff broke off into a forty-five-degree incline of gray soil. I was disappointed that the pageant was ending in this dull, lifeless bank. At second look I found the slope extended only fifty feet out to another blue horizon, another drop-off. I was on a *corniche* laden with fossils and waste that had fallen through the ages from the bustling metropolis above.

I hovered, contemplating the brink ahead. I stretched my arms and legs in space and greedily inhaled a lungful of thick, tasty air. Between the sibilants of my air regulator I heard rhythmic grating sounds and cycles of bubbles rustling overhead. Other human beings were alive nearby. Their commonplace respirations took on a cosmic significance. I was being seized by depth rapture. I knew it and I welcomed it as a challenge to whatever controls I had left.

The gray bank two hundred feet down was the boundary of reason; over the precipice lay madness. Danger became voluptuous. My temples pounded. Extending my arms like a sleepwalker, I stroked my fins and glided over the edge of beyond.

Hundreds of white walking canes stuck out of the vertiginous wall. I dropped slowly along a torment of life forms. Witches' heads stared at me. Pale gelatinous tumors grew on giant sponges ornamented with spider webs. As far down as I could see, untold populations clung along that wall. But they were denied to me. I trimmed off 240 feet down.

I heard a distant mechanical sigh—one of my companions opening his air-reserve valve. I paused. *Now I must soar out of here, pick up my friends, and obey the law of sun and air that rules my kind. Now? Why now?*

I stole another minute, clutching a white sea whip and looking down longingly. Then I knew I had an appointment with the second reef. I swore I would design, build, and operate devices that would deliver to me the sunken ridges of the silent world.

chapter
two   LA CALYPSO

          The story of *Calypso* began in liberated Paris in
1944, when theaters showed my four-reel motion picture about Aqua-Lung
diving. The film was called *Épaves,* or "sunken ships." The public liked it,
and so did the Direction Générale du Cinéma Français, through which the
government encouraged film production. I conceived the idea of an underwater feature movie that might enable me to build an exploration vessel, too,
so that I would no longer have to rely on trawlers and hired boats.

  For years Commandant Philippe Tailliez, Frédéric Dumas, and I had
planned the ideal vessel. She would embody all that we knew about plat-
forming free divers and submarine photography. The naval architect
André Mauric turned our sketches into designs for a 75-foot craft. I took
the designs and construction and operating estimates to Paris to solicit
governmental support. The Direction Générale du Cinéma was receptive and
recommended to the Crédit National that my feature picture be under-

written. This agency was willing to back the picture, but could not also provide the ship.

Thinking that a research vessel specializing in Aqua-Lung techniques would interest oceanographers, I went to the Ministry of Education, which administers French universities and national laboratories. I was met with polite, even sincere, interest but was told, "Exploration of the sea? That is the job of the navy. Only it can afford research vessels."

This seemed good advice, and I wondered why, as a naval officer, I had not thought of it. When I had jumped command channels in 1944 to get the service to commission our undersea group, Admiral André Lemonnier, chief of staff, had approved immediately. So I called on Admiral M——, chairman of a commission charged with studies of oceans and beaches. He listened, with encouraging nods, as I cited our diving record, including our participation with Auguste Piccard in the first bathyscaph trial. "Our team is ahead of everybody in putting man in the sea," I claimed. "The national interest is to keep us in the lead with a new type of undersea research vessel."

The Admiral said, "As a lieutenant commander you have no chance of getting a vessel. You'd have to get it on the navy budget and push it through parliament. My advice is to return to routine duty. Work for advancement! Become an admiral! Then you might get your ship." He was sincerely trying to help me.

I went to Admiral P——, in charge of navy personnel. He said, "The navy is in no position to give you a ship," and then leafed through my service file. "In eighteen years of duty," he continued accusingly, "you have been at sea for seventeen. This is far above average. It is high time you are assigned to staff duty ashore." I had appealed to my superiors to intensify my work at sea and was now in peril of being ordered ashore.

I felt cornered. I stood to attention. "With your permission, sir. From now on I have one goal—to give my country an undersea exploring vessel. I request three months' furlough to look after personal affairs."

The Admiral gave me leave, but he shook his head, saying, "Cousteau, this is hopeless. It will ruin your career." I left with no idea how I could make good my boast.

Back at our home in Sanary, Simone and I dined with Dumas and talked over the discouraging official attitude. "Who else do we know?" said Didi. I opened my address book and read off the first name on Page A. Simone shouted, "That's the man!" and I closed the book.

"Who's he?" Didi inquired.

Simone said, "We met him at Auron during the war. I was dying for a cigarette. There was no tobacco anywhere. A lady on the next bar stool took out a cigarette. I said nothing. She said, 'Why don't we share it? It's my last.' She cut it in half and we were friends. Jacques and her husband talked about the sea all night. Didn't he say something about the ship you wanted after the war?"

"Yes, he did," I said. "He told me to come and see him when I was ready."

Simone said, "Let's go!"

Monsieur A—— remembered the wartime encounter and took us to meet a hearty Englishman, who responded to my plans. As a veteran seafarer, he said, "It's not necessary to build a vessel. The one you have in mind could easily be converted from a surplus Fairmile." That was a mass-produced wooden coast patroller used during the war. "There are plenty of Fairmiles for sale in Malta," said my new friend. "I'll give you a grant to buy and refit one."

Overwhelmed by this offhand generosity, I said, "I won't know how to repay you." He said, "Forget it," and we agreed to place the ship under a nonprofit foundation, Campagnes Océanographiques Françaises.

I flew to Malta with a naval architect, Henri Rambaud, but we didn't like any of the Fairmiles. Then my eye landed on *Calypso,* and the search was over. Much bigger than a Fairmile, she was a 360-ton YMS-class mine-sweeper, 140 feet long, built in the United States in 1942 for the Royal Navy. After the war she had served as a ferry between Malta and Gozzo. Rambaud pronounced her wooden hull to be in A-1 condition.

Her price was a pleasant surprise. The Englishman's generous grant would cover it and an extensive refit as well. The former owner delivered *Calypso* to the Antibes shipyard, and I flew to Paris to see Admiral P—— again.

"I have my ship," I said. "I request the navy to detach me officially to Calypso Oceanographic Expeditions for three years without salary."

The Admiral said, "What is Calypso Oceanographic Expeditions?"

I said, "The expeditions I am organizing, sir."

He said, "Look here, young man, the navy cannot detach people for service to themselves. But possibly you could have the type of leave we give officers who want to make a trial in business."

I said, "I don't want to sell socks or radio sets. I am going to undertake nonprofit research." I stuck to the point because commercial leave papers would have created misunderstandings with institutions I was going to ask for backing. Admiral P—— gave me a three-year leave "in the interest of national defense," which implied the moral support of the navy.

But his bad day was not over. I said, "Sir, what would happen if the Ministry of National Education were to support the expeditions?"

He said, "I don't think that will happen, but if it does, come back to me. I give my word your leave will be transformed into an official mission."*

The navy detached René Montupet as my chief engineer, and I hired the rest of Calypso's first crew members: bosun Jean Beltran, formerly quartermaster of the Undersea Research Group; mechanic Octave Léandri; and a young photographer named Jacques Ertaud.

At Antibes the wrecklike carcass of the stripped minesweeper was replaced by a functional look. We enlarged the crew accommodations, planted a crane on the port afterquarters, and built three novel features originated during the evenings when Philippe, Didi, and I had imagined a ship.

The first novelty was a diving well down through the hull, entered through the galley, so that divers could go into the water midships—the most stable point on the hull. In bad weather they could avoid passing through waves at the sides. From cold dives they could climb into the warm kitchen. Where conditions made it necessary to dive without attracting attention, the well concealed our entrances and exits. The sea rose in the shaft to the normal water line, and the bottom was closed by a nonwaterproof hatch that served merely as streamlining.

Our next brain child was a high observation bridge spanning Calypso over the bridge house. Its two hollow aluminum king posts acted as ventilation trunks for the forecastle. The high bridge allowed several observers to scan the horizon for surface phenomena and assisted pilotage.

The most popular idea we brought to reality was an underwater observation chamber on the forefront of the ship, eight feet below the water line. To avoid weakening the vulnerable bow structure, we placed the steel chamber and entry tube entirely outside the hull. The tube, equipped with a ladder inside, measured thirty inches in diameter and ran twenty-five feet down from the forepeak to the chamber. We bolted it to the stempost and closed it on deck with a watertight hatch. The bulbous chamber protruded from the forefoot like the ram on an ancient Greek war galley. It contained a mattress for one prone observer—or two, if they were close friends. They could peer out five circular windows: two facing front, one

---

* Four years later the Ministry of Education did adopt Calypso. Admiral P—— was as good as his word and made me official. The navy, although furnishing no funds, has given Calypso many helpful favors.

angled down at forty-five degrees, and one on each side. Mounted under the chamber were *Calypso*'s vertical- and forward-beamed sonar transducers. The chamber had compressed-air ventilation and a phone to the bridge. When we installed it, the underwater observatory was a new idea. Today it is going into many research vessels. It gave *Calypso* an unexpected bonus as well. The projecting forefoot and rounded stem were unwittingly made to resemble the Maïerform bow, which gives a ship better entrance to the waves. Thus, the submarine room added a half-knot to *Calypso*'s cruising speed.

The broad open afterdeck, designed to handle cumbersome mine-sweeping gear, was an ideal platform for free diving, with plenty of room to lay out underwater equipment. There was no rail on the fantail to interfere with diving and equipment lowering. Down on the counter we placed a draw-bridge diving platform two feet from the water line. On diving stations it could be let down and fitted with a portable ladder with handrails that extended from beneath the surface to the afterdeck. Overlooking the deck was the divers' ready room with work benches and equipment storage. Near the door were compressed-air faucets from two free-piston compressors in the engine room.

As *Calypso* took shape, her battle gray changed to sprightly white. Manufacturers, sensing our testing potential, lent or gave equipment, and the navy let us have a ship's radio and other essentials until we could get our own. Ready for her adventures, *Calypso* put on her bonnet—a streamlined funnel topped with black and carrying her insigne: the white nymph Calypso of Homer's *Odyssey* swimming with a porpoise on a field of green.

I couldn't wait for every last detail to be finished before making a trial run. In June, 1951, Simone and I invited some friends, more or less experienced at sea, to serve as crew for a spin to Corsica. *Calypso* behaved beautifully—but I saw that I would have to find the money to hire a full professional crew. On one occasion, leaving the Marquis de Turenne at the helm, I went to my quarters, which open on both sides amidships. I looked out the starboard porthole and admired the moon. A moment later the moon was shining through the porthole on the other side.

Calypso was ready for her first working cruise in the autumn of 1951. We had long since decided that the maiden voyage would take her to the Red Sea. It was virtually unexplored, transparent, and not too far away. It had the reputation of being a nice hot bathtub full of sharks, and it was a coral sea. We sought out scientists who would like to use divers and submarine photography on a Red Sea project. Such an offer appeared to be completely unheard-of; for the first time a research ship was looking for scientists rather than vice versa.

Our first confrontation with oceanographers had come just after the war when Jacques Bourcart, professor of marine geology at the Sorbonne, was sent to the Undersea Research Group to get help in dredging sedimental samples from the sea floor. We awaited him with curiosity. To us, a scientist was an inscrutable type with a sad, doctrinal face and a stiff collar. We intended to give Bourcart the works in our rough, rolling tender, *VP-8*.

The scientist turned out to be a husky, black-haired, outgoing individual in a sports shirt. At sea Tailliez dropped anchor, turned to Bourcart, and said curtly, *"Maintenant, Monsieur le Professeur, à poil."* It meant, "Do your stuff." But by the end of the day we found ourselves gathered around Bourcart, asking questions. He told us fascinating things about marine geology and his special interest, sedimentology. Here, after all, was a real man, a worker, who knew so many things about the sea that we didn't. Soon Professor Pierre Drach affected us in the same way in the biological field. Scientists, with their clutter of instruments, specimen jars, and chemicals, had a great deal to teach us; and they, in turn, appreciated our direct knowledge of animal behavior and the morphology of a bottom they had never seen. We could not go very far without each other.

Drach leaped at the opportunity of working in the Red Sea and recruited a full-scale scientific party. In November the vision that had originated during the grim days of enemy occupation became a reality. *Calypso* was about to sail from the Toulon arsenal. Exhausted by years of effort and the scrimmage of sailing day, I walked on the quay and looked at my white ship glistening and humming in the searchlights. On deck *les savants* were helping the crew take on last stores and equipment. I joined Simone on board. We touched the varnish and the white walls. Her eyes were shining. She said, "Your eyes are shining."

We put the lights of Saint-Mandrier astern and steamed into a calm night. Nearly everyone jostled into the wheelhouse—which was to be the common urge on all *Calypso* departures. The optical engineer, Jean de Wouters d'Oplinter, who was in charge of the gyro, precision instruments, and stereocamera, switched on the automatic pilot. *Calypso* began her exploratory career as a robot ship with no one at the helm, cleaving a straight line through the Ligurian Sea. I turned on the echo sounder. *Calypso*'s song began, the hollow pinging of sonar. It was music that wrote its own score: a profile of the seafloor on a roll of paper. What had gone before in our

Lunch aboard *Calypso*.

underwater adventure was merely adolescence. The big years were ahead.

On this first voyage *Calypso* acquired a buoyant personality that has never left her. I decided from the beginning that those on board were companions in the adventure, whatever their jobs might be. There was no officers' mess; we all ate together. During the tumultuous and jocose mealtimes we discussed plans, made decisions, and learned from each other. No one shouted orders, and no one wore anything resembling a uniform. Pride of outfit began to develop, expressed in customs of our own: a bawdy *Calypso* song, a perpetual funny-hat contest, and a distinctive cry of recognition that sounded something like *Hooooooo* (falsetto) *Hop!* (guttural) —copied from the call of a Fiji Island bird. We borrowed the latter from a friendly Marseilles bark, *Hou-Hop,* that sometimes joined *Calypso* on diving stations. We greeted each other as *"Professeur"* or *"Docteur,"* unless the person addressed held such a degree, in which case he was called *"Monsieur."*

Our godfather was the Napoleonic marshal Pierre Cambronne, whose portrait hung in the mess. We chose him because of his reply to Wellington's demand for the surrender of the Old Guard at Waterloo. *"Merde,"* said Cambronne. It had no nationalistic meaning for us; it simply expressed the attitude with which we tried to meet adversity.

I invented none of these personality quirks of *Calypso.* In fact, the only time I tried to set a style, I was defeated the first day. In the French fashion everyone aboard shook hands with everyone else morning and evening. I suggested we ration ourselves to one clasp around in the morning, and my friends solemnly agreed. In the afternoon I encountered a photographer whom I had already greeted. He had both hands in a charging bag. He lifted his hand, bag and all, and I shook it without thinking. End of reform movement.

Calypso lacked certain ship's traditions, including rats. We have never seen one aboard, although once we had a rat scare. We were back in Toulon from the Indian Ocean, and Henri Plé was alone on board. He heard gnawing sounds belowdecks and traced them to the bilge. He found a big red coconut crab eating a champagne crate. The crab was from the Seychelles Islands, five thousand miles away. It had consumed six crates during the voyage, but could not broach the bottles to wash them down.

Calypso carried a three-ton stainless-steel wine tank, which amused foreign oceanographers, some of whom travel on wretched craft without a drop aboard. Calypsonians could drink as much as they liked: average daily wine consumption per capita was about a pint.

I wanted *Calypso* to be an international exploring ship with a French cadre. James Dugan was the first of many Americans to sail with us. Dr. Melville Bell Grosvenor of the National Geographic Society, a seasoned salt-water sailor, became interested in our work. The Research and Exploration Committee of the society voted financial support to Calypso Expeditions, which has been renewed annually in the decade since. The Edo Corporation, a key U.S. firm in aviation and marine electronics, contributed its elegant UQN sonar apparatus after its president, Noel McLean, read *The Silent World* and thought we should have one.

Our Red Sea program, the first to add a professional diving team to oceanography, was divided into three traditional aspects. Drach headed the team for biology. The geological party was led by the volcano expert Haroun Tazieff, assisted by Vladimir Nesteroff and Jean Dupas, the diving paratrooper whose knowledge of Arabic was to be vital in the Sea of Islam. The hydrological section, dealing with the chemistry and processes of water itself, was led by an ardent young scientist who had been quick to see the uses of free diving, Dr. Claude Francis-Boeuf. His assistants were Bernard Callame and Jacqueline Zang, the second lady aboard.

We didn't have the money to engage a complete crew, so the guests cheerfully accepted menial duties. They stood watches, they scraped, and they scrubbed. Coming upon a Ph.D. scraping a cookpot, Dumas dubbed it "scientific work," and the name stuck to kitchen police duty. Simone was supply officer, nurse, assistant cook, and sonarman. Skipper Saôut's navigational officers were the ship's surgeon, Dr. Jean-Loup Nivelleau de la Brunière, and de Wouters. In the mutual joy of heading for rare adventure, everyone pitched in where needed. One scientist, remembering the boredom of passenger ships, brought along a deck tennis set. The first day out, I found him slapping paint on the deckhouse and singing like a bird. Simone's dachshund, Scaph, was playing with the deck tennis rings.

On the third day the weather turned ugly. After several squally preliminaries the wind settled strongly northeast. This was the *meltemi,* a gale out of the Balkans that engulfs the Ionian Sea. By dinnertime *Calypso* was rolling violently. We had prepared for stormy meals by drilling hundreds of holes in the table, into which we stuck wooden dowels to fence in the dishes. The result looked like an oversized game for infants. This day *Calypso* took a big lurch and a pitcher of wine jumped the stockade, exploding at the end of the table and splashing half the room.

Tazieff made a dignified entrance to dinner. Then his foot encountered a patch of gravy. The ship rolled to port, and we saw a body going down the slide and out the portside door, which closed after it. The volcanologist re-entered, his poise somewhat impaired, and still unfortunately out of rhythm with the ship. He was thrown against Nivelleau, whose chair collapsed. The two carried six others with them in an avalanche against the starboard bulkhead. The rest of us shrieked with unfeeling laughter. Such Chaplin-esque improvisations were to enliven many a *Calypso* meal. Through it all, cook Hanen, never off balance, dourly produced hearty food from bottom-less pans.

That tempestuous night we crossed the deepest point in the Mediter-ranean, the Matapan Deep, charted as 14,500 feet. Simone got a sonar recording of 16,500 feet. We could hardly believe that previous soundings were 2,000 feet wrong, yet when we went back there later, we confirmed her sounding.

Toward morning the bow was coming out of the troughs as far as the antiroll keels and hammering the underwater chamber into the succeeding waves. I wondered if the chamber would stand these crashes. But this was a test voyage in which we had to find out how much *Calypso* would take. I maintained cruising speed. Montupet phoned from the engine room: "The fuel filters and pipes are clogging up. There must be dirt in the tanks and the sea is shaking it loose."

I said, "Do everything you can to keep the motors turning."

The wind began backing and *Calypso* swooped into twenty-foot troughs. The phone rang again. Montupet reported, "The fuel transfer pump has failed. I am forced to alternate the motors."

I said, "Don't let them both stop at the same time in this sea." It was going to be bad enough on one engine. Unfamiliar with what *Calypso* had in her, I judged our situation to be serious.

At all costs, we had to avoid falling broadside to the towering waves. Fearing we might lose both motors, I asked Saôut to round up all men off duty and rig an emergency sea anchor. If I lost all power, the ship would heave to with a sea anchor. Green seas were rolling over the main deck.

On the tossing afterdeck Saôut, Dumas, Beltran, and the two scientists, Gustave Cherbonnier and Nesteroff, assembled a sea anchor from a heavy life raft, planks, and spars. Application of the old maxim "One hand for the ship, one hand for yourself" slowed down this operation.

Both motors stopped.

The sea anchor was not ready. We were helpless. The ship would now broach to—the final test. *Calypso* fell off broadside to the waves. I yelled to Saôut's party to stop work and hang on hard. We reached for the strongest holds, watching the waves march over our side. A prodigious comber put *Calypso* over forty-five degrees. She shook off the water and rolled back gamely. Several more high waves crossed us. She recovered completely each time. We grinned at each other. "She can take it!" yelled Saôut. *Calypso* drifted swiftly, leaving calmer water to windward, manufacturing her own protective zone. Saôut and I were proud and astonished at the way she passed the storm test. This ship rolled uncomfortably in moderate seas but defied the big ones. Perhaps her seaworthiness had been improved by removal of the wartime weights on the maindeck—the guns and dredge drum. Montupet and Léandri gave me one motor and nursed it along until we could shelter in the lee of Crete. The engineers worked like tigers to clean out the oil systems as we traversed the Suez Canal.

At Suez, Dumas and I came back from a call on the French consul to find anguished faces at the rail. Montupet was stretched out unconscious on the mess table. The gallant chief, wearied with work, had fouled the sleeve of his coverall in a catch on the generator shaft. There was a long deep wound in his right arm. Nivelleau had anaesthetized him and was making sure the radial nerve had not been severed before he sewed him up. Simone was holding the wound open with two kitchen forks. I said, "But we've got a complete case of surgical instruments below."

She said, "We couldn't find it under the pile, so I sterilized the forks."

Nivelleau determined that the nerve was not permanently damaged. Montupet woke up as he had gone to sleep—without complaining. His only concern was that he had delayed the cruise.

The famous Red Sea began as a disappointment. In the Gulf of Suez the water was milky and turbid. I shivered in the northwest wind and wondered if the clear, warm, living waters we'd heard about were just another myth. The next day in the Zubal Strait we awoke in a deep, transparent blue sea. On the port hand Mount Sinai was a purple fleck at the bottom of a pink sky.

Calypso was a debutante in the coral paradise to which she would return again and again in the years to come.

chapter
three

RED SEA

AND

GREEN REEF

My interest in the Red Sea had been fired during adolescence by Henri de Montfreid's books about pearl divers, pirates, slaves, and hashish smugglers. This deep narrow ditch with its Biblical associations was not only teeming with marine life and perilous reefs but was bounded by some of the earth's most inhospitable coasts. The official Red Sea pilot books bore out Montfreid's cautionary tales. The *Instructions Nautiques* warned us not to go ashore save in a few harbors. The apprehensive note was underscored by a gloss on the chart for one of the bays: "Here natives have a mild disposition."

We conned *Calypso* down the central Red Sea shipping lane in a train of ships, mostly huge oil tankers, following each other as though on rails. Those going our way were mostly empty, but those in the northbound track were sunk to the Plimsoll mark with fuel bound halfway around the globe. The rigid file of ships made the Red Sea seem a 1500-mile extension of the

Suez Canal. *Calypso* was a scooter in this traffic jam of gas trucks. We posted double watches at night to be ready to change our track for colossi that would not modify their course one point to avoid us. High above, there passed lighted cities built on cisterns of petroleum.

We would have liked to get off the superhighway, but this is not encouraged on the Red Sea charts, whose soundings are almost entirely confined to the main track. Once off it we might encounter an unlit island or a coral bench crouching just under the surface. Generations of wrecks sat on reefs along the road.

The Red Sea, we learned on several voyages, is by no means a homogeneous body of water. The northern reaches (except for the Gulf of Aqaba) are poor diving grounds with hazy water, sparse fish, and dwarfed corals. In the center, however, on the Saudi Arabian and Sudanese shores, life abounds in bank after bank of exuberant coral structures, second only to those of the Great Barrier Reef in extent and exceeding it perhaps in splendor. Here there is deep clarity, blazing color, and active fauna living under the most arid and least populated of coasts.

The southern end of the Red Sea was again a disappointment. Off Yemen we dived into evidences of a recent coral tragedy. We swam through hundreds of yards of lacy gray stones falling in ruin with branches of broken dead corals strewn about. The fragments were lately snapped off—not yet pulverized and assimilated in the sand. This graveyard may have been caused by a sudden change of salinity or some intoxication furnished by the sea itself, for man could not have polluted the area. The oceans often have localized natural illnesses that we are not yet able to diagnose. In this deathly terrain we swam among hosts of fish, including many sharks, looking like wild animals of the prairie puzzled over a grass fire that has destroyed their pasturage—and covert.

Except for an occasional lofty sandstorm the central Red Sea is swept nearly all the year by a moderate north-northwest breeze, producing short waves that rolled *Calypso* disagreeably—but never to the point of swinging the clapper against the bridgehouse bell, which was our automatic warning of serious weather.

Sailing south in this latitude, the tail wind matched *Calypso*'s cruising speed, and the air stood still. It was almost insufferably hot, and we dragged ourselves from shade to shade, avoiding sunlight like an open furnace door. But when the anchor chain rattled at a diving station, the wind played refreshingly on our nearly naked bodies. Cruising north into the wind was

like being in an air-conditioned desert. Although the Red Sea's waters
are the hottest in the oceanic system, I have never found sea water that
was warm enough for me.

Many of my Red Sea memories center on *Calypso*'s high observation
bridge. While designing it, I was influenced by Montfreid's account of skip-
pering a Somali dhow that was being overhauled by a pirate boat. He sent
a boy to the topmast to call off coral heads and sailed through labyrinthine
reefs the pirate dared not enter. I used the wide crow's nest thirty feet
above *Calypso*'s main deck for the same purpose of invading uncharted reefs.
From the aerial balcony Saôut and I learned to read coral water. Brown or
white was danger—a reef near the surface. There was a wide range of subtle
greens from which to interpret depth, and dark blue was easy sailing.

As we became confident of our water lore, I ventured at one knot into
the outer breaking reefs of Shab Jenab. I read the colors wrong, and
Calypso ground her bow on coral. Divers went down while the rest of us
wondered how long the food and water would last. They came up with
good news: the bow was undamaged and resting lightly. Saôut backed off
and entered in the log, "0940: *Calypso* gave spur to a reef."

Encouraged by the incident, I tried to penetrate a lagoon on the west
coast of Abu Latt. From the high bridge I picked a tortuous course through
hundreds of coral heads that constituted a natural mine field. The afternoon
sun at my back beamed helpfully on the obstacles. We came to an apparent
cul-de-sac, where the ship scraped her port flank against a reef. We put
fenders over the side to save the planking. It seemed evident that we would
have to abandon the trip to the lagoon. I looked astern to pick out turning
room, but now the sun reflected from the water in such a way that the submerged coral tops behind us were no longer visible. It was impossible to
turn back, and it was too dangerous to stay in the pocket. We were forced
to continue and try to make the lagoon. *Calypso* eased through a bottleneck,
and we reached the lake as the sun was setting. In my nervous exhaustion I
had the pathetic notion that we were trapped for good, but I kept the idea
to myself. In the morning, as the sun searchlighted the reefs, we sailed out
rather smoothly.

We could not understand the geology of this phantasmagoria of submarine
coral structures and low, bare islands in the Far-Sans. Abu Latt, for instance,
is a slab of desert three and one-half miles long and a mile wide. The south
cape is a wrinkled plateau, the middle area is flat desert, and on the north
end there is a perfect cone one hundred feet high—the image of a newly

born volcano. Yet every ounce of Abu Latt is pure coral except for an admixture of pulverized sea shells on the beaches. The island, therefore, can be nothing but an ancient coral reef raised out of the water.

Walking around Abu Latt was pure harassment. Pipestone corals stuck up like overturned rakes. Everything underfoot was sharp and raspy. Embedded in the ground with their cutting edges turned up were sea shells perhaps half a million years old but ready to draw living blood through the sole of your sandals. Gaping open to the burning sky were fossilized giant tridacna clams—bleached effigies of the carnal monsters yawning in the limpid blue below.

In contrast to this bogus volcanic island, we found many others in the southern end of the Red Sea that are made entirely of lava. The Brothers and Zeberjed, isolated islands farther north, are ostensibly solid rock fringed with coral belts.

Among the unexplained reefs was Daedalus Light, a most dangerous table reef along the super highway. A lonely Egyptian lighthouse seemed to be floating in a green pond, which was actually the reef top spreading just beneath the surface of the indigo sea. Daedalus is a chimney standing a mile high from the floor. As *Calypso* inched toward the jetty, sonar showed the upper thousand feet to be just short of vertical. We dived to two hundred feet along the chimney flanks and found nothing but coral. As we crept sideways into slots just wide enough to get through, our air bottles chimed on the coral like the legendary carillons of the sunken city of Ys.

Perhaps Daedalus is a rock column only masked with coral, but it would take a costly drilling operation or a new means of plunging beyond Aqua-Lung range to determine how it was built.

Along the coast of the Sudan the reefs are strung in a fairly orderly line, providing a safe navigational channel inside. In this middle section of the Red Sea we returned again and again to the bay of Mersa Bela, a dustbowl with luxuriant undersea contents. I loved that place from the first dive. There was a magnificent series of deep water caves, their walls decorated with frosty bryozoans, fleshy orange and pink ascidians, and purple sponges. The vaults of Mersa Bela were pierced with holes through which shafts of sunlight struck tableaux of vibrant colors. Living threads looped across our course through the caverns. We often encountered candelabra of millepores, a "fire coral" that leaves a skin rash worse than poison ivy. The cost of admission was a livid itch on some part of our bodies. We made our way below like barefoot boys in a briar patch.

Once we came to Mersa Bela and found a deserted three-masted sailing ship skewered on the outer reef. As *Calypso* entered the bay, two trucks fled into the trackless desert, leaving behind a mound of crates and a couple of boats guarded by a Negro with a rifle. We invited him aboard for a meal. He said nothing to explain the wreck, the trucks, or himself. Perhaps we had stumbled onto piracy or a latter-day wrecking venture.

We nearly delivered *Calypso* to the fate of the three-master on the reefs south of Port Sudan. There the barrier reef thickens to seaward in a shambles of vaguely charted islets and coral *à fleur d'eau*. One feature named the Green Reef attracted us. It was noted on the charts as a peril of navigation. We set out for the Green Reef at noon to make brief dives and reach deep water before sunset. The intricate corals took longer to negotiate than I had figured. We arrived in the turquoise lagoon of Green Reef and saw black fins cutting the water. Two divers took the dinghy and rowed toward them. They made slow progress. Our time was slipping away. The sun was close to the sea when they returned to report a school of mantas. I wasted no time talking of mantas. Dusk was falling on *Calypso* in a coral ambush.

Saôut took the high bridge and I manned the sonar, each of us calling instructions to the helm. In order not to lose an instant of maneuver, I shouted direct orders to the man on the engine room telegraph. The bottom descended from two hundred to three thousand feet, but its sonar trace jumped abruptly, revealing uncharted pillars. The discolored patches of water ahead toward which Saôut was straining his eyes were the pinnacles of columns taller than the Eiffel Tower. My mind was split by our foolhardy predicament and the images of sunken towers. Their tops were sheared off at strikingly different depths. One would terminate eight hundred feet down, the next twelve feet under, its neighbor five hundred feet deep—and then Saôut would yell, "Reef dead ahead!" on one that shot to the top of my sonar graph.

Bathed in a fearful sweat, I called, "Both engines full astern!"

It took us two hours of frightening suspense to escape from the sunken city of towers. I vowed never again to risk *Calypso* in those alluring Red Sea reefs at night.

When my nerves recovered, I was left with the enigma of how the towers were made. The lower ones were far below the zone of photosynthesis, in depths where reef-building corals could not grow. I reviewed the sonar records of the Red Sea. Those from Daedalus and the Far-Sans bore a close resemblance to the bastions of the Green Reef. They varied greatly in height, yet had the same general silhouette; from their uniform flat tops they dropped vertically four to six hundred feet, then flared out in a forty- to fifty-degree decline for another fifteen hundred feet. Allowing for vertical exaggeration, they were the spit-and-image of Mont St. Michel.

What made these sea-scrapers? Geologists say that coral islands began to grow when constructor animals gathered on a rock jutting into the photosynthetic zone, where they could feed. While light and warmth gave them life, the mites began adding layer after layer of their skeletons. As the rock subsided into the sea floor, they built up faster than the rate of sinking. When the deep crustal rocks became stabilized, the polyps finished off the structure near the surface to crouch as a reef, a potential coral island. There must have been quite an uneven settlement of the Red Sea floor, with some plots subsiding faster than the next. Consequently, some coral animals could not build fast enough to avoid being pulled into cold, unlit depths. However, as their effort ceased, the next pillar continued to grow.

The wildest of all these reef complexes is the Far-San bank, 350 miles long and thirty miles wide, or six million acres of submerged reefs and isles along the Hedjaz and Yemen coasts. This demented masterpiece of outcrops, shoals, foaming reefs, and other lurking ship-breakers was created by societies of minute animals that have changed the aspect of our planet far more than man has yet been able to do.

The northern Far-Sans, an area of riotous marine life, are charted only on their perimeter. The central portion is depicted on the maps by a blank, upon which cartographers have written, "This zone, dangerous for navigation, is sprinkled with deepwater reefs without any practical channels." Here in the mid-twentieth century, a few miles from a great waterway, is a forbidden expanse of the globe. *Calypso* and her launches repeatedly invaded the blank space with a single restriction: never remain after nightfall. We found some of the most thrilling diving grounds of our years in the sunlit layer of the ocean.

Few had seen these lands and fewer still had dived there—only an occasional Arab pearler came into the reefs. It would take a lifetime underwater to feel confident of knowing a little about the architectural and biological variety of the northern Far-San Islands. They are bordered by curving reefs with a handful of sand that barely qualifies them as islands. From afar they seemed to us to be wearing pearl necklaces. The jewelry turned out to be thousands of electric light bulbs thrown from passing tankers.

An unruffled sea, a bright reef, and sheer underpinnings lured *Calypso* to the largest of the outer isles, Marmar. We berthed alongside the slightly submerged brink as we would at a stone quay, putting automobile-tire fenders between wood and reef and fastening mooring cables around coral heads instead of iron bollards. A sleeping Calypsonian, awakened by the cessation of the diesel lullaby, looked over the rail and saw coral eighteen inches underwater. He charged to the bridge, asking, "How did we go aground?"

Simone pointed across the wet reef to a distant dry hummock and said, "We'll spend the rest of our lives there, distilling water." I showed him the echogram: we had five hundred feet of water under the keel. *Calypso* rested uneventfully in her coral dock for two days while we probed the slopes of Marmar.

All the Far-San beaches were crowded with ghost crabs—square, long-legged creatures tinted a light ocher or pink, matching the color of the sand. Their eyes are placed on the ends of long stalks, which they use exactly like periscopes. When we landed, scores of long-eyed crabs came charging at us. If we made a threatening gesture, they buried themselves instantly, leaving only the tips of their eyes above the sand. Or they went clippety-clop into the water and submerged to the eyes. Scaph, the dachshund, played tag with them for hours, and sand flew from his forepaws as he tried vainly to dig them out.

Then Tazieff discovered an unfunny aspect of ghost crabs. He took an alpine tent and spent the night on an island with rare scrubby vegetation. He came aboard the next morning without sleep, vowing never again to stay ashore overnight. Thousands of long-eyed crabs had attempted to invade his tent, and he spent the night feeding dried bushes to a circle of fire around his camp.

There were signs on the outer islands that men had passed near the forbidden Far-Sans. On a sandspit called Malathu we came upon several graves surrounded by sea turtle skeletons. The coral headstones faced Mecca. We found more Islamic burials on the fringing islands, each decorated with turtle bones or sea shells. We wondered what misanthropic sect had chosen this wild, last exile, mourned only by birds, crabs, and turtles.

At Port Sudan, however, we found that the dead had not chosen their graves. At one time Saudi Arabia exacted a punitive head tax (not abolished until 1955) on Meccan pilgrims landed at Djeddah, the only official port of entry on the Red Sea. When African pilgrims came walking out of the interior in armies, carrying all their worldly goods to barter for passage from Port Sudan and Suakin to Djeddah, they learned only then of the Arabian pilgrim tax. Since it amounted to several years' income for most of them, the Sudanese waterfronts became great encampments of stranded pilgrims. Agents whispered to them of *zaroug* captains who would smuggle them into Arabia at places where there were no tax collectors. The ship-owners packed pious Muslims into their tiny craft, and many died during the voyage. Since the Koran forbids burial at sea and corpses could not be kept on board, the *zaroug* captains buried them in the outer Far-Sans.

We used Djeddah, the official pilgrim gate, as our supply and liaison base for mail and the rotation of scientific personnel by air. I went one morning to the local branch of the Banque d'Indochine to convert a bank draft into cash for *Calypso*'s payroll. When the French manager opened his counting room door, a gaggle of robed money-brokers burst in and grabbed his arms and ears. The most ferocious of the lot was a fourteen-year-old boy, who the manager told me traded as much as ten thousand dollars in a day. Silver coins were the only currency trusted in Djeddah, and businesses depended on heavy trucks to cart them about. *Calypso*'s monthly payroll was a bag of coin we couldn't lift.

Another precious substance in Saudi Arabia was black coral, from which the prayer beads for the wealthy are made. On Red Sea dives of from eighty to two hundred feet down, we found black coral and understood why it was rare. It comes in brown bushy trees, six to nine feet high, that resemble tamarisks. It is a variety of gorgonian, having trunks the thickness of a wrist and ramified, supple branches covered with a thick, tacky mucus. Often we found pearl oysters hanging from the black coral tree. It was beyond the strength of any of us to uproot them.

Dumas located a thicket of black coral a hundred feet under the Brothers lighthouse and took down a handsaw to collect a specimen. He exhausted a twenty-five-minute air supply while cutting a third of the way through the trunk. After he had rested, I went down with him. I took a stroll away from the patient woodman. When I came back, Dumas was seated on a branch, sawing away at it. He was in the fabled position of a man out on a limb, sawing himself off. The branch parted. Dumas remained seated without falling.

After he bore his trophy to the surface, it took him two days to scrub the mucus off his body. We towed later specimens behind *Calypso* and the sea removed the sticky coating. Calypsonians whittled and polished black coral paper cutters, knife handles, and cigarette holders. In Djeddah, Muslim dock workers asked to hold them. They smelled the black coral and pressed it against their hearts and foreheads.

Black coral has an air of magic. One time Simone and I and our friend Louis Lehoux paid a call on Pablo Picasso at his villa in Cannes, and she gave him a piece, explaining its holy significance to Islam. Picasso examined it from several angles and put it in the pocket of his baggy brown velvet trousers. From time to time during the gay afternoon we spent with him, he pulled out the coral and looked at it. Pinned on his wall were cartoons for details of his mural in the Unesco building in Paris. I pointed to the famous figure of a man plunging head down and asked what it meant. Picasso's eyes turned drolly to me, and he said, "The art critics have written kilometers of explanation about the symbolism of that figure. Some say it is the fall of Icarus. Others that it is Lucifer being cast out of heaven." He leaned closer and said *sotto voce:* "Don't tell anybody, Cousteau. I was just trying to paint a diver."

When I saw Picasso again a year later, he still had the black coral in his pocket. As he drew it out, I saw that the polish had been further heightened by the caresses of the most creative hand in the world.

During their stay in the green tent village on Abu Latt—our longest-lived shore establishment in the Red Sea—the scientists found that their first impressions of lifelessness had been deceptive. The "desert" island was the home of countless long-eyed crabs, rats, scorpions, snakes, and clouds of insects living in a place without vegetation.

The Far-Sans are a vast preserve of birds. Hordes of brown boobies nest in the blank space, bestowing puffs of white downy chicks on the seared land. Dumas found that he could swim up under a young floating booby and catch it by the legs. Pelicans swam ceremoniously in the channels. They took off laboriously, but once they had lifted their absurd architecture into the thermals, they flapped around like extinct flying reptiles.

Each afternoon at four we could expect an aerobatic show over an islet called Northern Goldsmith by a bird we named the clock bird because of its punctual daily take-off. The clock bird had a single long white feather for a tail. The flock would climb high and swoop into wild gyrations, drunk with speed and freedom, uttering shrill cries of *joie de vivre*. After their exercise the clock birds would disappear until the next afternoon's performance.

Less exhibitionistic were the grallatores, spoonbills, egrets, hoopoes, and herons of the Far-Sans. They stood in groups on capes or coral outcrops and were difficult to approach. Dumas and I obtained some photos of them by launching the dinghy into a favorable wind and hiding below the gunwales as the breeze carried us to them. One of the egrets, however, did not share the shyness of its kind. This bold individual would strut into the camp, walk into the tents, and have a look at everything. We called him the Inspector. There were a few owls out after dark, as well as huge flocks of the very spirit of night—a jet-black petrel that by day hid in crevices or even buried itself completely in the sand. One morning we found one on deck and offered it a dark corner in which to pass the day. The bird stayed there until nightfall.

The Far-San bank attracted us most to its dense underwater life. You could see a good deal of it without putting on a diving mask. The fish seemed impelled to go to the air. Elongated needlefish would break the surface in a series of ricochets that carried them more than three hundred feet. Half-beaks could do as well. Both these species sometimes took vertical flights fifteen feet in the air, which meant a take-off speed of about twenty knots.

Near the shore the top twelve inches of water were permanently packed with transparent fish smaller than sardines—the young of a species we have not identified. We called them "Plexiglas fish." For a diver they created zero visibility near shore.

These tons of food surrounding the islands in thick belts constituted a twenty-four-hour cafeteria for the carnivores of the air and sea. However, as is the case almost everywhere in the oceans, regular morning and evening mealtimes were observed. Then the ocean boiled. The dorsal fins of bonitos and jacks sliced the water like scythes. The frantic victims flipped into the air and rained back. Hungry jacks pursued them at full speed into the shallows and ran right up on the dry sand, flapping until the swell carried them back. At feeding time you could pick up four-pound jacks from the beach.

Boobies flew over the battlefield, swooping down and folding their wings near the water to make a clean dive. They swam underwater, stretching their bills toward the prey, snapping it up, and surfacing to fly it to the chicks. Pelicans managed to retain their dignity as they joined the kill. They boated through the splashing water, plunging only their long necks and outsized bills in a stroke that rarely missed. The feeding drama lasted about half an hour; then the satiated animals settled into a general truce and the surface flattened out.

Many times I tried to slip under discreetly and observe the orgy, but always in vain. As soon as my mask came through, however gently—even behind a coral screen—the excitement stopped in my locale. The little translucent prey would settle around me; while a good distance below, the jacks would take up station, waiting for the withdrawal of the invader.

We had a lobster preserve on an islet near Abu Latt. Although we never saw a lobster on a dive, they piled up in a single coral pothole, half in the water, half out. When my son Philippe, aged eleven, joined us by air at Djeddah, he was put in charge of lobstering for the cook. He filled the dinghy with crustaceans without even getting wet. There was no evidence that the lobsters were molting or laying eggs, and we could not learn why they resorted to the hole and why they were never seen below.

Lobsters on land, birds that dive, and fish that fly were not all the surprises of nature in this virgin marine jungle. There was also the bumpfish (*Bolbometron muricatus*). Imagine a flat fish four feet long, weighing more than sixty pounds, with powerful fins, a heavy jaw equipped with a parrot beak instead of a mouth, and on its forehead a white bump as prominent as Cyrano's nose—and you may approximate our surprise upon seeing the bumpfish. They swam to us in a flock of fifteen head and circled around, flashing blue-green and orange sides and looking at us with grave eyes. They looked as rugged as buffaloes, but when they turned tail to leave, the bumpfish was transformed into a ridiculously flat cut-out of itself.

We sighted them every day in the Far-Sans. They ventured into water so shallow that they could hardly swim. North of Abu Latt we once saw about two hundred bumpfish that seemed to be in pasture. Large, petrol-blue fins stuck out of the water and stretched in the sun. Was it their spawning season, or were they grazing? As we approached to find out, they slipped away. Neither Dumas' dynamite caps nor Dupas' harpoon ever brought us a bumpfish. Whenever I met the creature, I was either out of film or empty-handed.

On our last day in the islands Beltran, de Wouters, and I, after finishing a reel of deep photos, were swimming across the shallow shelf to the launch when de Wouters pointed to two large bumpfish in less than three feet of water. We approached them with gentle movements, trying to allay suspicion. They saw us but seemed to recognize our pacific intentions and permitted us to come along close enough to see what they were doing. They swam side by side in the sun-flooded surface layer, halted, turned head down, and with one fin stroke butted their heads into coral blocks with an audible impact. The beak removed a hunk of coral as large as an ostrich egg. The bumpfish chewed the coral, grinding it between powerful pharyngeal teeth. The animal's teeth were fused into the beak, which did not move after a bite had been taken. The sea bison moved through the stone pasture, grazing with heavy strokes of the head and sharp cuts of the beak. We could hear them pulverizing the coral like rock-crushing machines. According to the frequency and determination of the feeding that we witnessed, a bumpfish must consume several tons of coral a year. The sparsity of living matter in the coral heads means that they have to work remarkably hard to survive.

From time to time the bumpfish defecated a white dust cloud that filled fifty cubic feet of water. The first time we saw it, our masks were flooded from helpless laughter. But what was funny about it? Everything they swallowed had to go somewhere. I swam to a subsiding cloud and took some of the product on my palm. It was clean coral sand, no finer and no coarser than that covering the shelf. The bumpfish was a living sand mill. The common parrot fish, much smaller than the bumpfish but related to it, also grinds up coral to make sand. Possibly worms and shellfish do the same. Tide and wave erosion of rock and coral are by no means nature's only ways to make the sands of the sea. Nobody knows how much is manufactured by fish.

The chief concern in all underwater tasks was, of course, assisting the scientists. We went wading in two feet of water to net fish in coral basins. We also ranged the breakers separating the lagoon from the sea, where a great variety of creatures from both these environments were to be found. We not only collected all the species we could find, but sampled entire populations of an area to throw some light on the interrelationship of creatures.

Professor Drach led the underwater section devoted to fixed colonies on the reefs, while Dupas and the geologist Vladimir Nesteroff speared fish specimens for Dr. Cherbonnier. Dumas specialized in precision micro-explosions for taking population samples. He would dive, set a tiny dynamite cap at the proper spot, and come out before the explosion. Then back he went immediately to pick up every animal on the bottom while someone else gathered the floating specimens. Less than one-fifth of the fish killed in dynamiting come to the surface, so that widely as this collecting method is used by biologists, it produces poor results unless there is a diver to glean the bottom. Dumas' method gave Cherbonnier the assurance that he was getting a complete inventory of marine life from the chosen areas, and it gave the biologists a veritable fish market to sort out on the beach. They picked specimens and put them into jars like workers in a herring cannery.

Callame and Mlle. Zang took water samples from many depths and places, noting temperature, salinity, oxygen content, and percentage of nitrates and phosphates. Callame actively dived, carrying a highly sensitive thermometer to detect small temperature variations. From dawn to dusk our boatswain Beltran was recharging Aqua-Lungs, since relays of three or four divers were almost always below on one job or another.

All around Abu Latt, the depths were moderate, ranging from a few feet to a hundred feet. Isolated blocks of coral broke the monotony of a white, flat, sandy bottom. These blocks varied greatly in size and shape—some were low stone bushes, others were tall gothic cathedrals. One was a perfect coral fountain ten feet in diameter. In its center there grew a tall sheath of green algae. These buildings were tenements for tiny purple, orange, green, black, and white fish, which were usually encountered hanging in the water near their doors. When we approached, they vanished inside. The coral head gave the impression of a flower suddenly closing for the night in time-lapse cinematography. The biologists wished to have censuses of the populations of such corals, but a diver could not get at the tenants in their tiny caves. We solved the problem by breaking off the entire structure at the base and hauling it up to *Calypso*. During this operation the little fish stayed in their homes and only emerged when the coral was on the deck, where they cascaded out with a jewel-like glitter.

The energetic young oceanographer, Dr. Claude Francis-Boeuf, arranged for a four-seater airplane to conduct our liaison with Djeddah and to make photomaps of Abu Latt. Unfortunately the plane was grounded at Benghazi with mechanical troubles that could not be overcome while *Calypso* was at the island. Then unexpectedly at Djeddah airport a young man alighted from a Beechcraft. He was Tony Besse of Aden. I knew his father, Antoine Besse, who was a rare combination of a businessman and a humanist. Tony was now running the family steamship line, a department store, an automobile agency, and a shipyard that built traditional Arab dhows. He also operated a trucking line in Ethiopia and handled most of the frankincense and myrrh exported from the Imamate of Yemen. He spoke perfect English, French, and Arabic. He volunteered the Beechcraft, its Swedish pilot, and his own services as a diver for a few days.

First we had to build an airfield on Abu Latt. The most likely terrain was littered with sharp corals, and had a pilgrim tomb in the middle. We all fell to work with pick and shovel, leveling the strip but preserving the grave. Simone even swept off the runway with a broom. When the Beech-craft flew over, Tony saw on the ground in whitewashed letters, ABU LATT. He also saw a warning marker on a tomb in the middle of the strip, and a wind sock consisting of smoke billowing from burning cotton waste that had been collected from *Calypso*'s engine room.

Tony proved to be a modest, unaffected comrade, a calm and clever diver, and a willing hand at physical labor. Between aerial surveys the Swede perched silently on the back of the diving launch, fishing with a huge assortment of rods, reels, and hooks.

We left a cache of aviation gas on Abu Latt for Francis-Boeuf's use when his plane was fixed. Later he and his assistant, Mlle. Zang, and their pilot, M. Ivernel, completed the aerial survey and flew to Addis Ababa. There, on a take-off in the high, thin Ethiopian air, the plane crashed, killing all three. French oceanography still feels the loss of the brilliant, driving figure of Claude Francis-Boeuf.

One day inside the Far-Sans, when most of us were away on launch expeditions, Simone sighted a modern trawler coming toward *Calypso*. This surprising vessel was flying the colors of Sweden, Saudi Arabia, and of the United Nations Food and Agricultural Organization. As it stood off *Calypso*'s rail, Simone waved to the skipper, a man with an Oriental cast of countenance. The rest of the crew was Arab. The skipper spoke to Simone in German. She did not speak that language and replied in English. He did not know English. He tried Tagalog, and Simone answered in French. As they seemed to have exhausted the tongues trying to communicate, Simone said laughingly in Japanese, "Well, we haven't tried Japanese." The skipper replied in Japanese. He was a Filipino fisheries expert in charge of a Swedish trawler chartered by the FAO to experiment with better fishing methods on behalf of the Arabs. He had learned Japanese during the wartime occupation of the Philippines. Simone had acquired hers in a convent school in Japan, where she grew up.

Sailing south, *Calypso* got her first glimpse of the Southern Cross. The next morning we came to the Zebair Islands, also called the Seven Apostles. These shunned and arid volcanoes jut from the Red Sea within sight of the incense groves of Yemen; the black Apostles seem to cast reflections of evil rather than light on the jade sea. We were especially interested in one called Djebel Teir, which unlike the rest had once been inhabited. Nearly a hundred years before, in the halcyon days of the Ottoman Empire, a French contractor had erected a Turkish lighthouse on its pinnacle—the most important light north of Aden. Our landing party on Djebel Teir could barely walk upright on the twisted lava. Painfully we climbed to the abandoned light and went up rusted ladders to the lantern itself. The windows and the prisms were broken. Sea birds fluttered around the tower. As a sailor, I felt a chill over the loss of the light, which had spared many a ship from crashing into the Seven Apostles. As *Calypso* left the volcanoes at night, tankers and liners were sternly watching each other by radar, jamming our screen with interference patterns. In the radar age the Turkish light was no longer needed. Its ruins will be forgotten forever.

It was in the Red Sea that we first tried out *Calypso*'s underwater observation chamber. During a long and complicated trip through coral hazards, Dumas and de Wouters went into the chamber while we were traveling at ten knots in shallow channels. Sunlight reflected from the sandy bottom, lighting the observers' faces like green gargoyles. In the sixty-foot visibility, pillars and walls of coral materialized and reeled past in four seconds. As the big steel snout with five eyes drove toward schools of fish, they scattered in wild flight. Along the reefs other animals twitched and fled into their caves.

In the deeper stretches Dumas and de Wouters felt as though they were in an airplane crossing a dusky blue land. When the bottom climbed again, throwing towers at the chamber, they shrank back, expecting to crash into obstacles that passed ten feet below. The observers came up for lunch raving about the ride, and people lined up at the hatch leading to the submarine room.

On a night anchorage along the cliffs of Zeberjad Island I went into the chamber while the others lowered powerful lights to a position outside my window. Many tiny creatures appeared in the light, brought like moths to a summerhouse lantern. Copepods, worms, larvae and very young fish jigged crazily in space. The micromob swelled until the lamp became invisible, replaced by a sort of halo. I peered past the central glare. On the outskirts large, dim forms sluggishly moved about, never venturing into the limelight. I could distinguish jacks in the perimeter. Other large creatures made lightning dashes through the jacks, too fast to be identified. Perhaps the big ones were waiting for the light to go out before raiding the careless fry dancing in the night club.

While we were under way in the open sea, the chamber had few occupants. That was when I most enjoyed using it for undisturbed hours of watchful meditation. I saw schools of mackerel crossing the bow, shining like swords, swimming in a stiff mechanical way, and rolling their eyes awarely. One day I encountered a surpassing sight—groups of dorados, a fish that wears most of the colors of the spectrum. The dorado is the most radiant creature of the sea. The females are beautiful, but the males cause an intake of breath. They seem to be wearing Punic helmets set with emeralds, sapphires, diamonds, and rubies. They eyed my window aggressively and even swam toward it as if to demonstrate their fearlessness. I knew how well they fought a hook and how their colors faded in death. It was inspiring to see their unmatched splendor in their own environment.

Sometimes my observatory plowed beneath what seemed to be a school of sardines about a foot deep. They were suddenly replaced by a sprinkling of froth. It took me some time to realize that *Calypso* was startling flying fish into the air.

I was in the chamber as we left the Red Sea for the Indian Ocean through the Strait of Bab-el-Mandeb. The sea was high, and *Calypso* capered at her best. I rattled around like a die in a cup. Waves threw the stem aloft, pressing me into the rubber mattress. When she plunged into the trough, I experienced Zero G, or perhaps even negative gravity, as I toured the steel walls. The windows came up through blinding sunlit foam and crashed back into the blue. No fish appeared, even during the short interludes when the chamber stayed under. I was in a volume of nothingness, under a thrashing ceiling, riding in the booby hatch of a drunken ship. When I limped back topside, I took a close look at the helmsman. He was sober as a judge, enjoying the tiff with the naughty strait.

chapter
four

THE RIDDLE
OF
THE URNS

In a spanking breeze on a bright midsummer's day
Calypso approached a chain of forbidding white islands as devoid of life as
the Far-San bank, although only ten miles from Marseilles. She anchored in
a narrow pass between the commanding island of Riou and its smaller sister,
Grand Congloué. We came to this unlikely place because of a tip picked up
by Frédéric Dumas.

Earlier at the Undersea Research Group at Toulon, Dumas had helped
to cure an emergency case of the bends incurred by a free-lance Aqua-Lung
diver named Gaston Christianini, who earned his living gleaning crustaceans
and salvaging scrap from the sea bed around Marseilles. The patient's toes
had to be amputated, but his life was saved. Dumas visited him in the hospital, and the secretive operator said, "I'll never dive again, so I want to tell
you about all the places I have visited downstairs." Since no one knew the

floor of the region so well, Dumas took out his notebook and listened patiently.

"I will tell you where the most *langoustes* [lobsters] are," said the disabled diver. "In the big sunken freighter off Île Maîre, and some by the rock arch under Grand Congloué, near the pile of old jars." Dumas started. The "old jars" could only be amphorae, earthenware cargo containers that were the jerrycans of antiquity, used to carry wine, oil, grain, pigments, ores, perfume, tessera tiles—anything that would flow through a five-inch neck.

It had taken years of our underwater lives before we appreciated what a group of amphorae on the bottom meant. In the early days when Dumas and I quizzed veteran helmet divers, they spoke of "old jars" without comprehending the secret they held. One old-timer, describing a row of amphorae sticking out of the bottom, said, "Probably there was a jar factory on the shore and a landslide swept it into the water."

But now we knew that heaps of old jars indicated a buried cargo ship of early times. And today we had come to Grand Congloué to have a look at Christianini's amphorae. We had long wanted to excavate an ancient sunken ship. Aboard *Calypso* with us was Professor Fernand Benoît, Director of Antiquities for Provence. He got into a launch with Marcel Ichac, the Himalayan explorer and film producer, Dumas, myself, and Albert Raud, our new boatswain. Raud started the outboard motor, moved over to the northwest cape of the precipitous islet, and stopped to let Dumas into the water with a triple-bottle lung. The diver sprawled, feeling his buoyancy, then somersaulted and plummeted down through the transparent sea. I took the tiller and steered behind his bubbles crackling on the surface.

Occasionally I glanced up at the overhanging folds of tormented white rock. Our motor raised gulls that were creaking in the air. The sky promised rising winds. It was a dangerous place. After twenty minutes a pallid form loomed up from below and Dumas heaved himself aboard, grimacing with exhaustion, the white stamp of the mask encircling his eyes and nose. "I found the arch right away," he said. "I searched on both sides of it but saw no amphorae."

If Dumas' sharp eyes saw nothing, there was probably nothing there. Yet, I hated to abandon the search and dismiss Christianini's confidences as no better than a fisherman's tale. I felt compelled to go down myself, spurred by Professor Benoît's silence and the skeptical slant in his eye. Raud motored to a windbreak in the northeast cape. I tried a pressure gauge on several tank blocks, shouldered the one with the most air, and slid in.

I had been out of the water most of that summer of 1952 and was not in condition. I drove into the fifty-foot zone, where the unfit diver strikes the sharpest Eustachian crisis, and was surprised at how good my ears felt. The depths were exceptionally clear. As I stroked down the wall, I regained the exhilaration of our first submarine manflights, as if the experience were brand new. I passed from wave-shattered sunlight into an ambient reful-gence, the place without shadows. I swam over an escarpment of morose yellow algae to a drop-off into deeper blue and saw below in diffused gray light a gradient of vague boulders covered with gorgonians. I went into the boulder country.

My compressed air tasted mechanical, and my thoughts began to blur. I raised the wrist depth gauge to my mask: 170 feet. The lay-off was telling on me. I had to force my thoughts into orderly sequences: *My right hand means south.* I looked in that direction, and there were no amphorae in the hundred-foot range of visibility. *I have only ten minutes of grace left at this depth. My left means north.* I struck out on that course through the boulders, intending to round the northeast point in the time I had left. *My friends in the launch, whatever the state of the sea, will stick to my bubble track. Remember, no effort, no haste, no exertion.* I rationed my foot strokes and rhymed them with deep exhalations, turning my head from side to side like a radar scope. The northern reach revealed no artifacts. My eyes were growing tired from looking down the gray bank. Suddenly I saw a long dark object. *It is deeper. Should you go down? It may be an amphora.* I emptied my lungs and, without kicking, drifted deeper. The object was concealed in a sea wig. I clawed at it and uncovered an ordinary chunk of limestone. My depth gauge read 240 feet. *Stupid! Up you go, quick!* I timed a big scissors kick with a bumper intake of air and soared back to 170 feet, escorted by a squadron of large silvery *liches* (leer fish).

I rounded the cape as planned and found that there the gray slope rose to my strata. My intakes of air grew harder. I turned on the reserve valve to gain five more minutes' credit. My hope was about gone. I had to save most of the remaining air for underwater stage decompression. Ascending the slope, I saw before my mask the gracefully rounded silhouette of a solitary, half-buried amphora. *I can't leave without making a landmark.* Gathering what strength I had left, I wrenched the amphora out and punched it upright into the magma.

The effort upset my breathing. I inhaled deeply and trudged up the slope. Then, in the half-seen field ahead, the truth arose. I was alongside a high tumulus of sand and rubble, looking at a cascade of broken pottery. Never before had I seen as large an ancient ship mound. The wreck ascended the bank and broke against the base of the island. A lolling dogfish grudgingly gave way to let me work loose a stack of three cups resembling chalices.

I went up the wall like a sleepwalker, my heart pounding erratically, and hung to a gorgonian ten feet from the surface, to decompress there for as long as I had air left. I clutched the cups to my breast, while the launch circled loyally above in the dazzling foam. My air sputtered out. I surfaced, thrusting the cups ahead in my hand. Benoît, his white hair blowing in the mistral, saw a hand bearing gifts from the sea. "They're Campanian!" he cried.

I stretched out in the boat, eyes closed, and listened. The archaeologist announced, "These cups resemble Campanian ware that were found in the *oppida* of Provence. It is enough evidence to assume that the wreck is as old as the second century before Christ."

Dumas asked, "Do you think it is worth an all-out digging job?"

"Absolutely," said Professor Benoît.

The buzz went through *Calypso* from engine room to bridge, and people crowded the mess to see the finds. With a ritualistic manner, Ichac lifted the cups. "They are stacked with the twin handles at right angles to each other," he said, separating them. "I am now taking apart objects that an expert packer arranged this way twenty-two hundred years ago."

The remark stirred the company. The cups had been turned and packed by living people whose deftness carried from their hands to ours across two millennia. We were not going to dive merely for museum pieces, but for news of these artisans, of the way their delicate wares came to the waters of Gaul, and above all—for sailors like us—of their ship and the seamanship of her crew. What kind of ship was she? How was she built? What manner of men had sailed her? Clues might come out of the mud below to tell that tale.

We would dig the wreck out from the geological and biological accretions of centuries. We would unload her long-overdue cargo jars with minimum damage to the buried hull and then remove the hull, leaving no trace of the ship. Benoît wanted to take it all to a single repository—his large Borély Museum in Marseilles—where experts could ruminate all the evidence of an antique cargo ship. They would reassemble the hull and—who knows?— perhaps the rigging and top hamper. It would be a serious contribution to marine archaeology. This young science boasted few recoveries, and most of them had been on land—prehistoric boats embalmed in bogs, Egyptian and Viking vessels entombed with dead kings, and showboat galleys of the age of Caligula that were uncovered by draining Lake Nemi in Italy in the 1930's. Only four seagoing ships of ancient days had been partially excavated from the sea floor. The first was the Antikythera wreck off Greece, raided by hardhat divers in 1901 for its cargo of bronze and marble sculptures. The second was Alfred Merlin's Roman argosy off Mahdia, Tunisia, which also yielded plundered Greek statuary, and from which Dumas, Tailliez, and I had taken marbles in 1948. The Italian salvage ship *Artiglio II* had made bucket grabs into a first-century B.C. wreck off Albenga, Italy, devastating the mound to fetch up oddments. A wreck of the same century off Anthéor, France, had been partially surveyed by Dumas, Philippe Tailliez, and divers from my former navy command, *L'Ingénieur Élie Monnier*. On the evidence of the Campanian cups, none of those ships was as old as ours; and none had been salvaged thoroughly as we intended now to do.

I committed *Calypso* for two months to exhume the antique ship buried 130 feet under her keel. How naïve that schedule seems now! The wreck was to take five years and one life. She was to drain our expeditions near to bankruptcy and force us to establish the first human settlement on the island.

The ancient ship also became a school of manhood. She forged our diving team into an oceanographic instrument and obliged us to establish our own shore-based research and development center for underwater technology, the Office Français de Recherches Sous-Marines (O.F.R.S.). She overthrew impractical notions about working underwater and taught us better ones.

However, on the evening of discovery we sailed to Marseilles in fruitful ignorance, spinning plans for our season below. The Campanian cups had an immediate effect on the Director of Antiquities of the Ministry of National Education, who made a large grant from his frugal archaeological budget (it proved to be a tiny fraction of the cost of digging up the ship). The National Geographic Society responded with a subsidy, as did the Préfecture des Bouches du Rhône and the Marseilles Municipality.

The harbor authorities and the Marseilles Chamber of Commerce contributed material and services to the submarine dig. Most exciting and encouraging, from every part of France came dozens of divers to volunteer for work on the wreck. Most of them were competent; all were enthusiastic. Among them was Albert Falco, a son of the sea from the village of Sormiou near Marseilles. Although seasoned since boyhood in the underwater world, Falco had been denied the basic able-bodied seaman's papers he needed to become a *Calypso* diver because of our rigid social security system. He had lost three fingers of his left hand in the explosion of a German mine detonator while working as a postwar volunteer to clear the harbors.

I took Falco to a merchant navy social security doctor to get him A.-B. papers. The physician found him a superior physical specimen in all respects and was about to sign the permit when he noticed Falco's hand. He said, "I'm sorry, Monsieur . . ."

I said, "Don't be ridiculous. Try to think of some way to pass him."

The medico gave Falco a permit confining his employment to *"le navire océanographique Calypso"* and shoreside fishing. (Today Falco is the chief pilot of a jet submarine that roams a thousand feet down.)

Falco recommended another good diver to me, Armand Davso, an employee of the Marseilles sanitation department. The city fathers detached him to *Calypso* while continuing to pay his salary. Davso was a *ramasseur de vides, deuxième classe,* that is, a specialist in gathering empties from the streets. He began picking up their antique counterparts from the bottom of the sea and has remained with us—a versatile submarine technician.

With a good ship and an eager diving team, we returned to Grand Congloué to form a plan of operations. Dumas and I reconnoitered the wreck mound. On top of the grave lay boulders that had fallen from the island in recent epochs. Water had so cushioned their fall that they had not crushed the wreck. We found one rock, weighing at least two tons, resting on top of unbroken amphorae. Our first step was to clear them off. François Juniet of the lighthouse administration sent his rugged tender *Léonor Fresnel* to lower slings from a powerful winch and tumble the bigger boulders down the slope. *Calypso* lifted the smaller ones. We could not budge the largest rock, a thirty-ton menhir at the lower end of the wreck. This housecleaning indicated the enormity of the task we had undertaken. Broken amphorae and shards of cups, bowls, and dinner plates were embedded in sand mixed with stones and sea shells. Moreover, the working depth was just about the limit for safety—the top of the site was 125 feet deep; the bottom, 140. As we dug down, we would be diving deeper. The place was the edgeland of depth drunkenness. Dumas and I had to think out a logical attack on this disorder.

Our first clue came from a series of amphora necks protruding about ten inches from the slag heap. They were standing in a line that indicated the

longitudinal axis of the buried ship. We took down a calibrated rope and
wondered what to measure from. Taking random line-ups and guesses, we
estimated the vessel was ninety-three feet long and twenty-seven feet wide,
which later proved fairly accurate. It was a ten-thousand-amphora ship,
one of the largest of ancient times.

On *Calypso's* messroom wall we tacked a plan of the wreck site, on which
we entered the location of important or characteristic finds. In order that
we could all speak the same language, we blindly labeled the wreck as to
stern and bow, starboard and port; and the dig began. First the divers
removed amphorae that would come loose by hand—three hundred of them
in the first fortnight. They also cleared off stones and broken crockery.
This period of trial and error lasted longer than we had estimated, because
of a series of unseasonable mistrals that drove *Calypso* away from the island.
We also made a serious tactical mistake. Instead of picking systematically
at the upper end, or stern as we called it, and working down, we blurred
the archaeological picture by gleaning all over the mound. The error we
could correct, but we could do nothing about the mistral.

This screaming wind of the Mediterranean descends dry and fierce from
the cold north along the Rhône Valley and roars out to sea, driving the
warmth before it. In the seething water *Calypso* heaved at her reins to the
island. We envisioned our new research ship piled up on top of a 2200-year-
old disaster and wondered why we had been mad enough to try the
salvage.

The mistrals came suddenly. We would recall the divers and joust for
hours with anchor chain and hemp cables taken out by men in boats to
sheer us off from the inferno. In those times we had very much in our
minds the men who had lost a similar battle against Grand Congloué. During emergencies, however, there was a certain wry comfort in seeing Professor Benoît nervously pacing the deck and pronouncing over and over to
himself, "It's dreadful."

To help us cope with mistrals, Juniet again lent the *Léonor Fresnel,*
which anchored a mooring buoy big enough to calm a battleship 250
feet off the island. We had no idea this reassuring buoy would bring a
tragedy upon us.

Calypso then had twenty berths, and we often had thirty-five people
aboard. In the atmosphere of exhilaration and ever-present danger, no one
complained of poor feeding and sleeping accommodation. Sometimes we had
sixteen divers engaged. Our rules allowed each man three descents per day

with an average of fifteen minutes' work on the bottom. Between dives the men rested for three hours, if they could, to pass off accumulated nitrogen and regain energy. Two-man teams rotated on the bottom almost continuously. They were called to the surface by a timekeeper firing a rifle into the water. When coming up, the divers took a three- to five-minute decompression stop ten feet down before re-entering the atmosphere.

Rifle shots, the deafening roar of compressors, the lashing of the sea, screeching winds, whistles of compressed air, the popping of our obsolete diesel winch, instructions howled against the gale, the squawk of gulls— all these made an intoxicating clamor in this lonely place at sea. Nevertheless our efficiency was disputable.

The lure that had fetched divers from afar also brought sightseers. Flotillas of barks, lateen-rigged sailboats, yachts, and power cruisers came out to Grand Congloué to watch. One day the most exotic sightseer arrived, "le Comte Renoir de Dong," having swum the ten miles from Marseilles. He carried a spear gun, a pack on his back, and a bottle of wine in the bosom of his diving dress. When he started to swim back, we insisted that he accept a lift in the *Calypso*. He jumped overboard a half-mile from Riou Island and swam to the deserted rock. A fishing tartana brought him in that evening. He was carrying a rabbit he had shot on Riou with his underwater gun.

Fishermen, plodding past our noisy operation in an area heretofore shunned by vessels, had only one explanation: "A fabulous treasure. The gold is piling up in their holds." In a way they were right; we were working a treasure—but a priceless one. Instead of bullion and gems we were recalling gossip of an overdue ship in some old agora which was becoming today's headlines.

At first we raised amphorae by stringing a dozen of them on a trawl line attached to the winch. Some fell off, endangering men below. We winched them up bunched in a cargo net, but it crushed the jars. Pierre Labat suggested a method that pleased everybody. He took down an air hose, turned an amphora upside down, and scoured out the sludge with compressed air. The buoyant jar took off and spiraled to the surface, where Raud in a dinghy fished it out. But we could not send up broken amphorae in this way, and cracked urns leaked and fell back on the site. We adopted a steel lift basket with a twelve-jar capacity, which was the average number that a trained diving pair could gather in one work shift on the floor.

Wet amphorae arrived on deck coruscating in the sun. Their purple and gold biological encrustation faded soon into dun and drab and dried into a patina of white fossils and iodine stains where shellfish had been attached. Biologists Jacques Picard and Roger Molinier of the University of Marseilles seized the fresh amphorae and stripped off the living blankets for study. They found one species unknown to science and several new associations of fixed marine life. Their colleague, Jean Blanc, dived to the wreck to study its sedimentation and measure the oxygen content of the mud and ambient water. These young scientists shared the spirit of *Calypso*. On week ends they spontaneously showed up at the Marseilles dock and helped our men scrub and paint the ship.

Mealtimes on board were jovial exchanges of ideas for improving our working methods. We also talked and argued a lot about the identity of the wreck. Benoît maintained that she belonged to the third century B.C. His assistants, Henri Médan and Ferdinand Lallemand, claimed the evidence was not strong enough; they felt that the ship went down in the first century B.C. Dumas belonged tentatively to the latter school. I knew little about archaeology, but I hoped that she was older than the first century, because the previous remains of classic vessels found in the sea were from that ship-wrecking century. Little by little the finds from the gray slope told us more about our freighter. We were living an engrossing historical detective story.

After loose stuff on the mound was cleared off, we dug with our hands to penetrate the next layer. The artifacts seemed embedded in cement. When we tried to rock a jar by the handles, we either ended up exhausted or broke the specimen. It was imperative to remove the sediment packed around the jars. A month after work began we introduced the needed system —a suction pipe, operated from a mammoth pump. The flexible metal pipe was five inches in diameter and two hundred feet long. Lashed to it was an air hose, its lower end turned up inside the pipe near the nozzle. Compressed air traveled up the pipe, increasing in volume and speed, gobbling up everything small enough to pass through the nozzle.

You must calculate diameter, rigidity, air volume, and depth in a submarine *suceuse*. The specifications for our depth required the compressor to furnish four thousand cubic feet of compressed air an hour in order to lift four or five hundred cubic feet of product. Such a suction tool literally devoured the bottom. It swallowed mud, sand, shells, shards, fish, and stones larger than a fist. If we had accidentally placed a section of our flesh squarely against the mouth, it would have sucked our blood away as well.

The pipe emptied into a wire mesh basket on deck where an archaeologist examined the siftings. The roaring pipe poured out fragments of wood fitted with oak dowels, iron and copper sheathing nails, bronze treenails ten inches long and shining like new, bits of crumpled leaden sheathing with a zigzag pattern of short copper rivets, and fishermen's sinkers and hooks from various centuries later than the wreck. The foaming basket drained off to reveal a bronze finger ring, which I called the captain's ring and wore for several days before handing it over to Benoît. The pipe and the basket convinced us that no clue, however small, was going to escape.

On deck it was fashionable to refer to the "underwater vacuum cleaner." But when we had hold of its attacking end, the pipe was a galloping Loch Ness monster. Handling the nozzle was hard, thrilling, and dangerous. We went down the diving ladder in pairs, nosing into the blue along the pipe and clearing our ears as quickly as we could. A hundred feet down we saw the wreck and the pipe was waiting, coiled motionless and menacing, for our next bout. The first diver grabbed both handles of the brass nozzle and heaved it to the work spot. It was heavy and difficult to bend—the penalty for the large diameter and rigidity we had chosen for the sake of productivity. The operator, making sure the second diver was clear of the nozzle, turned on the aircock, and the ride began. The pipe vibrated like the neck of a wild horse as he tried to tame and feed it. When its muzzle struck sand and silt, the pipe chewed in, changing the topography before our eyes.

Much of the time, however, the pipe struck the hard belly of an amphora; the wreck mound seemed to be one block of fired earthenware. Then he would probe gingerly for the mud packing between the urns and carve out their graceful forms from the mother material like an inspired sculptor for whom the clay shapes itself. These creative moments ended all too soon when the sucker choked on something too large—a pottery shard or a stonelike organic concretion. Then suction power prevented the operator from pulling it out. The second diver might break it up with a hammer, but usually he had to shut off the air to get rid of the obstacle. With the aircock closed, the onrush of material slowed down, pebbles gathered slowly into the mouth, the roar diminished, and overhead was heard the clatter of the previous deliveries falling back down the pipe. Rather apologetically, the *suceuse* belched and became incredibly heavy before it regurgitated the bone from its throat.

One day two divers came up laughing a little too noisily, like guilty schoolboys. The filter basket showed their appalling act—thousands of freshly crushed pieces of fine potteries. Lallemand scooped his hands in the rubble, shouted, and pulled out a beautiful Campanian wine cup. The fragile specimen had survived overseas shipping, the impact of the ship against the rock and the floor, the boulders falling from the island, the diver's hammer, and the trip up the pipe. The debris consisted of other dishes ruined by our carelessness. We had not realized that small, intact potteries were entering the pipe to be smashed to bits. The unexpected surviving cup proved it. I could not blame the divers. The previous day I'd had a touch of nitrogen narcosis while riding the pipe.

The little cup created a crisis for our operational plan. For some time it had been evident that we would have to lift thousands of tons of sediment, but the pipe seemed to be doing it well. Now it became apparent that the pipe, however careful the divers were, was smashing what might be the most important things in the ship. It was up to me to decide whether to crunch away, incurring such losses, in order to fulfill the time schedule, or to slow down in meticulous concern for the delicate Campanian wares. We decided to slow down and do it right, no matter what the cost nor how long it would prolong the ordeal. We instructed the divers accordingly.

The amount of work ahead was frightening to contemplate. But we were buoyed by what had been learned. The ship carried two distinct types of amphorae. The upper layer consisted of elongated jars carried as deck cargo. They resembled the finds from the Albenga and Anthéor sea excavations, which Benoît attributed to Magna Graecia, the Greek culture in Italy. They had long necks, and impressed on the clay rim was a common mark, "SES," followed by a trident or an anchor symbol.

On the deep port flank of the top layer of the ship mound we found the second prevailing type of cargo jar. It had a full tapering belly, short neck, and nicely modeled handles—a style more refined than its cylindrical sister's and one suggesting Greek influence, if not origin. These "Greek" jars seemed to have been loaded in the hold beneath the long "Roman" ones and had erupted from the starboard hand when the wooden side collapsed.

The crest of the mound yielded clusters of small potteries that had been stowed between the necks of the amphorae. After we adopted cautious methods, there came up hundreds of specimens of forty standard shapes: *kylix,* or drinking cups with double handles; bowls and cups of various sizes; platters and fish plates with a center well for sauce; perfume flagons;

ointment and rouge pots; and a ravishing miniature amphora that the ancients used to collect human tears. All the dishes were of a similar mode, like those of a contemporary dinner service. As we carved out deeper nests of potteries, we found some with patches of intact black varnish, stamped on the bottom with rosettes or palmettes. Lallemand longed for unchipped Campanian blackware with varnish unmarred. Dumas took a worn bowl, daubed it with shoe polish, and slipped it into his collection. "Here it is!" shouted the assistant, rapturously transferring shoe polish to his hands. Before long the joke became true. Deeper in the ship's hold we found thousands of black dishes in their original glossy state.

In the Anthéor ship mound we had found amphorae with mouths still sealed with stoppers made of pozzuolana, or volcanic mortar. It was a long time before we dug out wine jars at Grand Congloué with the stopper in place. Each of them was empty and had a small hole drilled in the neck, as though naughty seamen had broached the wine cargo. "Perhaps that's why they sank," Dumas observed.

Under one of the pozzuolana stoppers we found an inner cork lining hermetically sealed with resinous pitch. There was liquid sloshing inside. We had found the "wine layer" of the excavation. I asked, "How are we going to keep *Calypso* sober with thousands of gallons of wine coming aboard?" We drew off a quart of transparent pinkish liquid in a flask. I couldn't resist drinking wine 2200 years old. I tasted the mustiness of the ages in that wraithy wine. It had been de-alcoholized, but contained no taste of salt. A shipmate saw the expression on my face and inquired, "Poor vintage century?" At the bottom of the jar we found resinous purple lees. Originally the insides of the amphorae were coated with pitch to prevent evaporation through the porous clay walls. This practice of ancient merchants gave the wine a taste of resin.

Among the thousands we took from the wreck, we never again found a jar that contained wine. By every circumstance, she had a full cargo of red wine aboard when she came to grief; but except for that single amphora, the sea had consumed it all.

Most of the containers had lost their stoppers from sea pressure and the play of ages. In many of the ones that had been standing upright, there were pottery fragments mixed with sea shells and pebbles. As more jars were hosed out on deck, live octopuses emerged, slithering and blinking. Here were the magpies that had collected the shells and shards to construct doors for their homes. The venerable cargo was a housing project for the octopus.

<table>
<tr><td>chapter
five</td><td>PORT

CALYPSO</td></tr>
</table>

The mistrals increased. By the close of the second month's work on the antique wreck I was afraid to risk *Calypso* in the working anchorage with her stern crane thirty feet from the rock. The harbor and lighthouse people sank new concrete moorings in addition to the three-ton battleship buoy, and Falco and Davso swam down to tighten a chain around the rock arch to which she could make fast.

Calypso was in an odd predicament. We had struggled for an oceano-graphic research vessel to explore all seas, and here she was shackled over the grave of an old wreck that threatened to demolish her any day. This was a job for a barge. Or why not for an installation on the island? We decided to inhabit the grim rock and liberate *Calypso*. An archaeological diving station could be planted on Grand Congloué. We could hang an engine platform and diving station above the wreck. There was no time to lose if this unconventional facility was to be built before winter.

With a heartening outburst of confidence, Marseilles authorities, institutions, clubs, and business firms again came forth to help us. Six borrowed soldiers and a young engineering officer built the engine platform in three days in waves rising to their waists. The platform held a winch and compressed-air storage bottles filled periodically by *Calypso*. Roger Gary found a sailing ship mast, and we hung it out eighty-five feet from the rock to let a lifting basket and the suction pipe into the wreck. We laid the top end of the pipe around a corner of the island so that the residue would pass through a filter basket into the sea at a spot where mud clouds could not drift back over the wreck site.

Early in November a furious mistral blockaded *Calypso* in the old harbor at Marseilles. It was blowing at sixty-five knots when two cheerful, husky youths stepped aboard and asked me for jobs as divers. They were Jean-Pierre Serventi and Raymond Kientzy, recently discharged navy combat divers who had come through two years of amphibious action in Indo-China. I said, "I'm very sorry, but we don't have the money to hire you." Serventi said, "Think nothing of it, Commandant. We still have some discharge pay left, and we'll work a month for nothing before we go ashore to find jobs."

I welcomed these experienced men, who were volunteering for the hardest time, when our student divers' holidays were over and our financial commitments were expanding to build the island base. The new men sailed with us to the island in abating winds. At Grand Congloué we were dismayed to find that the battleship buoy had floated five hundred yards to the east, making it impossible to anchor *Calypso*. This big float was the key to doing anything with the wreck or the new settlement ashore. What conceivable force could have displaced it? No gale could have moved the buoy's overweighted anchor hundreds of yards around the northeast cape. We had to go down and find out what had happened.

The new divers wanted to prove their ability, so I sent them off in a launch with Falco, while Saôut and I kept *Calypso* hovering off the buoy. After a half-hour dive Serventi and Kientzy surfaced and reported that the buoy had parted from the anchor. They had followed the dangling chain to the bottom and found it wedged in a rock spur. The storm had pulled the anchor chain apart at a shackle. Half of it lay on the floor, still attached to the big anchor, while the buoy had dragged the rest of the chain away until it fouled in the rocks. The divers thought the drifted chain was stuck in the rocks firmly enough to hold. We put back for Marseilles, dining

Excavating the ancient wine ship.

over the problem and often invoking the *Léonor Fresnel* and her giant winch.

Serventi said, "I observed the end of the chain very closely. It left a deep track in the mud until it caught in the rocks. It would be easy to follow the track back until we came to the break in the anchor chain."

I said, "But the working depth is very difficult—probably 200 to 230 feet."

Serventi said, *"Oui, Commandant.* But we can use three or four divers in succession, planting marker buoys along the chain track when they have to come up. I suggest using a cork float with a reel of fishing line and a small weight that we can drop when one of us becomes over-extended. The next man can go down the fishing line and take up the search. In two or three dives I'm sure we'll find the anchor without trouble."

I liked our new friend's ingenuity. "Okay," I said, "if the weather's right tomorrow, we'll try it."

Serventi said, "I volunteer as first diver."

Overnight we assembled several Serventi marker buoys. Next day, November 6, the weather was propitious, and *Calypso* sailed for Grand Congloué. Since we were shorthanded and Saôut was on leave, I decided to risk anchoring between Riou and Grand Congloué. Most of the eleven people aboard would be needed on launch operations, leaving too few to maneuver *Calypso* on station.

I went in the launch with Raud, Falco, and the new pair, who had been with us less than a week but were already solid members of the team. At the battleship buoy Serventi put on the triple-pack Aqua-Lung, strapped a depth gauge and chronometer on his wrist, and secured the marker buoy to his belt. I said, "Remember, you are not allowed more than ten minutes at that depth. If you tire sooner, drop the buoy and come up. You must decompress for three minutes at ten feet."

"Oui, Commandant," said Serventi. He molded his lips over the mouth grip, hurdled into the water, showed his flukes, and drove down the chain. The mistral was dying reluctantly; the water was still choppy. I stood at the bow, watching the diver's bubbles. Falco, the next man to go down, checked his lung and joined me in the always anxious scrutiny when an agitated surface threatens to smother the breathing track of a man below.

About three hundred yards from the can buoy we became unsure of distinguishing his bubbles. I called on Raud to look sharp from the helm, glanced at my watch, and said, "He's been down eight minutes." The boat was in line with Serventi's previous course, but we could not find his breathing track. At nine minutes my throat went dry. A half-minute later, I had to hold onto myself firmly to avoid becoming rattled. Something warned me that the worst had happened. At ten minutes I said, "Falco. You understand. Hurry up if you want to bring him back alive." Without a word, Falco went in.

I had too much experience to have any hope for Serventi. Whatever had happened, had happened too deep. He would be very hard to find. I suppressed the dreadful images crossing my mind and took automatic actions. "Raud!" I said. "Go to *Calypso* while he's down. We need more divers." We sped to the ship, and I called on Yves Girault and Jacques Ertaud to get ready to dive immediately.

As they were donning their suits, I dashed to the bridge and found Simone alone there, looking pale. *"Zut, alors,"* she said, "a couple of minutes ago our anchor pulled out and we went toward the rocks. I got here just in time to order the engines started and get the bow into the wind."

With a quick, proud look at my wife, I took *Calypso* toward Falco's presumed position. He surfaced off the side, struggling for breath, and gasped, "He's unconscious. Very deep. I ran out of air. Quick! Quick!"

"Girault," I said, "try to empty his lungs by bringing him up head down, holding his feet." This was his last chance for life. Girault brought him up in that way. We put Serventi into the one-man recompression chamber and rocked it rhythmically to provoke artificial respiration while *Calypso* ran to Marseilles at top speed, radioing for a truck to meet us. We put the chamber onto the truck and raced to a big recompression chamber. There Dr. Nivelleau went in with Serventi and tried every known method of reanimation. After agonizing hours we had to abandon our efforts. Kientzy, Simone, and I drove away to tell Serventi's mother.

The medical examiner gave heart failure as the cause of death. Girault had found the diver 220 feet down, apparently stricken while trying to affix his fishing line to one of the concrete-block anchors laid by *Léonor Fresnel*. Serventi was buried at Hyères with a Grand Congloué amphora on his grave.

© *National Geographic Society*

Docking *Calypso* on a Red Sea table reef, half a mile of water under the keel and eighteen inches off the starboard rail. Diving party on afterdeck prepares to plunge down the vertical reef wall while a snorkeler starts across the shallow table.

© *National Geographic Society*

Dreamlike flight down the table reef. Opposite page, a diver passes a hanging jungle of alcyonarians, which are actually colonies of animals. Above, deeper in the velvet darkness—two hundred feet down—surgeonfish glide among white sea whips.

© National Geographic Soc

Digging up the wine ship. A mighty freighter of the third century B.C. gives up it wrecked cargo of amphorae from a depth of 130 feet of Marseilles. These six-gallon wine jars once held the vintages of the Greek Islands and the hills of Rome, ten thousand amphorae in a single ship on its way to Marseilles The freighter rammed Grand Congloué Island and san only ten miles from port.

The archaeological basket comes up from the excavation of the ancient hull with the elongate Roman jars from the deck lading and the round-bellied Greek containers from the hold, telling us that the wine ship sailed from Greece and called at Italy on the way to Gaul. One jar still contained the residue of red wine almost 2200 years old.

© National Geographic Society

© *National Geographic So*

The delayed cargo of Amphorae finally reached Marseilles after five years of exertion by our digging team. The wine jars and thousands of other finds crowd the Borély Museum. The boy holds a bronze treenail with which the wooden planking was made fast to the ribs of the ancient ship.

Television plunges into ancient history. We helped non-diving archaeologists understand the wreck of the wine ship by taking down a high-definition TV camera built by our group. It transmits by cable to the surface, and the underwater operator has a small TV monitor in front of his eyes in order to frame his shots. Powerful flood lamps bracket the camera.

© National Geographic Society

© National Geographic Soc

The S.S. *Thistlegorm* lies a hundred feet down in the Red Sea. She was sunk by Axis planes in 1941. Above, Falco swims over the stern gun. Below, along the deck, is a wrasse, one of the hosts of fish who dwell in the *Thistlegorm*. Opposite page, a gray porgy passes the radio direction-finding loops, while above it a spotted surgeonfish nibbles at a coral bouquet that has grown on the antenna.

© National Geographic Soc.

Angelfish browse on the living mantle of the *Thistlegorm*'s bell. Opposite page, Luis Marden tries to get a caranx to hold a pose for the camera. Below, a friendly tête-à-tête with our noble friend Ulysses, a grouper, companion of our days in the Seychelles, the Isles of Return.

© National Geographic Soc

Ulysses the grouper was the star of our underwater movie studios in the Seychelles. Amiable and omnipresent, the giant fish was all over the set. Dumas' shark billy floats upright.

In the background Delmas is carrying Ulysses' dinner as Falco lights the shot.

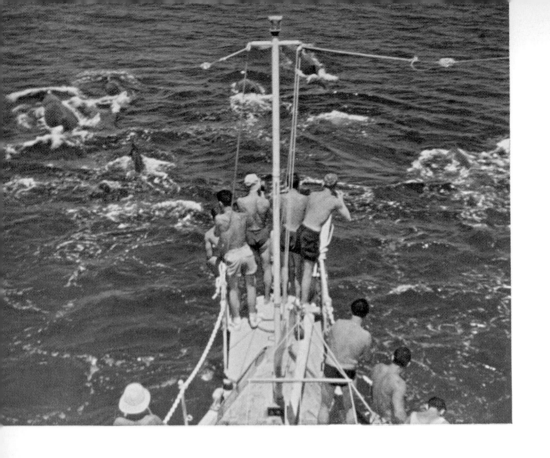

© National Geographic Sc

Sperm whale and shark drama in the Indian Ocean. Near the Equator a pod of unhurried sperm whales permitted the *Calypso* to follow them closely. A baby whale drifted back into our propellers and was badly lacerated. The adults tried to shoulder it along, but the little one was too weak. We got a line on its tail and brought it to our stern, where Dumas administered the *coup de grâce*. From nowhere, the sharks came and began rending the whale. Movie cameramen quickly went down in the antishark cage to film this rare glimpse of the sharks' feeding behavior.

National Geographic Society

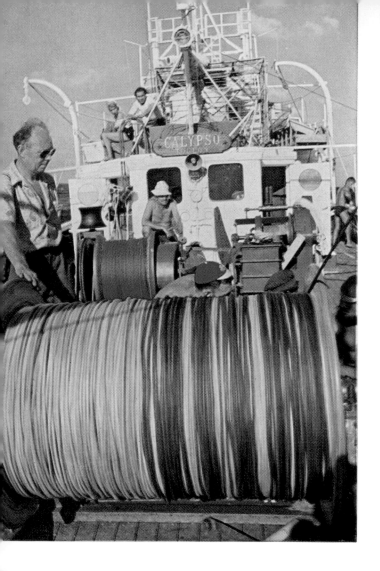

© National Geographic Soc

Romanche Trench: Atlantic Ocean: the deepest anchoring. "Papa Flash" Edgerton (upper left) wanted to lower his electronic flash cameras into the Romanche Trench, 4½ miles deep. In order to hold station over the abyss, we tried anchoring there with 5½ miles of ⅜-inch braided nylon cable, since metal cable would be hopelessly heavy. The thin line, which was in varicolored segments to tell us how much had been paid out, held the 360-ton *Calypso* firmly anchored for 72 hours against a 1.2-knot current and a 15-knot wind. The anchor was 24,600 feet down.

© *National Geographic Society*

© National Geographic Soc.

Off West Africa, we capture a rain bow runner, a fish hitherto un known in the eastern Atlantic Sorbonne biologists Claude Maurin and Jacques Forest examine the specimen in a *Calypso* lab.

Philippe jigs a big squid. At night over the Romanche Trench an army of squids rose from the depths to feed on flying fish around *Calypso*. Spearing squids over the side became a contest, won with this whopper by Philippe Cousteau, aged fifteen.

TORCH DIVE INTO THE BLUE
(opposite page)

Crossing under the Equator (below). King Neptune usually sets up court on deck to initiate voyagers traversing the Equator for the first time. When *Calypso* crossed the line in the Indian Ocean, we decided that our sort of crew should swim beneath the Equator. A ship's launch made the line of Zero Latitude with green fluorescent dye, and five novices Aqua-Lunged under it.

There goes the diving saucer (opposite page). One of the first test dives in the Caribbean of our little jet-propelled continental shelf submarine, *DS-2*, was photographed by Tom Abercrombie of the *National Geographic* with an "in-and-out" camera that recorded the aerial and underwater scenes on the same exposure.

© *National Geographic So*

© National Geographic

Amphitrite, the world's largest inflatable vessel (65 by 27 ft.), an experiment of the *Calypso* group and the National Geographic Society. The U-shaped hull is made of rip-resistant nylon-neoprene fabric with nine sealed compartments. When fully-laden for a two-thousand-mile voyage, the fast, skimming ship draws only fourteen inches of water. *Amphitrite* is a prototype of speedy, pneumatic, jet-propelled marine research vessels and commercial fishing craft. Future developments of the design may lead to good-sized vessels that can be deflated, taken apart and boxed for airlifts to remote places, where they can be reassembled, pumped up and launched from beaches on pneumatic rollers.

A jet submarine that carries two men a thousand feet down. The Diving Saucer is the climax of our efforts to put a pressure-resistant hull around a diving team and penetrate the continental shelf with an agility approaching that of the free diver. The saucer provides for direct observation by both men inside, still and motion picture photography, the collection of specimens from the bottom, and external tool-handling by a mechanical arm. She has three sonar beams and can spend six hours one thousand feet down.

© *National Geographic Society*

The tragedy seemed the end to my underwater endeavors. I went about like an automaton, dissociated from my speech and acts. The unbearable taste I had felt since Minute Nine remained in my mouth. Did I have the right to risk lives to bring up old jars? The unarguable answer was, *No*. I sat with Simone in morbid apathy, too listless even to begin dissolving the expeditions. A telegram arrived. I mechanically opened the folded blue form. I had to read it twice. It said, "Share your grief over Serventi loss. May I have the honor of replacing him to further your work? (Signed) BESSON."

I passed the telegram to Simone. Neither of us spoke. No words were necessary. We knew we would carry on. I wired Henri Besson to come ahead. He was a capable and intelligent diver who had worked at Grand Congloué on week ends. When he heard of Serventi's death, he was about to start a month's vacation. To his manly heart, it seemed the right thing to offer help. His gallantry saved Calypso Oceanographic Expeditions.

The next morning the *Léonor Fresnel* and *Calypso* went to the island to reconnect the big buoy and its anchor. To do this we would have to attach a line to the end of the anchor chain and pull it up. First we dragged a small sharp grapnel across the ocean floor, 240 feet down, and hooked the length of heavy chain fastened to the anchor. Then I got ready to go down and attach a stronger line by which it could be pulled up. The sea was cold, so I put on my constant-volume dress, which gives good insulation at the cost of some mobility. I took a line from the *Fresnel* and sank with it along the grapnel rope. I told myself to be very languid and not overexert myself in such a depth.

Halfway down I entered a slight current which tugged on my trailing line like a sail. At two hundred feet I had to pull strenuously on the belly-ing line to keep going. I wondered if those above were feeding me line smartly enough. I saw the anchor chain a hundred feet away and tugged my line toward it, feeling some relief, which was probably nitrogen narcosis.

I went as slowly and evenly as possible, taking deep breaths, but spend-ing energy I wanted to conserve. My heartbeats were disorderly, and my consciousness was flashing with images of Serventi smiling and Serventi dead. When I arrived at the chain, I saw I was at the middle of it. My legs

© *National Geographic Society*
Diving saucer *Denise* takes her dazzled crew into the Caribbean netherworld

were so exhausted that I hauled myself along the chain by pulling on the links. Halfway to the goal, I reached the limit of my strength. Very deliberately I knotted the line on the chain, clamped my hand over the exhaust valve in my hood, blew my exhalations into the suit, and ballooned aloft, trailing my spent limbs. Once out of the realm of rapture, I felt pleased at having successfully completed my task.

Fifty-five feet from the top I took my hand off the exhaust valve and trimmed off neutrally to slow my ascent so that I would not miss the decompression mark hanging ten feet from *Calypso*. After ten minutes on the line I surfaced, feeling that I had accomplished something. Captain Jean Jeres was leaning over the *Fresnel*'s bows. "We winched up your line," he said, "but it was not fast to the chain. Nothing came up."

I dragged myself aboard *Calypso* and swore to Falco, "That knot was as good as any I've made in my life. Tell them on *Fresnel* that I will take three hours to get rid of nitrogen and then go down and do it again." I went to my quarters and slumped in bed. Simone was ironing. She asked no questions, for which I was grateful. I turned from side to side in a doze until it was time to be powdered with talc and wriggle into the constant-volume dress again.

On the second descent, instead of trying to tow a line, I took along a 300-foot coil of rope. Water conditions were poorer this time; a stronger, clouded current was running in midwater. I was in deep fatigue and rapture when I reached the chain, but so defiant that I made a triple knot and shook it violently. Something was whispering, "You said this risk was not worth an old jar. Yet you are doing it for a secondhand anchor?"

I inflated and soared up. The *Léonor Fresnel* fished up the anchor chain and refastened it to the battleship buoy. *Calypso*'s spirits rose. As I was recovering, Davso and Besson asked me if they could make a really deep dive.

Storms lashed at the island through December. One night the sea leaped on the engine platform and swept away the winch and the rack of air bottles. Working all night in surf climbing over their heads, the men managed to save the long boom and the suction pipe. When the sea went down, they dived and recovered the winch and storage bottles. Although we had quick recovery possibilities, we could not afford such interruptions. We built a heavier platform higher on the rock face, enclosed the machinery in a hut, and fixed a steel ladder to the cliff leading to a shelf of rock fifty feet above the water surface. On this escarpment the newest village in France, Port Calypso, was founded. In Marseilles we found some disused tin hutments left behind by the U. S. Army and fashioned them into a yellow house with the aid of army engineers. The billet had five beds and a combined kitchen and dining room, with a propane refrigerator for a touch of chic. The islanders, by courtesy of the avuncular Marseilles Chamber of Commerce, even had free radiotelephone service to the mainland. They built a stone terrace and adorned it with amphorae. Then they settled in to a daily diving schedule right through the winter. And *Calypso* was now freed from her dangerous commitment to the ancient ship. Lighthouse tenders volunteered to provision Port Calypso, remove accumulated finds from the wreck, and exchange diving parties from time to time to give the workers shore leave.

During storms the islanders would look down at waves pounding twenty feet high against the rock and think what it must have been like for the crew of the old freighter when she crashed into Grand Congloué. "The poor devils never had a chance," they agreed. "There is no place to pull yourself out of the water."

Calypso's last chore of the first year of excavation was to deliver a powerful medium-pressure air compressor to the island engine house, so the divers could run the suction pipe themselves. As we were about to take it there, another storm confined *Calypso* to Marseilles. We held a Christmas Eve party on board for the crew and a half-dozen staunch friends, including Yves Girault.

At midnight Davso stuck his head out on deck and called, "Look, the wind has died."

Before I could make the obvious suggestion, Girault said, "Now I know why you invited us to the party." He gestured toward the heavy compressor and said, "Cheap labor." Everybody howled.

We put out for Grand Congloué. An hour later in the rays of a searchlight the Christmas partygoers were puffing away at the compressor on the afterdeck. They lodged it in a niche in the rock, from which it was winched up to the engine house on Christmas Day.

For New Year's I offered to put all the islanders ashore, but they counterproposed that I bring their parents and girl friends to Port Calypso instead. There were twenty people packed into the flower-dressed hut. In the midst of the party, Pierre Labat said, "Let's dive for the first amphora of 1953!" He and Kientzy got into their suits. At midnight they stroked into the cold depths. We saw nothing in the black graveyard below but the distant emerald gleam of their flashlights. They brought back a superb amphora, which we greeted with cheers and toasts.

When we had dug down to the second tier of deck cargo jars on the crest of the ship mound, we ran into a stubborn compaction that slowed the work. The wreck was listed to port, and the amphorae were jammed tightly on that side. We had to dig another section and work our way down into the midships jam. We went to work at the stern—the shallowest section—and in a few days made a deep cut, removing three layers of jars. Underneath, the suction pipe suddenly revealed the main deck of the wine freighter. There lay the planks that the old seamen had trod. The wood was saturated and fragile but lifelike in appearance. The pleasure of this discovery was lessened by the realization that under the deck was the main hold, undoubtedly full of even more layers of jars that we had to get out.

On the starboard side of the main deck we uncovered leaden sheets, large intact expanses of the shriveled scraps that we had found earlier. This hull sheathing was possibly torn off as the sinking ship scraped the rock. The copper rivets in the sheathing were capped with lead, showing that the ancients understood how to prevent the corrosive action of different metals touching each other in the salty medium. The shipwrights had not been able to explain galvanic effects, perhaps, but they knew how to prevent them. We estimated that there were twenty tons of lead plating on the argosy.

Other finds added information about the ancient seamen. We found a heavy marble mortar, a long piece of slate, a thick tile plate, an oar counterweight, a small earthenware stove, an iron ax, and stout crockery unlike the Campanian blackware. As we had guessed earlier, this was the stern section of the ship, for ancient crews cooked and ate on the fantail. Here we also found a drinking mug. Scratched on the side in crude Greek letters was the legend "TO YOUR HEALTH."

The pipe fetched up a lot of polished black volcanic pebbles the size of peas. This was not material indigenous to the sea bottom in the area. It had to have been in the ship. Was it ballast stone? Or perhaps an exportation of mosaic tiles spilled in the hold on a previous voyage?

All this time Lallemand had been waiting impatiently at the end of the pipe for coins to come up. Girault gave him a momentary thrill by feeding some modern coins into the nozzle. We did not find a coin on the entire dig.

One day our ship's surgeon, Dr. Nivelleau, had finished his stint on the suction pipe and was leisurely swimming up the cliff wall, admiring the red gorgonians. Sixty-five feet from the surface he came to a small ledge that no one had particularly noticed before. There directly under our engine house lay a leaden anchor stock of the old ship, now painted flaming red by a nation of small animals. The anchor had probably snagged there and been ripped away as the ship went down. The position was above the bow of the wreck. Later we found the other anchor stock buried among amphorae near the bow. The close vertical proximity of the anchors to the hull seemed to say that they were catted to the sides when she sank, and that the crash had been so sudden that nothing could have been done to save the ship.

The wooden elements of the anchors had been dissolved by biological processes, but Italian and French archaeologists had already established a convincing picture of ancient Mediterranean anchors. The post and hooks were made of hardwood. The top crossbar, or stock, was made of lead, as was the collar brace by which the hooks were fastened to the post. Unlike the modern anchor, the antique one had the heaviest weight at the top, necessitated by the fact that the old sailors had no chain and used rope on anchors. Rope would stretch taut in a wind and drag the anchor if it were not weighted at the top.

The wooden elements of the wreck made us admire the virtuosity of the shipwrights. They applied differing woods according to various structural demands. Planking, sheathing, keel, and main timbers, knees, ribs and dowels were an interplay of Aleppo pine, Lebanon cedar, and oak. Several other species have not yet been identified because the wood is rotten and tunneled by shipworms. The timber had become rubbery. In the air it dried into shrunken flaky matter. However, we found techniques for embalming sections of the hull.

When spring came, our island exploded with wild flowers, gull chicks, and exuberant young men. The divers had toiled all the harsh winter long on the shaded north side of Grand Congloué, and now the sun poured over the peak into Port Calypso, lighting the white rocks and yellowish *maquis*. Lizards basked on the warm stones. We held a spring party. It began as a sort of magazine stunt. There was a photographic session on the terrace with the divers dressed in Greek robes, feasting from the Campanian dinner service. But the banquet turned into something else entirely—a communion with the past. Amidst the wine and hilarity, we were conscious that the dishes were once again serving their natural purpose. We were handling real things and not museum pieces. The use of mysterious dishes was solved naturally. One small bowl, whose function the experts had been unable to determine, was spontaneously filled with green olives. It was nothing else but an olive dish. Black dishes marvelously set off the colors of meat, salad, and fruit.

Our high-spirited photographer, Jacques Ertaud, who was to be married to Marie-Jeanne Herzog, sister of the famous alpinist, asked that the marriage ceremony be held at Port Calypso. I was delighted to have our pioneer village assume this important civic function. I took the wedding party out on *Calypso*. The diving ladder was unsuitable for receiving matrons in long gowns and high heels. The only other way to climb onto our island was up a steep fissure in the west end. The islanders wedged themselves into the vertical gully and handed up the guests. Maurice Herzog, who had lost his fingers and toes on the ascent of Annapurna, refused aid and scrambled up the crack like a chamois. The officiating clergyman tucked up his skirts, revealing a pair of blue hiking shorts, and followed him aloft.

Diver Henri Goiran, acting as altar boy, handled the communion cup, a black *kylix* from the wreck. The bride carried a bouquet of scrubby island flowers. After the ceremony, without explanation, Marie-Jeanne walked away from the party to the edge of the cliff and tossed her flowers into the azure sea.

On May 15, 1953, we reached the keel of the argosy. It was a joining of oak, twenty inches wide and thirty inches thick. The pipe spun out more information, including the rough itinerary of the fatal voyage. The hold contained amphorae from the Greek island of Delos; therefore she probably set out from there. The top lading was Roman amphorae and Italian pottery; therefore the vessel had called at a Campanian port. It seemed almost certain that her destination was Marseilles, which was at that time the bustling Greek colony of Massalia, entrepôt of Hellenic culture and trade moving up the Rhône River highway into the wilds of Gaul and Germany.

The archaeologists found that the virgin dishes now coming from the ship mound had a striking feature. A dozen examples of the same kind of bowl carried identical circular indentations that could not have been left by a potter's hand. They had been shaped by a wooden matrix on the potter's wheel—evidence of mass production two centuries before Christ.

Professor Benoît was not a diver and therefore could not see the most important excavation of his career, so the O.F.R.S. televised it to him. The submersible TV camera was a high-definition unit with a lens corrected for underwater work. It transmitted images to *Calypso* through multiconductor cables. The artificial lighting system consisted of a bracket of two reflectors containing 6000-watt overvolted lamps. The cameramen pushed the barrel-like camera and flanking lamps into the excavation, and Benoît's party got their first glimpse of the old wreck while sitting comfortably in a darkened room on *Calypso.*

Without telling the cameramen, engineer Henri Chignard wired a loud-speaker into the camera housing. Jean Delmas was next to operate the rig below. Chignard said into the microphone, "Delmas! Correct your focus." The startled diver almost dropped the camera. Instructions from the surface sounded down there like the commands of Poseidon.

Delmas then settled a heated dinner argument. The archaeologists had accepted the evidence that the ship was sheathed in lead but would not believe the divers' assertion that there was also lead plating on the over-heads. The TV camera proved the underwatermen right.

Ever since he had seen the hallmark "SES" on the lips of many jars, Professor Benoît had been trying to find out what it meant. It was obviously the owner's mark, but who was SES? Since the Greeks and Romans were great abbreviators, he thought the mark was probably the first syllable of the owner's surname. He ransacked classic genealogies and epigraphs throughout Europe. One day he came to me with a big smile and announced, "The name of the man who owned the ship was Markos Sestios. He lived on Delos." It was a stunning accomplishment for the dry side of our detective story. Benoît had found records of a powerful Roman clan named Sestius, the most prominent of whom was a merchant and shipowner named Marcus. According to Livy, the Roman historian, Marcus Sestius had lived during the second half of the third century B.C.—the period in which the evidence of our pottery had placed our wreck. Livy says he settled on the Greek island of Delos and set up a shipping business in the sacred city. Furthermore Benoît had the text of an inscription on stone dated 240 B.C. that had been found on Delos. It set forth that Marcus Sestius had received Delian citizenship (*isopoliteia*) and had changed his name to Markos Sestios.*

During the second summer of excavation, *Calypso* sailed past Grand Congloué and hooted a greeting to the divers, which they returned on a trumpet. *Calypso* was on her way to Sestios' home port in the Greek isles. We arrived at Delos on a honeyed morning to find the harbor silted up, so we had to anchor offshore.

---

* Prof. Benoît has not ventured a definite date for the sinking, but it seems almost certain that Sestios' ship went down in the last quarter of the third century B.C.

Delos had fallen in the first century B.C. to Mithridates the Great and was never rebuilt. Where once pilgrims to Apollo's shrine had strolled through marble colonnades in green groves, we walked through sere grass, thistle, and rubble baking under the cobalt sky. Broken columns and monuments stood here and there on the treeless, lion-colored sacred mount of Kynthos, once crowned by Apollo's temple.

The present-day population of Delos, consisting of thirty-five people, was attached to the Delian archaeological project of the French School of Athens. The young chief archaeologist, Jean Marcadé, invited us to look at his study collection, which might contain further information on Markos Sestios. Leaning against the outside of the archive house were amphorae shaped exactly like those in the wreck. But neither they nor any of the thousands of shards inside had any sort of inscription related to the merchant. There were only his stone "citizenship papers" in the collection.

Marcadé led us to the Roman traders' quarter where our shipowner had lived. Several villas had been cleared of rubble down to the mosaics on the ground floor. In one large house we came upon mosaics showing sea waves and an amphora. Robert Edgerton, an American youngster who was with us on the cruise, called out, "Look at this one!" The design depicted a dolphin entwined with an anchor shaped like the mark on the "SES" jars. "And look at this one!" The second mosaic had a beribboned trident recalling the fork symbol on our jars. Dugan made two sketches and handed them to me. The first was a copy of the trident, which was shaped like a Roman *E* with two *S*-shaped brackets between the tines. The second sketch showed the brackets removed and placed on either side of the *E*. The cipher spelled "SES."

In the dust around the villa I kicked up black volcanic pebbles the same as the pea-sized pellets we had taken from the pipe at Grand Congloué. However, for our excitement at these discoveries Marcadé had only an indulgent smile. The archaeologist said, "There is no proof that this was Sestios' villa. You know, we found evidence that the building was never quite finished."

"Perhaps Sestios went broke when he lost his big ship," I said.

The skeptical *archéologue* grinned and invited us to his house for a cool drink. I took a glass of iced Greek wine. It had the same resin flavor as the 2200-year-old wine from the ship. Although for centuries now the Greeks had been putting up wine in casks and bottles, they still demand the *retsina* flavor imparted originally by the pitch lining in amphorae.

Some of us left the sacred isle with the unscientific and unproved notion that we had seen Sestios' house as surely as we had seen his big ship.

In five years of toil the men of Port Calypso removed more than seven thousand amphorae from the ancient wreck, and as many pieces of pottery. These and other associated finds—hull sections, tools, fittings, and leaden sheathing—weighed some two hundred tons.

Ten years after our archaeological adventure began, Professor Benoît published his thick, lavishly illustrated, scholarly report of the findings at Grand Congloué. I leafed through it in my quarters on *Calypso* during a biological survey of the east coast of South America. The cups and amphorae had been measured, sketched and classified. The wood structure was discussed, elaborate dry theories were proposed, and the account of the underwater excavation was intermingled with references to land diggings. I closed the book with disappointment. There was nothing in the tome about the way Markos Sestios' crew lived and sailed and died. It was not the bridge across the centuries from my seamen to his. I closed my eyes and visions drifted across my mind. . . .

The Mediterranean was seething in the mistral. A clumsy, pot-bellied sailing ship was in distress near Massalia. With helpless horror her men saw a white island looming in the tumultuous waves. She crashed. The ship sank into calm green, turning slowly and splintering her poop as she went down the wall past glorious gorgonian fans. She landed upright on a sloping shelf—the pedestal of the island. Her starboard bower anchor lay on a ledge above the ship. She rested with her bow pointing to the sacred isle of Delos, her crumpled stern framed in a rock recess that almost fitted her lines. Some of her deck cargo jars cracked on impact, and a purple cloud of wine enveloped her.

The wreck lay below the working of swell and surf, partially embraced by rock, so that she did not break up and scatter. Worms attacked the wood, and the lead sheathing worked loose during centuries of settling. Sponges, calcareous algae, ascidians, and sea urchins settled on the wreck. These sedentary creatures attracted nibbling fish. Octopuses writhed along the rocks to take shelter in the amphorae.

As the ages passed, a steady rain of surf-made sand and rain-scoured soil from Grand Congloué fell upon the ship. Centuries of fossil diatoms sifted into the site. The man-made building was merging with the sea. Under the weight of the long sea snow, the overloaded main deck sprang its knees and collapsed on the hold cargo. The port flank opened like an oyster and

ejected cargo jars down the boulder-strewn slope into the deep. The mistral
hurled island rocks down on the wine ship.

In a few more centuries no trace of the tragedy would have appeared on
the floor. But before she was buried forever, Christianini came swimming
along looking for lobsters, and *Calypso* followed to put time in reverse.

Today, Port Calypso, like Markos Sestios' ship, is gone. The rock has returned to solitude and the gulls. If you care to risk your vessel against Grand
Congloué you will find no reminders of human occupation except a rusting
ladder on the wall of the eastern cape and a plaque beside it bearing the
name of Jean-Pierre Serventi.

chapter
six   THISTLEGORM

It was raining at Port Calypso. Summer had gone
and our volunteer divers with it. The sun was arching lower each day.
Before long, shadow would prevail on the working side of the island. In
the yellow tin hut the hard core of archaeological divers—Jean Delmas,
Henri Goiran, and Raymond Kientzy—talked at dinner of the winter ahead.
Autumn storms were due. It was September 29, 1953.

Calypso was in Marseilles. She would be around a few weeks more before
she went into the dockyard to prepare for her winter cruise. After that the
divers would be cut off much of the time, dependent on other supply vessels
and the radiotelephone. As they cleared the table, they discussed what would
happen if one of them were seriously hurt during a storm when boats could
not come out of Marseilles. It was Delmas' turn to wash the dishes. Kientzy,
the cook of the day, lit his pipe and scratched his guitar. Goiran looked out
and said, "It's stopped raining." They went outside. Above the cliffs of the

99

Marseilleveyre, the red afterglow of sunset was packed with black clouds; more squall was coming. With a premonitory shiver for the months ahead, they went inside, pulled down books from the library shelves, and got in bed to read, restore their caloric energy, and take a long sleep.

Rain came tom-tomming again on the tin roof. "Listen," said Kientzy, "is that somebody yelling?" They sat up and heard far-off human cries. They went out with flashlights into the thunderstorm. The shouts came from under the cliff. They shone their torches down the wall and saw a small lifeboat with two men who were calling out in Italian. Delmas waved them over to the archaeological boom. Goiran ran out on the long spar and took a line from the boat. The divers helped the Italians up the ladder to the hut and gave them dry clothes and brandy. The story was pieced together in fragments of French and Italian.

The pair were from the motorship *Donatello D* of Reggio, which had left Marseilles that evening and lost her way in the blinding rain. She had run aground on Riou Island, the big sister of Grand Congloué. The rest of their crew had got ashore on the uninhabited island. These two men had volunteered to take a boat for help, and the first light they had seen was the window of Port Calypso.

As the tale unfolded, Delmas' eyes glittered. "It hasn't changed at all," he said. He shook his fist at Grand Congloué and Riou. "You one-eyed whores, you! You took Sestios' ship and you're still taking them!" The Italians were puzzled by the laughter that followed. Delmas tried to radiotelephone Marseilles but the storm had blanked the radio. He put the shipwrecked men in spare bunks and sat by the phone until the atmospherics had cleared.

Toward morning the Marseilles radiotelephonist brought the news to *Calypso*. Saôut sailed immediately. Several miles from Riou, the Calypsonians smelled turpentine. At dawn they arrived at the *Donatello D*. The new freighter was hanging by the stern from the rocks and her bow was sinking. Ten minutes later the *Donatello D*'s steel plates scraped and screamed; she went over to port and slid under to join the wine ship. A whaleboat ripped loose and was battered by flotsam shooting up from the wreck. As the rain ceased, the sea was covered with oil, cotton bales, barrels of turpentine, dunnage, and three-foot cakes of industrial wax.

As it always does after a heavy rain, the mistral came screeching in. Saôut sighted the *Donatello*'s crew waving their shirts on the ridge of Riou Island. Weaving in and out of wreckage in the rising sea, he took *Calypso* around to a small beach and lowered a launch, which brought them off safely. He gave the miserable Italian skipper the solace of his own quarters and put Goiran ashore with a tent and a rifle to guard the flotsam until the Coast Guard came.

The winds were down next morning and Falco went out in his bark, *Hou-Hop*. He found Goiran firmly enthroned as king of the island. They put on Aqua-Lungs to visit the freshest wreck in their experience. Seventy-five feet down they found the *Donatello D* lying over to port. They were disturbed at the sight of the shipshape, freshly painted vessel that, except for her list, looked as though she were in drydock at dusk instead of a total loss at the bottom of the sea. Rather than evoking the usual pensive and lyrical mood of a sunken ship, this one was as shocking as a corpse on a slab. The *Donatello D* did not yet belong to the sea.

There was still a certain amount of air trapped in the vessel, and she moved with the swell, groaning and creaking as if bemoaning her fate. Falco swam in the open starboard bridge door while Goiran went outside. They looked at each other through the clear windows. Falco was at the helm of a ship that would never move again. Goiran collected the ship's bell. Falco went into the captain's room and was startled when he saw himself in the bright full-length mirror. The divers left the *Donatello D,* caring not to go back again. Within a few hundred yards of each other they had seen their oldest and newest wrecks, divided by two millennia.

On the late summer day in 1956 that the *Andrea Doria* sank after colliding with the *Stockholm* off Nantucket, Massachusetts, I was thousands of miles away in the equatorial Atlantic. I did not know that two Calypsonians, Louis Malle and James Dugan, were organizing an expedition to make motion pictures of the sunken liner, or I would have cooled down their enthusiasm. Diving at least 160 feet in the open sea at the beginning of the autumn gales with an improvised outfit was too dangerous and expensive for even the optimum results that could be expected.

Dugan chartered a small diving tender, the *Samuel Jamieson,* in Hyannis and Frédéric Dumas flew to the States to lead the underwater team. The *Jamieson* was held in port by bad weather for six weeks. When the Calypsonians finally sailed for the wreck, they could expect to spend days finding her. But they had the luck of a glassy sea, and Dumas guided the tender along sinuous trails of oil bubbling from the *Andrea Doria*. Late in the afternoon he lodged a grapnel in the sunken ship.

With time for one reconnaissance dive before night, Malle loaded the camera with sensitive black-and-white film and went down the grapnel line with Dumas. He wanted to test exposures before starting four days of filming. They reached the white port flank of the liner, exulting over the unexpected clarity of the water. Malle shot Dumas swimming along the promenade deck, past empty lifeboat davits, and turning down into the open promenade to pick up an ash tray. They surfaced. While Malle developed the end of his film, Dumas reported, "Down there you are stupid with narcosis. You can only keep a small fire in your brain to get you out alive. She is deeper than she seems on the echograms." Malle came out of the darkroom, rejoicing over the clean-cut images on the film.

The *Samuel Jamieson* anchored over the liner for the night and raised wreck lights to warn off vessels. The boat was parked in one of the world's busiest ship crossroads. The crew pieced out the top of the anchor chain with hemp and placed a fire ax nearby. If a ship bore down on the *Samuel Jamieson,* they could cut and run. In the middle of the night a storm blew up so quickly that they had to cut away the anchor and retreat to Nantucket.

The wind blew for six days, during which time the *Samuel Jamieson's* charter expired. The owner had another charter that could not be postponed. Dugan borrowed a twin-motor sporting cruiser from an Ohio banker for the second attempt. Its echo sounder was not working. At the wreck area they found that their grapnel buoy had been blown away in the recent gale. Dumas studied the oil slicks. He spotted a cocktail olive in the water and said, "There she is." He put another grapnel in the *Andrea Doria.*

In contrast to the fine transparency of the first dive, this time Dumas and Malle found the wreck enveloped in a thick dark layer "like black coffee." Groping down through it, they met a strong current, which nearly blew them off the grapnel line. At the depth where they should have been landing on the white side of the *Andrea Doria,* their hands encountered nothing. They wondered if the wreck had collapsed or subsided in the storm. The brown fog could have been raised by resettlement of the ship. Dumas led on down into the zone of rapture.

Two hundred and fifteen feet down, Dumas halted. Just below was the giant dorsal fin of a whale or a basking shark moving along slowly in the particle-laden water. He lowered his foot and touched it. The object was a hard bronze screw blade. The particles were flowing past it. The divers were in the propeller cage of the *Andrea Doria.*

The screw was entangled with cables. They had enough cognition left to realize the danger of fouling themselves. It was hopeless to try to expose film in the brown murk. They started up. The ever-experimenting Dumas got out a small packet that was advertised to increase a deep diver's buoyancy for emergency ascent. He pulled the release to inflate it with CO_2, but the "safety pack" did not swell up. The pressure was too much for it. Dumas batted it ahead until the pack finally inflated.

On deck Malle stripped off his rubber helmet. His companions gasped. One side of his head was matted with blood and powder. The pressure had perforated his ear drum. The *Doria* expedition was finished. It had obtained eighteen seconds of underwater film.

Dumas said, "The sea owns the *Doria* now. She's a real wreck. The first film of algae has settled on the paint. She will never be raised. I don't think divers will ever get into the only important places—the first-class bank and the purser's office. They are on starboard, pressed against the bottom near the big collision hole."

The Nantucket shoals of antiquity, where shipwrecks were most numerous, were unquestionably the home waters of early commerce and naval warfare among the Greek and Turkish islands. In the summer of 1953 *Calypso* made an archaeological reconnaissance in the Aegean Sea.

On the way our sonar registered a 13,000-foot deep southwest of Zante Island in the Ionian Sea. In order to survey it, we steamed on to make a fix on a lighthouse on the south cape of Zante. We found a cape but no lighthouse. I said to Saôut, "According to the chart, this must be the place. Log it as the lighthouse, and turn back to the deep." After two days of charting we reached the island of Antikythera to begin archaeological scouting. There we learned that Zante had been devastated by an earthquake that toppled the lighthouse a few hours before *Calypso* arrived. In our preoccupation with things at sea we sometimes miss events on shore.

Antikythera is an impoverished island with one claim to attention—it was the cradle of the infant art of submarine archaeology. In 1901 Greek navy men and sponge divers recovered Greek bronzes and marbles attributed to a Roman plunder ship that sank fourscore years before Christ. The shrine—it seemed that to us—lay deep under a cliff in the most transparent water we have encountered in the Mediterranean. Through a mask on the surface we could see the buglike Aqua-Lungers crawling across the floor 172 feet below.

Dumas and I went down to estimate the size and position of the wreck. While I hung overhead, Dumas swam around the ship mound, picking up a pottery shard, planing up fifteen feet for a general view, darting back down to turn over another artifact, and re-creating the outlines of the ship with gestures. We rigged a short submerged suction pipe and excavated shallow holes that confirmed his guesses. However, we were not trying to resume the old excavation. We were merely pilgrims to the scene of discovery. It was evident that the hardhat divers had thoroughly skinned the site but had not done much excavation. Later we saw their recoveries in the museum at Athens: the famous bronze Ephebus, and tons of marble gods and nymphs, allegorical figures and horses. The marbles were disfigured by shellfish, which showed that the carvings were found lying on the bottom exposed to water. They had simply been slung to the surface. It is likely that the Antikythera mound still contains virginal Greek sculptures.

To find Aegean wrecks, we followed the old trade routes. Any reef or cape that looked treacherous to us may have been fatal to the ancients, so we dived on it. At every spot we found the litter of an old ship and, on several, signs of two or more. Under one frothing reef, the story of Grand Congloué and Riou was repeated by a small iron steamer resting on a field of amphorae. In anchorage, when we went for a mask swim in the evening, we looked down on potsherds scattered on the rocks. These shallow wrecks were beyond salvage; surge and wave had long since ground the ship to pieces against the rocks.

On a single dive off Crete, Falco swam through perhaps four thousand years of history. At a depth of 125 feet he came upon a heap of spherical Byzantine amphorae and, along the slope fifteen feet deeper, another mound of cargo jars associated with an earlier Christian century. Around 150 feet down he found piles of bronze dishes. He did not disturb them, wishing to leave *in situ* evidence for future archaeologists. At a depth of 170 feet Falco encountered a mass of round-bellied amphorae, identical with a type Sir Arthur Evans dug up at Knossos. The half-hour descent through liquid time—from *Calypso* to the Bronze Age—symbolized for us the lavish opportunity for archaeology in the Aegean.

Professor Benoît asked me to salvage a first-century B.C. wreck discovered in 1959 off St. Raphael on a flat bottom 115 feet down. He was afraid that looting would erase the ship before archaeology could intervene. I told him, "Seagoing research is *Calypso*'s business. I can't tie her down as an archaeological hoist boat. But I'll assign the *Espadon* to you for two months." She was a new research vessel, an ex-trawler, refitted for our laboratory in Marseilles.

The project was carried out by our O.F.R.S. team, with Alexis Sivirine as technical director and Henri Goiran as chief diver, working with archaeologist J. M. Rouquette. They took Dumas' advice on how to gain the most knowledge in the least time. The divers first picked up the broken potsherds and placed them in sorted piles beside the wreck. This revealed the outlines of the buried vessel, a modest craft of the 1500-amphora class. They rigged a suction pipe and cut thirteen feet down through the keel amidships, bringing up only unique and type specimens and setting duplicate finds aside on the sea floor. The O.F.R.S. completed a neat job within two months, systematically photographing and charting as the trench went down. The St. Raphael wreck gave valuable new information on the joinery of ancient wooden ships.

Because so little state money is available for marine archaeology, Benoît had to be content with Sivirine's report and abandon the St. Raphael ship to souvenir hunters. Today, after less than two decades of Aqua-Lung diving, it is an unprepossessing Riviera restaurant or villa that does not have a classic urn from the sea. Once a Hollywood art dealer cabled me to quote prices on three hundred amphorae. Collectomania may thwart the future of underwater archaeology before those who could sponsor it are aware of what opportunities are slipping by.

While *Calypso* called in at Bizerte, authorities of the French Naval Base in Tunisia asked us if we could dive and report on a French submarine fallen south of the Kerkenna Islands during World War II. Delmas and I took along my thirteen-year-old son, Philippe, who already had nine years of Aqua-Lung experience. Before we went down the ladder, I told the boy, "This is a serious dive. The submarine is one hundred feet down. You must agree to stay with me at all times." The water was milky, and Philippe restrained his impulses to break away like an adolescent porpoise. He swam alongside me, imitating the languid leg strokes of Dumas. Near the floor the water cleared, and we saw the submarine below.

She was broken in two in front of the conning tower. The fore section was torn open in a chaos of pipes, trunks, and plates, which had become the nursery of hundreds of lively ten-pound groupers. Unabashedly they swam with us, taking playful nips at our foot fins. Philippe hooted and pointed to an exploded torpedo lying in the sand alongside the wreck, only recognizable by its intact counter-rotating propellers. It had struck the submarine amidships. There lay our report to the navy on what had happened to the submarine. The after section—conning tower and control room—

was undamaged. The hatches were closed; many of the crew were still inside. Gray triggerfish thronged around the stern, metrically waving their dorsal and ventral fins like a funeral chorus. I looked at my watch and grabbed Philippe's arm to go up. Delmas stayed down awhile longer. When he came aboard, he carried the submarine's bell. He had found it in the sand twenty feet from the wreck.

We had long anticipated looking at a wreck deep in coral seas. Our experience had been limited to half-sunken hulks that had run up on Indian Ocean reefs. At Providence Island we had found large groupers living in the toppled hollow mainmast of a flattened wreck. At Farquar, an older ship had been peeled down to the rusted boiler and steam engine, crouched like a prehistoric beast in the blue water. Swimming under these purgatorial wrecks was dangerous. There was a blinding sunlit surge that could drive one against jagged plates. I wondered how the residents—long tiger fish with horizontal yellow-and-black stripes—could stay so phlegmatic in the thrashing water. However, as for tropical wrecks, Providence and Farquar were just appetizers. We wanted a big deep one.

During a *Calypso* southbound passage through the Gulf of Suez, Dumas and I red-penciled promising wrecks shown on the nautical charts. The main problem with charted wrecks is that they are sometimes shown as much as six miles from their actual position. We found a promising wreck on the chart; it was in 103 feet of water on a flat bottom off the Sinai Peninsula.

Laban prepared a large-scale chart with polar coordinates centered on the tongue of the outer reef at Sha'ab Ali. There we anchored a launch with a barrel radar target that *Calypso* could pick up seven miles away. We made zigzag sweeps, correlating radar distances and gyrocompass bearings every half-minute to pinpoint position on Laban's concentric chart.

I supervised the six-man search team. Henri Plé, eyes buried in the black rubber radar hood, sang out distance and direction from the barrel target. Saôut manned the telegraph and relayed Plé's data to Laban at the chart table. Dumas was on sonar. I called maneuvers to Maurice Léandri at the helm. *Calypso* plodded back and forth for several hours, occasionally running over a bump rising on the floor, but none high enough to be a ship. The chart maker's nice flat floor was liberally supplied with coral mounds.

I said, "If the wreck is big enough to be marked as a menace to navigation, it must stand fairly high."

Dumas and I had a simultaneous thought. He expressed it. "Of course! We should have a man in the underwater chamber. You can probably see the top of the ship from there."

I said, "Why not go down yourself? I'll stay on sonar."

He disappeared down the tube. On the intercom he said, "I'm set. We have about sixty-foot visibility."

"We can't miss it," I said.

Fifteen minutes later, I got a steeper and higher shape on the echogram. "Dumas, do you see anything?" I said into the microphone.

His voice came back, hollowed by the steel cell. "No. But the color of the water changed for a while. It seemed to be lit from below."

"It must be her," I said. "Look sharp. I'll turn back on a close parallel run."

On the reciprocating course, before anything showed on sonar, Dumas said, "There she is. I see her topmast." Laban drew a triumphant red circle on his chart, and we threw a marker buoy over. *Calypso* crossed and re-crossed the wreck several times to assemble her dimensions and position from the echograms. The wreck was over three hundred feet long. I had the impression she was fairly intact. We anchored alongside her.

The sun was low in Egypt. There was time for only one dive before dark. Dumas and Falco got into Aqua-Lungs. "Just take a good look," I said, "and decide whether she's worth some time on our way back." They went down the ladder, and the rest of us idled at the fantail, awaiting the news. After twenty minutes the reconnaissance team surfaced, slipped their mouth grips, and started laughing. They ignored us while they roared over some secret they had shared.

The twosome climbed the ladder and walked past us, shaking with laughter. They took their gear off. "What goes on?" I said. "Let us in on it." This started them off on a fresh round of guffaws.

At last Falco said, "The Thing! It's enormous!"

I said, "That shows on sonar. What's funny about a big ship?"

"Not the ship," Dumas said. "The Thing. A fish."

The two men realized their audience was on tenterhooks, so they gave a straight report. "The top hamper is still standing," said Dumas. "She is almost upright with a small list to port. There are a bunch of railway freight cars on the foredeck."

"Did you look over the afterquarters?" I asked.

That set them off again. Between chortles Falco managed to say, "No, Commandant. The fish wouldn't let us."

I asked, "What, a shark?"

"It's not a shark," Dumas answered.

The story finally came out. They swam over the wheelhouse, and looked aft. There the deck had been mangled in an explosion. They dived off the wheelhouse for closer inspection.

Then they saw the Thing. It was a prodigious dark-green wall of flesh, a single slab-sided animal that barred their progress aft. Dumas and Falco were stupefied. It was beyond the remotest connection with any fish they had ever seen. Dumas said, "There were army trucks on the deck. When the Thing passed near them, it seemed as big as a truck. I'll give you a very sober estimate that it was twelve to fifteen feet long and seven to eight feet high. Eh, Falco?"

The other reliable man said, "At least. Its height was formidable. When I swam toward it, each scale of that fish was as big as my hand. When I got to about fifteen feet away, the fish turned toward me."

Dumas continued, "It started toward Falco. We backed into the alleyway on the mainhouse where it couldn't get at us."

I said, "How do you mean?"

Dumas said, "I mean the fish was too big to pass into the alley."

Falco said, "When it came quite close, its lips looked as big and fat as a life buoy. It had lids on its eyes and a very dangerous look."

The divers ran out their depth time peering at the colossus; they swam forward in the alleyway and surfaced, bursting with emotions engendered by the Thing.

We hauled anchor. We had to sail on. After dinner I took Dumas and Falco to my quarters and pulled out atlases and catalogues of the world's marine fishes. They paused for some time over a picture of the large Red Sea parrot fish we called the bumpfish. "No," Falco said. "That's not it."

Dumas added, "The silhouette is something like it, but this is not the bumpfish. Anyway, we have never seen a bumpfish more than four feet long."

By this time we were calling the Thing the truckfish. Dumas turned from the reference books and sank into thought. "I hesitate to say it," he said, "it's so ridiculous, but the truckfish looks a lot like a wrasse."

Falco added, "That's exactly what I think, but I've never seen a wrasse more than three feet long."

"It's out of the question," said Dumas. "It's a truckfish, that's all."

Falco mused, "He acted as though he owned the wreck."

"Well, maybe we'll have some fun with him when we come back," I said.

Three months later we hit the Sinai wreck on our first sonar pass, thanks to Laban's chart, and lowered the hook. I staked out three days to explore and film the wreck—and also, we all hoped, to film the truckfish. There were some people on board who grinned crookedly when they said "truckfish," which irritated Falco and Dumas. I paired with Dumas for three film dives a day. While I was handling the camera, preoccupied with choosing angles, framing, panning and pushing it along on the free-following shots you get in the sea, I could still enjoy a thrill that had been mine for twenty years— Dumas, the manfish, in all of his experience and grace, swimming in our new haunt. He appeared above the bow, hovered with his arms to his sides, and headed languidly across the petrified ship.

The windlass on the foredeck had been turned into a garden; the hard edges of the gear teeth were softened by fronds and filaments. Just abaft the capstan, the bronze bell hung from a standard that was thickly dressed with bryozoans. On the bell grew a single perfect pearl oyster. Dumas drew his knife and rapped the bell. A chime rang through the sea, and a blue angel-fish jumped out of the bell. Around us in the plankton fog there were masses of crumpled metal—railway tank cars lashed down on the well deck, which had imploded under water pressure.

The main hatch cover was missing. It had probably floated off during the sinking. Didi gave himself a pull on the hatch coaming and glided, motion-less, thirty feet down into the hold. I followed his bubbles. The place was jammed with war matériel: sea-changed trucks fender to fender, filled with motorcycles hub to hub, and inserted between, fighter aircraft wings. We shined our flashlights and brought coral colors out of the dark. From every-thing we touched there scurried frightened fish—the rats of this forsaken garage.

Dumas turned upward and I followed his footbeats into the light. He swam straight up before the bridge house and stopped at the builder's plate. He wiped it off and we read:

> Joseph L. Thompson & Sons, Ltd.
> North Sands Shipbuilding Yard, No. 599
> Manor Quay Works, 1940, Sunderland

She was a British vessel, a wartime product quite new when she was sunk.

We continued to the top of the wheelhouse, where there stood a tall radio direction-finder attended by vigorous and fearless gray porgies. An aviary of damselfish fluttered through the loop antenna. We turned around the bridge wings and found the port and starboard wheelhouse doors closed. The square bridge windows were broken, but the circular ports were merely cracked in star shapes, as though struck by hammers. Dumas grasped the knob on the starboard door. It seemed odd that he should expect the door to open, but open it did; the hinges gave way and the door fell toward him in slow motion.

He held on to the doorframe, and we looked into the tenebrous wheel-house, not quite ready to push further into this mysterious tragedy. The traditional tidiness of the bridge was replaced by the disorder of a major explosion. Wires hung in garlands from the overhead, the compass was shattered, and the deck was covered by a foot of debris—chronometers, sex-tants, binoculars, and uprooted electric switch boxes, mingled with years of sea-dust. The wheelhouse was not uninhabited. In the corners there were scorpion fish and groupers swimming in and out through the broken windows. We gave ourselves a pull on the doorframe to slide in without kicking up sediments.

We came to the door of the captain's quarters, leading aft from the bridge. It would not open, so we forced it off its hinges. The door sank slowly into a pitch-dark room. Again we hesitated, like children about to dare a haunted house. After all, a ship that held a truckfish might be the home of monsters of the dark. Shining our flashlights ahead, we entered the captain's quarters.

His two rooms were in wild disorder. On the floor in a layer of sludge were scattered porcelain dishes, bearing the owner's flag, and corroded silver-ware. There was a litter of bottles, some of which, corked and half full of air, were clinging to the ceiling. As we looked up at the captain's aging cellar, our exhalations pooled overhead in a quicksilver mirror that distorted our reflections. Dumas ran his hands over a solid rectangular object attached to the bulkhead, and we exchanged a glance of recognition; everything else may have come loose in the explosion, but the captain's safe was intact, still bolted to the wall.

We left the bridge house and dived into the open alleyway leading aft. The deck was almost solidly paved with pearl oysters. They hung from the standing rigging and clung to the rails, distorting the form of familiar things. It reminded me of one of the "Pearly Kings," a button-covered costermonger that I had seen in London when I was a boy.

Behind the wheelhouse we crossed the wide explosion hole. Dumas ex-tended his arms and pantomimed an enormous shape, and I understood that this was where he and Falco had met the truckfish. But it was nowhere in sight today.

A hundred-foot expanse of the afterdeck was almost unrecognizable as a ship. The explosion had almost cut her in half. The mutilated plates were twisted and rippled like kelp. Here and there we saw shining black automobile tires and sea boots, unimpaired by the fire, the sea and the years. A four-inch gun had been gaily converted to peace by nosegays of polyps; its shells were cemented to the scuppers by coral. We swam over the devastation to the after section, which was twisted to port and tilted up.

We arched over the stern and saw the great propeller plunged in gray sand. Fish swirled around it like waves of the sea. We returned to the foremast and ascended it slowly, our exhalations mushrooming overhead around the tall pole. From the crow's nest it was only fifteen feet to the sun and *Calypso*.

Relays of men went down to the wreck from first light to dusk. Toward evening of the first day Malle and Luis Marden saw the truckfish near the explosion hole. This time the vast animal was not inquisitive. It left the ship before they could photograph it. Their observations, added to those of Falco and Dumas, convinced us that it was in truth a wrasse, *Cheilinus undulatus*. Why in the world had this commonplace animal taken such a Brobdignagian leap in size? The general behavior pattern of the wrasse was to move off the rails when we appeared and circle the ship restlessly, waiting for us to leave. On the third morning two divers came up shouting that another truckfish had joined the giant. It was smaller—only eight or nine feet long to the other's thirteen feet. The big one and the "pickup" truckfish remained together throughout the last day.

We made up four-man camera teams, with two divers to carry flood lamps, to record close-ups of the dated organic growths on the freighter. The last movie sequence called for Dumas to unveil the name of the ship. We trained the lights on the ship's bell, which glowed rich and rosy in its coralline robe. Dumas scraped away the oyster, corals, and sponges, bringing out the inscription: S.S. *Thistlegorm,* Glasgow.

Later Marden wrote to the builders, asking for information on the *Thistlegorm*. Thompson & Sons replied with an account by the surviving Third Engineer, H. A. Bansall. The ship met her end on October 6, 1941, while carrying vital arms to the British Eighth Army. Because the Axis then practically controlled the Mediterranean, the *Thistlegorm* was routed from England around the Cape of Good Hope through the Indian Ocean to Egypt.

Moving up the Red Sea in convoy with twenty other supply ships, the *Thistlegorm* was forced to anchor in sight of Mount Sinai to await admission to the Suez Canal.

German planes from Crete raided the anchorage and dropped two bombs on the *Thistlegorm*'s afterdeck. They exploded in the munition-packed afterhold. In the blast nine of the forty-nine-man crew were killed. The others jumped overboard. A wounded gunner was left behind on the flaming deck. Able-bodied Seaman Angus McLeay ran to him barefooted over the red-hot plates and carried him forward to a lifeboat. For this act McLeay was awarded the George Cross, Britain's highest honor for a noncombatant deed of valor.

As I was about to haul anchor to leave the *Thistlegorm*, Delmas said, "Quite a few of the fellows would like to bring up the captain's safe before we go." I had been afraid of this ever since Dumas' avid hands had first caressed the strongbox. Bringing up treasure was contrary to the spirit of *Calypso*. I had often discussed this treasure-chest business with Dumas, Laban, and Dugan, who agreed with me that it would only bring complications. But there was a splendid glow of cupidity in Delmas' eyes, and over his shoulder I could see his anxious partners hanging on my reply.

"We don't have time to bring it up," I said.

Delmas replied, "I have everything lined up. I guarantee we'll do it in a half-hour."

I didn't think they could do it in a half-day, so I said, "Okay, I'll give you an hour. Then we sail." With that, several treasure hunters plunged into the water while the rest whipped down cables and rigged the winch. They really had it planned. The captain's safe was on board in twenty minutes.

As they stood around it, licking their lips, it was my move again. I said, "Of course you realize our responsibility. We are not pirates. If we open this safe, we must report to the naval authorities and account for everything we find in it. Then we must wait for a court to adjudicate the salvage award. You must name delegates to see that it is done fairly and honorably." They elected a committee headed by Henri Plé and settled on equal shares for all. René Robino moved in with a chisel to force the strongbox. It was covered by a stinking, black, gluelike substance and, soon, so was Robino.

He knocked the door off. Forcing his hand through a wall of human heads, Plé reached in and pulled out a cylinder of soggy paper. He peeled off the outside layers, exposing a roll of sonar charts. The treasure hunters giggled nervously.

Plé removed a small drawer. In it was a rotten leather wallet. With trembling fingers he emptied one of its compartments. It contained the captain's membership cards and some receipts for port dues. From the last fold Plé drew a Canadian two-dollar bill and an English pound note. There was nothing else in the safe.

I said, "Now, draw up your declaration. If you are ever awarded the usual half, you'll have $2.40 to split among yourselves." Plé smoothed out the wet notes on a lab table. In the morning he found the money dried into tiny flakes.

chapter
seven

PULSE
OF
THE OCEAN

In the Mediterranean, night comes swiftly after sunset. On this particular nightfall *Calypso* was sailing east along the Île de Levant. I cut the engines a mile south of Titan light, the rays of which swept a glassy sea. On the intercom I said, "Fantail. Engines stopped. Depth, three thousand feet. Get ready for Station Twelve." The floor was etched heavily on the sonar graph. Above it there were several less distinct streaks in the water, and they were rising, as they do every evening. The climbing lines were the oceanic mystery of the century.

I went out on the bridge wing. The surface of the dark sea was ablaze with phosphorescent spatterings. Uncounted hordes of tiny bodies were leaping a few inches in the air and falling back with a soft sizzling sound. It was like rain turned upside down. Most likely the creatures were infant squids or octopuses that had risen to feed in the superficial layer during the night. At dawn they would flee to the deeps again. Station Twelve was another attempt to understand such daily vertical migrations of marine life—migrations that had been established by echo sounding as the pulse of the animate sea.

During World War II, when sonar spread through the world fleet, a ship would be pinging along a six-thousand-foot floor when one or more "false bottoms" would suddenly be registered at, say, five hundred, eight hundred, and eleven hundred feet. They were called "deep scattering layers" (DSL), and they occurred unpredictably everywhere and nowhere in the oceans. Detailed sonar probes revealed that the DSL rose at night and descended by day. Theories about them were as prevalent as evidence was absent. Those who suspected that echo-sound impulses were being scattered by chemical or thermal rifts in the water were overruled by biologists. Since the DSL went up and down rhythmically, responding to penetration of natural light, it must be animal. The layers were deeper on bright days than on cloudy ones. When the DSL climbed at night, it stayed deeper at full moon than in other lunar phases or on cloudy nights. Military experts became fanatical about the DSL; often its trace was thick enough to conceal a submarine from antisubmarine sonar on the surface.

When first attracted to the DSL, I knew that Aqua-Lungers, because of their two-hundred-foot limit, could not contribute to the question. I was then actively supporting Professor Auguste Piccard's bathyscaph invention, which could sink men to the average depth of the sea—about thirteen thousand feet down. The French navy was building the first practical model, *F.N.R.S.-3*, and Piccard was constructing the bathyscaph *Trieste* in Italy. However, it was questionable whether or not these clumsy and expensive deep-boats could solve the mystery of the deep scattering layers. I thought cameras should be sent ahead of bathyscaphs. Americans were already lowering depth cameras several miles. I looked into this activity and found the answer in Boston, Massachusetts.

Melville Grosvenor introduced me to Harold E. Edgerton, Professor of Electrical Measurements at the Massachusetts Institute of Technology. Edgerton was the main innovator of electronic flash photography, with which he had been stalking tame prizefighters and wild hummingbirds. He was already involved with undersea applications, too. Our first meeting established a lasting friendship.

Calypso's campaign to understand vertical migrations and the mysterious DSL began near Corsica in 1953. Professor Edgerton, his son Robert, engineer Laban, and electrician Paul Martin were on the afterdeck, puttering with the depth cameras. Each camera consisted of a frame holding two steel tubes. In one tube were the electronic flash lamp, capacitator, and batteries; in the other was a camera loaded with a hundred-foot spool of movie film. The tubes were angled toward each other so that the flash would light a water area six feet from the lens. Shutter and flash were synchronized to click off eight hundred shots at fifteen-second intervals.

When Edgerton was ready, *Calypso* moved out to a depth of six thousand feet, where three tiers of DSL showed on sonar. The thickest layer was 514 feet down. We lowered a camera and tracked it on sonar. When it reached the five-hundred-foot layer, we stopped the winch, and the DSL completely swallowed the camera trace. We soaked the camera for a half-hour, then lowered it slowly into the deeper DSL. Then we hauled it up and stored the negative for a professional darkroom ashore.

That summer we made seventeen DSL camera stations from Sardinia to Greece. Since Edgerton rated the camera's pressure-resistance at three thousand feet, he sent one to that level as a practical test. He got back a flash tube flattened by pressure. Edgerton accepted the fact with a smile. He disassembled the wreckage, including two softwood lathes that he had used as wedges. Sea pressure had turned them hard as ebony. He rattled the wedges—and afterward used them as castanets in the ship's orchestra. By now these two cheerful Americans, father and son, were known on board as "Papa Flash" and "Petit Flash."

Camera lowerings at night were spectacular. Leaning over the side, we could see the explosions of light below to a depth of five hundred feet. When we hauled the rig to the surface, the flashes came like submarine lightning. I tried to imagine the effect of these light bursts on creatures in the eternal dark below.

After the cruise Papa Flash and I tackled the job of cataloguing thirteen thousand midwater photos, the results of our first inner-space survey. We ran the reels through a film editor; while one called off the contents of pictures, the other took notes. Since neither of us was a marine biologist, the notes went something like, "Reel five, Matapan—Shot 427—bugs." We used such terms as "strings," "dots," and "grapes." Experts could later give proper names to them. "Bugs" were tiny copepods. "Strings" were filaments of siphonophores. "Dots" were anything from eggs to dead matter.

We found a number of genuine deep-sea monsters in the DSL. True, they were only small, silver-plated *Argyropelecus*, or hatchet fish, but a photo enlargement of their bulging eyes, saber-toothed-tiger jaws, and bellies covered with luminous nodules would scare a side-show crowd.

A DSL station in the Villefranche canyon produced an astonishing inventory from a stratum one hundred feet thick and one thousand feet down. The statistical evidence was that there was one pretty medusa per cubic yard in this DSL. Evening shots showed them all oriented upward—they were rising. In the morning pictures their crowns were inverted—they were going down. They were accompanied by crustaceans, arrow worms, and other unidentified creatures in the endless rise and fall of life layers.

Further down, darkness prevailed day and night and we did not expect such a density of animals. Yet when we put Edgerton's cameras in the black depths, we found that *density of plankton increased* below the DSL, in the 2300- to 3500-foot level, but this did not show on the echo sounder. The photographs were crammed with white corpuscles—the very image of outer space as seen through a large reflecting telescope. I remembered that two men—and two only—Dr. William Beebe and Otis Barton, had seen this layer with their own eyes from Barton's bathysphere. Both had reported that the density of micro-organisms increased with depth. Science had paid no attention to this upsetting datum. Our cameras seemed to confirm it.

Of course, a goodly percentage of the white dots were lifeless—molted shrimp shells, excreta, corpses of diatoms, and other waste matter that was barely heavier than water and might take months to settle on the floor. Once they were settled, bacteria would transform the dead matter into nutrient salts; then deep currents, the plows of the sea, would return them to the cycle of life.

Edgerton and I were disappointed by the scarcity of larger aquatic animals in the midwater photographs. I found an explanation for this in the Indian Ocean. One evening the sonar graph reported a very thick scattering layer in four hundred feet of water. I stopped *Calypso* and shot Edgerton's camera into it. I watched the winking tube sink down the graph paper. As it neared the DSL, the thick trace vanished. I had the winchman continue lowering deeper. The 400-foot DSL returned to life as thick as before, erasing the camera's image. Here were animals that quickly dodged the alien camera and reassembled when it went deeper. I could not believe they were the usual feeble medusas or drifting plankton and siphonophores. The flash may have alerted them, or perhaps the faint hum of the camera motor, sounding like a fire alarm to them, or even the slight pressure waves ahead of the descending rig. At any rate, here was proof that closely-packed, fast-moving creatures also formed a DSL.

Over the winter we installed an air-conditioned professional photolab on *Calypso* in order to look at DSL results immediately. In Boston, Papa Flash built new weapons. He turned up for the second campaign with a silhouette camera in which the flash and camera tubes faced each other at a one-inch interval. His idea was to produce a sharp outline of any micro-organisms that drifted into this small disk of water. We put the new rig into the populous half-mile layer. In eight hundred pictures we caught only one small copepod and a number of indecipherable dots. What in the devil was wrong? We had a crazy thought: were the little creatures avoiding the aperture because it looked like a mouth?

At once, Edgerton remounted the tubes at right angles, so that the flash crossed the short-focused lens. We ducked the revised camera, and it brought up plenty of little animals. But the enlargements presented a new riddle. Many of the dots were blurred. Looking closer, we saw that they had comet tails. They were moving. Edgerton's electronic flash lasted about three-thousandths of a second, and the "bugs" were one to four inches from the lens. He computed that they were traveling at a velocity of three to ten feet per second! Even the midges of the ocean were fully capable of dodging the camera. High-speed micro-organisms and athletic fish alike kept clear of lowered instruments. Where did this leave the oceanographers who relied on plankton nets to give them an idea of life distribution in the dark below?

For several months I thought of how to counterattack these artful dodgers. I proposed to Edgerton a new camera adventure: "dynamic depth photography." Instead of lowering cameras that telegraphed their presence ahead, we would sneak up on the crowd with a camera mounted on a glider towed by *Calypso*. Edgerton's M.I.T. laboratory turned into a camera factory, working up still, stereographic, and motion picture cameras for the dynamic flash experiment. At the O.F.R.S., Commandant Jean Alinat and André Laban built a glider assembly—a streamlined affair with a powerful downward thrust furnished by a hydrofoil like that used on a minesweeper's cable cutter. *Calypso* could tow it at a speed of six knots.

The first tests of the camera glider produced plenty of empty black water, but from time to time we surprised dense assemblies of shrimps and obtained a movie of a deep school of squids dispersing into flight twelve feet ahead of the camera. Now we were breaking through into the bigger mobile crowd in the DSL.

Along came another ingenious recorder to dangle into the sea—a device that measured bioluminescence. It was virtually an underwater photomulti-plier, built by Dr. George L. Clarke of Harvard University and his assistant, Lloyd Breslau.

Papa Flash sent them to *Calypso* to try it out in the Mediterranean. The light meter's support wire contained electrical cables to transmit its findings to the surface. The tiniest flash of light from the weakest bioluminescent animal could be picked up instantly. Clarke had already recorded phos-phorescent animals two miles under the Atlantic, close to the mean depth of the oceans. We placed both *Calypso* and a smaller research vessel, the *Winaretta Singer*, at his disposal for lowerings between Monaco and Corsica. It was fascinating to stand in the chart room and watch Clarke's recorder stylus leap up and down at different intensities and intervals, which were apparently related to depth. A surprisingly large volume of lighted animals registered on the graph. Even in the poorest area of luminescent life—below six thousand feet—hardly two seconds went by without a flash.

Clarke also wanted to see what manner of animals were setting off the fireworks, so he and Breslau made a rack for his meter and an Edgerton flash camera, with the lens oriented toward the same phenomenon as the meter was recording. The two instruments were linked so that a light hitting the meter would simultaneously trigger the flash camera. Thus the luminous animal would take its own picture. We put the rig down. Clarke's dials reported showers of meteors pouring into the light meter. Bernard Marcel-lin, our radio engineer, who had helped connect the camera, was rubbing his hands over what we were going to see in the photographs. When they came from the darkroom, however, there was no sizable form of life in a single one of the several hundred photos.

Completely at a loss to explain the disparity between what the meter felt and the camera saw, we continued to drop the rig, but always with the same glaring contradiction. One night the meter really went crazy, reporting several times as much light below as we had seen before. *Calypso* was rolling in a rough sea, but everyone crowded around to see the needle jump. I took a lurch with the ship, and it shook a clue loose in my head.

As a diver, I was familiar with passing through *Noctiluca* and other zooplanktons that created constellations around my body. The slightest physical contact or pressure wave lighted them up. Dr. Clarke's device, I thought, might be recording not only the animals that lighted up spon-taneously in the water, but also the light coming from the irritation that it, an alien body, was producing in the phosphorescent creatures. Because of the rough sea, the meter was jiggling up and down in the water and tripling the effect. There was a simultaneous rhythm to the bounce of the ship and the sweep of the needle.

To see if this was true, I docked *Calypso* at Calvi in placid water at night. We submerged the meter from the hydraulic crane and went under water. The craneman dipped the unit up and down, simulating the pitching of the ship. A glowing nebula formed around the meter when it was moving and faded when it was stationary. That's the sort of thing you are up against with robot depth devices.

As our DSL evidence accumulated, we became aware that a moving layer sometimes broke into a series of layers, as if several schooled species were separating, each according to its own sensitivity to light. The vertical migrations never started deeper than 1500 feet, beyond which hardly any light ever penetrated. There was no reason at the time to suspect the rise and fall of layers below. However, we had to change our mind about that, too, when we reached Madeira.

To most visitors Madeira is a charming holiday island. To us it was a small mountain range marooned far at sea, crowded with 350,000 people dependent for life upon a deep-sea monster, a single species of fish, *Aphanopus carbo*—or the "espada," as the islanders called it. The immediate coastline of Madeira was practically fished out many years ago. The men were forced out to the deep, where they found the espada at night. We accompanied three men and a boy in a graceful sailboat on a nocturnal hunt. Four miles out, where the base of the island slopes to ten thousand feet, they furled sail and set two lines a mile long and weighted with stones. One hung from the bow, one from the stern, and they were baited with squid on hundreds of hooks. During the three hours the lines were down, the fisherfolk kept a torch lighted to attract squids, which they jigged for next day's baits.

On each line they hauled up at least twenty-five espadas weighing an average of ten pounds each. The fish was satanic; it looked something like a black barracuda with fiery glints on its hide. It had saber teeth and huge green eyes. The espada, the only deep-sea monstrosity of economic significance, has been fished only near Madeira. Some of the fishermen have been induced by the Portuguese government to try for it in the Bay of Biscay and other places, but practically none were caught. A most interesting thing about *Aphanopus carbo*—and a lucky thing for the Madeirans—was that for generations past it had been yielding the same reliable harvest every night.

There was no moon the night I was out with the espada fleet. The skipper said, "When the moon is shining, we have to fish fifteen hundred feet deeper than this. But when the moon goes behind a cloud, we have to haul back up to a mile depth to find the fish." This staggering announcement was made in matter-of-fact tones by a man who had fished espada for twenty-five years and fished nothing else. It upset my notions about vertical migrations. Here, apparently, pale moonlight was affecting the behavior of fish a mile down, while far brighter sunlight had no effect more than a half-mile down. How did the espada respond to moonlight that did not possibly reach its depth?

I wondered if the fish's climb might not be induced by a chain of movement above it. For instance, plankton in the upper layer could be moving up and down according to the brightness of the moon, while below, at the edge of complete darkness, fish that prey on plankton might be following it up and down. Therefore the espadas, who feed on the second or third layer of fish, would be responding to the pattern although moving in total darkness below.

Temperature also influences the vertical displacement of fish. In the Mediterranean the temperature below one thousand feet is a uniform 55½° Fahrenheit all the year round from the Pillars of Hercules to the Golden Horn. The Gibraltar sill, one thousand feet deep, seems to form a dam of permanently stable bottom-water temperature. In the upper layer, however, the temperature varies sharply from 40°F. in winter to as high as 80°F. in summer. In mid-April there occurs what is known as the Day of Homothermy—an event of surprise and tragedy. On that day the temperature from the surface to the floor is equalized at 55°. On the nights before and after Homothermy, deep dwellers come to the surface from the second and third life layers. Most of them die of decompression. The sea is strewn with miniature dead dragons, as nature, on this single day, removes the guard rails that have kept fish safe in their own depths.

chapter
eight

BLOOD
LIKE
OURS

Simone and I turned out, feeling underfoot the
first long, indolent swells of the Indian Ocean. We went to the port
rail, yawning and stretching, and looked at the burnt, bare-boned Hadramaut Coast of Arabia. *Calypso* was on an easting in the Sea of Oman.

The phone rang in my quarters. In urgent tones, unusual for him, Saôut
said, "Can you come to the bridge?" I found him thumbing through our
largest-scale charts. "There is no reef here," the skipper announced.

"What reef?" I demanded.

"A tremendous reef—thick, white water dead ahead," he replied.

I bounded to the wheelhouse and took up my binoculars. Some miles
ahead, there was a barrier of foam across the horizon. "There can't be a
reef here in the ship lane," I said.

"Then what is it?" Saôut asked.

I replied, "Stay on course. We'll find out."

The reef seemed to sway. A half-mile from it we saw that the splashing breakers were composed of leaping dolphins, the most formidable host that either Saôut or I had seen in a quarter of a century at sea. He rang the bridgehouse bell to rouse out everyone to see them. The dolphin army wheeled and charged toward us in a storm comber that erupted twisting black bodies into the air. A nation of dolphins had gone mad before our eyes.

Dolphins, of course, are air-breathing mammals, and we were familiar with their light, measured prancing into the air to breathe. But these were shooting vertically high out of the water, bending and contorting in the leap. It was a mass high-jump contest, a bridal feast, or a frenzied victory celebration after some unknown war in the deep. We jostled each other in the companionways, running for cameras and scrambling for the high bridge and the underwater observatory.

For the rest of the day *Calypso* was steered by dolphins, obeying the whims of the flying phalanx spreading before us to either rim of the ocean. I took a rough sighting on their jumps. The tails were clearing twelve to fifteen feet. As they fell, they twisted into awkward postures, as if vying to smack the water in the most ungraceful way. I tried to estimate how many there were. At a given minute, there were about a thousand out of the water on jumps that averaged three seconds. For one in the air, there must have been nineteen in the water. Perhaps twenty thousand dolphins formed the living reef.

The massive crescent of foam and flying bodies, glistening in the sun, moved along the Hadramaut Coast with no apparent destination, given up to some titanic collective joy. We shouted like children and bet on leaps. Two dozen amateur cameramen tried to anticipate and film the record high jumps of the dolphin Olympic games.

From the underwater chamber the sight was apocalyptic. The radius of transparency was about a hundred feet, a sphere packed with streaming bodies, effortlessly maintaining the pace of *Calypso*. Some dolphins hung close to the windows of the observatory, eying the men inside. The escort was crisscrossed by dolphins charging across the bow with flickering speed. Through this fleeting, crosshatching pack there was also an astounding vertical movement. Dolphins sped straight up from the deep, threw themselves into a sort of secondary rocket-booster stage in front of the windows, and shot through the glittering ceiling. They belly-flopped back into the water, collected themselves, and sounded, printing a white trail of exhalations in the blue. Down there on their vapory launching pads, these living missiles began another take-off past the windows into the sun.

We were so enthralled by the three-dimensional carnival that we did not hear imploring yells from the top of the entry tube: "Hey, you people have been down there long enough! Give somebody else a chance." At dusk the pack left *Calypso,* and she got back into the business of being a ship instead of a plaything for dolphins. We waited for the stars to come out to tell us where they had led us.

On many occasions in the Atlantic and Indian oceans we have come upon hundreds of porpoises or dolphins, but no herd as large or as tirelessly berserk as the legion of the Hadramaut. In all other encounters they were moving in orderly formation, apparently agreed on where they were going. They would detour from the route march to satisfy their invariable curiosity about *Calypso,* then take up course again. It was quite rare to see one perform a high jump. Nor did we understand the goals of these migrations, for several times we saw two disciplined packs passing each other in opposite directions with no apparent fraternization.

Dolphins like to play in the late afternoon and occasionally they remained with us some hours after dark. When night found them around *Calypso,* I was selfish about the underwater chamber. Then their show was written in sparkling sequins of plankton. As the dolphins arched their backs, a ghost animal formed in the water and streamed back to the window in a glowing contrail. This black-and-jade farandole had a bewitching visual rhythm and a lively orchestral accompaniment. The resonant chamber amplified their twittering patter of song.

Dolphins *may* be able to speak. However, if it was conversation that we heard on sonar, hydrophones, and in submerged chambers, it was not articulated like human speech. The dolphin does not have a throat, tongue, and lip equipment to pronounce words, but makes shrill, modulated sounds. There are at least two places in the world where men still use a modulated type of language. In the Pyrénées and the Canary Islands there is a whistling speech that carries much further than glottal expression. Canary Island shepherds on crags three miles apart converse in a whistling language that has a considerable vocabulary. This *may* be the dolphin's technique as well.

In a school the usual flow of high-pitched dolphin chirps was interpolated with distinctly different grunts and croaks in low register that did not seem to belong to the "language." The bass tones may have been echo-ranging impulses, as distinguished from gossip.

Considering their complicated social behavior and the growing suspicion that they might talk, some specialists do not rule out the possibility that the dolphins, porpoises, and toothed whales have a folklore, an oral preceptorial and storytelling tradition passed from generation to generation in the deeps of time. *If* they have a language and we can someday decipher it, man may learn something of the history of the sea. *Calypso* often induced such indefensible dreams of the space below.

Sometimes on nights of dead calm I stood on the foredeck and spotted ahead, a hundred feet or so, a frightened splash and an opalescent trail coming toward me. I looked down at a dancing wraith, a dolphin or porpoise—followed by more mammals streaking to the ship. *Calypso* had awakened a tribe sleeping on the surface. Like many wild animals, dolphins probably sleep with one eye open in the direction of predators—in this case sharks—and close the other on the secure side, the air. By day the lightning dolphin need fear no rival, but in bed it is vulnerable and maintains a highly-tensed alarm system. I imagine sea mammals have many restless nights.

The young dolphin stays with its mother until grown about half her size, then it leaves and joins a gang of other adolescents. These youthful packs are full of vigor, eager to devastate the sea. *Calypso* often chased them but was never able to get among them. They are not interested in playing with ships.

In the Amirantes we had a rare glimpse of the dolphin's private life. I was taking a diving party by launch along the north cape of Daros Island when two dozen adults swam around the corner and stopped to fool around the boat. We harnessed up and dropped in with them. The dolphins were not at all disturbed. Indeed, they seemed to welcome an opportunity to show off some stunts. Several pairs marched away like duelists, turned, and drove toward each other. At the last moment, they avoided bashing heads. The rest lolled around, resting flippers on a friend's back, lazing in the shallows, or turning up their bellies to scratch their backs on the rocks. At Daros, the tireless racers of the open sea seemed to be on vacation.

The well-organized marine circuses of Florida and California use dolphins as performing animals and also make important studies of their psychology. Dolphins, porpoises, and a few other cetaceans are the only known creatures with brains comparable in size to man's. Out of the trilogy that made the human adventure possible—brain, hand, and language—only the hand is not developed in toothed whales (*if* we accepted the proposition that dolphins can talk). This failing bars them from using tools; otherwise, man might have rivals in the sea.

At the Oceanographic Museum in Monaco I installed a large acclimatization tank for dolphins and asked Albert Falco to capture some without injury. He devised a humane spear. Instead of a barb on the end, he fitted padded tongs that sprang shut when touched. Falco stalked dolphins from the *Espadon* every fair day for a year. When the *Espadon* got into a school, he picked one out and fired at the slender junction of its body and flukes. In approximately fifty shots, he tonged twenty-seven live dolphins.

With the captive secured, Falco let it have three hundred feet of light line with a free float at the end. The *Espadon* put about and overtook the buoy. With mask and fin, the captor went over the side, grabbed the buoy, and went along the line to the dolphin. He tackled it in a friendly fashion and the animal surrendered to his embrace. (All of them squeaked pitifully, however, about the unfairness of fate.) Falco put the captive in a sling and the *Espadon*'s men hoisted it aboard, taking care not to abrade the tender skin. They placed it on an inflated mattress and covered it with wet rugs to avoid sunburn.

Falco spent hundreds of hours tracking dolphins from the forepeak of the *Espadon*, and their behavior endeared them to him. He noted that when they came to play around the stem, it was always the largest and strongest dolphin that took up the direct frontal position. The others gamboled in and out on its flanks. Once he gripped his tongs on the tail of a mother and drew her out of the school. An infant remained with her. Abruptly and hastily the calf ran back to catch up with the others—by direct order, Falco thought. He thinks that mothers adopt orphaned young; he often saw three babies with one nursing female.

One day while watching a group of mothers with many calves, he saw one of the females and a brood of young swim toward the *Espadon*. Fifty feet away, the babies broke off and returned to the herd. The solitary dolphin looked the *Espadon* over for a while and then rejoined the others. Often Falco witnessed a young one coming toward the bow, followed by a swift adult, which conducted it back to the tribe. One time he clamped the tail of a youngster. He cradled the captive, which weighed about twenty pounds, in his arms. From below he saw a female that outweighed him, approaching rapidly. She was screaming. A twitter of unmistakable anguish sounded in his ears. The diver did not know what to do. He was underwater, and his hands were engaged in holding the baby that we had asked him to catch, while its mother or foster parent was angrily upon him. The big dolphin didn't touch him. She passed under him, over him, around him, everywhere at once, filling the sea with cries. The mother seemed not to be threatening him but to be calling on the infant to come home and appealing to Falco to let it go. He couldn't stand it. He opened his arms, detached the spring clamp, and watched the mother and baby sound with chirps of joy.

After he boated a live dolphin, Falco accompanied it on a truck to the museum and into the pool, where he held the animal, teaching it to avoid the walls. When it seemed resigned to imprisonment, the diver got out of the water, and a veterinary surgeon went in to start twice-daily examinations of temperature, pulse, and respiration. The doctor administered antibiotics and vitamins and even made encephalograms.

Some solitary animals after several days in the pool literally sank in despair, drowning or suicidally ramming their heads into the wall. However, when two or three captives were together, each gained morale and accepted food after a fast of five or six days. They would eat only fresh sardines—the most expensive fish on the market. The keeper of the tank, Étienne Gastaldi, rewarded them with a sardine for bumping a balloon into the air. I could not help thinking that the dolphins did this cynically, despising their slavery. The keeper introduced cheaper pay in the form of whitings. The dolphins would not eat them. Gastaldi showed a sardine to a dolphin. The animal headed the balloon into the air and raced back to collect its salary. By sleight-of-hand, the keeper substituted a whiting for the sardine and the animal gobbled it. The dolphin gave Gastaldi a look and splashed water furiously on him with its flippers, sending him away drenched.

This self-respecting species, *Delphinus delphis,* has a bottle-nosed cousin, *Tursiops,* that dearly loves show business and often stars in oceanariums. *Delphinus* is equally intelligent, but despises captivity. When we understood that, we liberated them into the sea. Falco was the happiest of us all to see them go back home.

In glassy water off Stromboli, *Calypso*'s high watch called out a dark object floating in the sea. As is our custom, we changed course to inspect it. It was a solitary dolphin, alive and moving feebly to keep its blowhole out of the water. Kientzy swam to it. The dolphin kicked spasmodically to avoid him and then stopped, fatalistically accepting the diver. Kientzy stroked the animal and helped it hold its vent in the air. He reported, "It's not wounded. Nothing seems to be wrong."

I remembered tales of the sea, as old as Greek myth, of dolphins rescuing drowning sailors. It seemed due time for sailors to return the compliment. I joined Kientzy in the water and verified that the dolphin was unhurt. We worked a blanket sling under it and placed it in a water-filled launch on deck. Dr. Nivelleau began medical ministrations and *Calypso* sailed on, a hospital ship for dolphins.

It was a young female in the prime of life. Nivelleau injected a heart stimulant and straddled it in the boat to give artificial respiration. Two hours later, he lost his patient and began an autopsy. Organ after organ seemed perfect—none gave sign of disease or internal malfunction. A diver ventured the opinion that the high-strung animal had died of heartbreak after being rejected by the school. Nivelleau said, "Or of unrequited love."

Near Corsica, I sent Falco and seaman Antonio Lopez in a launch to try to lasso a dolphin from a pack overtaken by *Calypso*. Lopez is a valiant little man who has followed the sea since boyhood. The dolphins gave them a merry chase. Lopez raced his outboard, following pantomimed directions from Falco in the bow. Falco shouted, "Hard left, quick!" Lopez veered away from what looked like a smooth black rock. It showered him with a stinking mist and receded into the sea. A whale three times the length of the boat had unaccountably risen amidst the dolphin pack.

Still, some biologists downgrade the Mediterranean as a "sterile" sea. I like to take men of such opinion on *Calypso*. Between the Côte d'Azur and Corsica we have often encountered what seemed to be resident packs of big blue whales. A dozen times a year we passed and always located at least two big ones humping about in a proprietary manner. A half-century ago, Albert I of Monaco, "the oceanographic prince," took European royalty out for a day's whaling and rarely disappointed his guests.

Our sterile sea can produce mammalian comedies such as the one *Calypso* wandered into one morning between Corsica and Messina. We spotted a pod of blue whales sleeping on the surface and slowly approached them. I was on the bow as the ship nudged toward them. The sleepers awakened with a thrash of water and sounded, leaving the sea stained red. The whales had been sleeping off a banquet of scarlet shrimps. When *Calypso* came, they unpacked their bowels in fright.

Whenever *Calypso* overtook whales, we manned the submerged observatory to watch the movements of the largest animal alive. From this underwater room we were the first men to see a pod of whales swimming beneath the open sea. It is an awesome sensation to see tail flukes as big as a banquet table, fanning up and down in front of your window. From the chamber we gained a possible explanation for the persistent reports of white whales in literature from Melville to Heyerdahl. Several times in my own career at sea I had seen white shapes through the surface when approaching a whale pack, but never an albino whale breaching into the air.

One day in placid water *Calypso* was passing the Lipari Islands in the Tyrrhenian when she entered a sea of floating stones. Gravel paths meandered over the surface of the deep blue sea. We scooped up buckets of pebbles: aerated bits of pumice shed by neighboring volcanoes. As we steamed on, there came a shout from the high bridge, *"Baleines!"* Two blue whales sixty feet long were ambling along just beneath the paths of pumice. They offered no objection to our putting *Calypso*'s bow between them. They spouted calmly and dipped a few feet under between aspirations. A man at the bow yelled, "One of them is a white whale!" I rushed down into the chamber.

Both whales were the same dark color. But when they went under, they played with each other, often rolling on their backs and showing their gray-white bellies. This observation may relegate the white whale to the roster of bankrupt monsters in which underwatermen have now placed the moray, devilfish, and octopus. Today the dread once attached to them has fastened onto the horrible, bloodthirsty "killer whale," or orca.

The orca is the largest variety of dolphin. It is clever and agile and not seen very often, which helps its ogreish reputation. Whaling literature regales us with scenes of carnivorous orcas ravaging a big whale and biting away its lips to seize the tongue, which is the *pâté de foie gras* of "killer whales." Such things certainly happen once a whale has been harpooned and has become easy prey. But a healthy blue whale or sperm whale is quite capable of dispelling orca attacks and has often been observed doing so. The most reliable evidence comes from Antarctic whaling controllers who fly over the grounds low and slow. The airmen have often seen massed orcas approach a small family of whales, such as a bull, cow, and calf. The bull drives the orcas off without undue effort, and the pack does not persist.

But the storytellers are right about the high intelligence of orcas. Along the New Zealand coast offshore whaling was practiced well into this century. When whales were sighted, men went out in boats, harpooned them, and towed them into the beach for butchering. Packs of orcas came into the bloody surf, where the whalemen threw them the offal, including whales' tongues. At night the orcas roamed up and down the shoreline. When they encountered whales, they came in to the beach and barked to awaken the fishermen. In order to feed on whales, the orcas had to enlist the help of the only truly bloodthirsty creature in nature's kingdom. If "killer whales" lived up to their reputation, they would have long since destroyed all the whales in the oceans. The rarity of orcas indicates that they are not such a successful species, as compared with sharks, for instance, that have infested the seas in countless numbers for millions of years.

To me orcas are just bigger and more beautiful dolphins. The male attains a length of twenty-five feet and has powerful jaws and large teeth. He could easily tear a swimmer to pieces, but there is no record of his doing so. Trustworthy divers in Morocco who have encountered "killer whales" reported that they came to the men and swam around them for a while. When their curiosity was appeased, the orcas swam away just as ordinary dolphins would have done.

South of Socotra Island in the Indian Ocean *Calypso* sighted what we thought was a school of pilot whales. When we drew closer, I recognized *Orcinus orca,* or the orca, from their tall, black, scythe-shaped dorsals. As we came up to a cable's length from them, *Calypso* slowed to their pace of six knots. They swam quietly in the lapping waves. We got close enough to see the snow-white patterns on their black flanks. The largest male was about twenty feet long. Four shorter adults swam with him, undoubtedly his harem. There were two calves that wandered a short distance off course and then ran back to their parents. As the ship closed up, the orcas bunched nearer to their leader.

I picked up speed. The male left the herd and doubled back toward *Calypso.* I thought he was going to play around our bows like a dolphin. But, no, he stayed a hundred feet ahead and increased his speed to match ours. *Calypso* was full ahead following him before I tumbled to his game. He was luring us away from the family, which was pursuing a course tangentially away from ours. Then he sounded deep and did not reappear. We searched the flat sea for five minutes before we saw the family again, about two miles off. Because of the undeveloped swimming ability of the infants, *Calypso* was again able to overtake the orcas. Now the chief was really irritated with us. He cut out from the pack in the opposite direction to his original maneuver, but we trumped him by following the family instead. The females and infants sounded simultaneously, much as though they had heard an order from the boss. This left us with nobody but his lordship to chase. He led us on all afternoon. His shrewd and heroic maneuvers kept us from his wives and children. During the episode there were a few shark fins to be seen on the outskirts. We always see sharks near a herd of sea mammals.

A hundred miles north of the Equator, Saôut rang *Calypso*'s bell to call out the faithful. In the offing we saw the long, low, dark silhouette and slanting misty jet of the sperm whale. Three of them were swimming across our course at a prosaic seven or eight knots. We turned, brought our bow up to them, and began a day of wonder and tragedy.

From the underwater observatory, Louis Malle saw them treading the ocean and rolling over to reflect sunlight from their pale breasts. When *Calypso* drew too near the whales, they sounded for ten minutes, but returned to the bow area. From the forepeak we looked down upon huge black leather backs scarred with old gray weals. For an hour we marched companionably with them on the broad ocean.

The whales returned from a dive very near the ship and inexplicably crossed the bow. Collision was unavoidable. *Calypso* ran at ten knots over the flank of a twenty-ton sperm. The underwater chamber took the brunt of the impact. Malle popped out of the hatch like a jack-in-the-box, shaken but unhurt. "The chamber took it. It's not leaking," he called. Men ran aft to see what had happened to the whale while I put on the sonar earphones and listened to its anguished, mouselike squeaks. Before the crash I had heard the whales conversing in a subdued, modulated piccolo, but now there was counterpoint—the nervous, plaintive cries of the whale we had hit and the piercing replies from its two companions.

Calypso slowed down. Its companions reached the stricken animal, which was apparently in a trauma. They put their shoulders under it on either side to lift its blowhole out of the water. During the first days of life the mothers of whales, while teaching them to swim, support them in this way, and the memory apparently lingers on. From all quarters of the compass whales converged in groups of two to four on the wounded one and its bearers. I shuttled between deck and headset to listen to the chatter of the gathering school. The cries became more normal. Apparently the distressed sperm was catching its wind again. *Calypso* was now following thirty-seven whales, including five or six babies averaging about twelve feet long. It was easy to keep up with them because of the slowness of the invalid and the calves. We sailed tightly with them.

One of the playful young turned back to have a look at *Calypso*'s black belly. The little whale drifted under our hull to starboard. I heard the emergency whistle from the engine room and an almost simultaneous telephone ring from René Robino. "The starboard engine has stopped," he said. I looked back. *Calypso*'s wake was red with blood. The calf had been swept under our twin propellers.

"Start the engine, Robino," I called, and I listened for vibrations. There was no evidence that the collision had knocked the screws or shafts out of alignment. I took *Calypso* into a sharp turn back.

The little whale, spurting blood, its body scored through the white fat by our bronze screws, was swimming toward the tribe. Malle returned to the underwater observation chamber and looked out into a stream of blood looming before his forward windows like the trail of an aircraft set on fire by flak. From above we saw that our propeller had turned five parallel slices in the whale.

The infant regained the pack, and we sensed a mass emotion there. The biggest whale among them rose vertically out of the water and by an extraordinary thrashing of its flukes stood quite a while with about a third of its length above the waves. It stared at *Calypso*, measuring the enemy that had harmed two of its subjects. The leader slid back in, tail first, and a moment later the pack sounded or scattered, abandoning the mortally wounded infant.

From the whaling pulpit under the bow Saôut hurled a harpoon into the bleeding whale. He climbed with the line to the maindeck and ran precariously atop the port rail the length of the ship, in danger lest a convulsion of the animal should topple him into the ocean, where sharks were already gathering.

Dumas killed the whale with a rifle shot in the brain, and from the diving platform under the stern seamen got a bight around the flukes. We tried to winch the whale to the deck. On the diving platform Maurice Léandri was drenched with blood—warm blood like ours. Nobody said a word. The whale was too heavy for our tackle. We stopped the winch with the whale partially out of the water. It was sixteen feet long and weighed about 1500 pounds. Léandri stuck his head up over the fantail and said, "There's a brown shark about ten feet long right under my feet."

The shark, barely submerged, circled *Calypso* in a leisurely way. Another shark arrived, then two more. Soon there were twenty brown sharks, all more than six feet long and several running to twelve feet. They were joined by a splendid thirteen-foot blue with a long pointed snout, an elegant silhouette, and large vacant eyes.

Where did they come from in this expanse of open ocean with three miles of water under our keel? What brought them? The smell of blood? Pressure waves from the struggling whale? Or did they always follow whales, scavenging leftovers from their meals and waiting to pounce on a sick or injured one? As the sharks cautiously, even timidly, patrolled the ship and the whale, I felt that they had been more or less permanently attached to this whale pack. It was a constant danger to them and also an irresistible chance for food. Sea mammals can kill a shark by ramming it at high speed, as dolphins have demonstrated in oceanarium tanks. Perhaps this was why sharks kept well clear of whales, as well as the origin of their shy behavior in general and their great deliberation and dithering before they struck at even a dead whale.

The hesitation of the sharks gave us time to rig the antishark cage, load cameras, and charge Aqua-Lungs. Dumas and Laban entered the cage, and we lowered it into the water near the whale. After a while Malle and I replaced them in the human zoo. The pack, now numbering about three dozen, ventured closer. We did not feel so safe in the cage. Although the stout iron bars were spaced close enough to keep out a shark, the cage hung from a wire cable that might possibly break. If it did, we would have to get out of the door before the cage sank beyond the compressed-air range and then make our way up through the sharks. This present fear was accentuated by the growing boldness of the sharks. The heavy brutes swam to the cage and stupidly banged their noses on it. Each carried at least a half-dozen remoras stuck to it, generally to the lower jaw. Escorting them were many pilot fish, whose gay stripes belonged in an aquarium rather than in this blood-drenched wilderness.

The shark ring skulked around for an hour before the bravest ones ventured along the flanks of the whale, still without biting. They slid along the cage in the same way. When they seemed about to begin feeding, I held the cage door open to give Malle a better field for his movie camera. I was prepared to close it fast in case a shark headed for it.

Hundreds of times the sharks caressed the dead whale with their muzzles before one suddenly took the first bite. Pounds of leather and blubber came off the whale as though sliced by a razor. The orgy began. No man had ever seen its like before.

Being only a few feet from the saturnalia, we were able to learn exactly how a shark bites. Because of the long overhang of the upper jaw, it had been assumed that sharks turned on their backs to feed. That is not necessarily the case. We saw them approach the whale upright and open their mouths not so much by dropping the lower jaw as by snubbing the nose at an acute angle, so that the gaping mouth was in front of the head and no longer under it. The open mouth, bristling with sharp-honed teeth, resembled a steel animal trap. The shark set this apparatus into the whale's hide and clamped it. Then its entire body shook with frantic convulsions, in effect turning the teeth into saws. The powerful sawing action was over in a twinkling, and the shark turned away, leaving a deep, clean concavity in the whale. It was terrifying and loathsome.

Perhaps, now that these Indian Ocean sharks were bloated on whale blubber and beef, it might be possible to film an unprotected diver swimming among them. Falco and Malle went down in the cage with a movie camera. The pack was slowing down, swollen with blubber and flesh; they had practically finished feeding. Hanging motionless about thirty feet from the cage was a twelve-footer that Falco thought might be dozing. He opened the cage door and swam out while Malle moved into the opening with his camera to record what happened. Falco swam toward the shark's snout. Its eyes were staring at him. Six feet from the shark Falco could not hear the movie camera clicking and shot a quick glance back. Malle gestured that the film was jammed. The shark moved toward Falco. He rushed back into the cage. Malle slammed the door behind him and the shark's nose crashed heavily against the bars. It was evident that no diver could fool with this lot, even after they had fed to the bursting point.

On deck our men had watched them devouring the whale and were overcome with the hatred of sharks that lies so close under the skin of a sailor. When we finished filming, the crew ran around grabbing anything with which they could punish a shark—crowbars, fire axes, gaffs, and tuna hooks—and they got down onto the diving platform to thrust, knock, slash, and hook sharks. They hauled flipping sharks onto the deck in a production line and finished them off. Delmas yelled, "Death to the blue!" and hauled the big blue shark on board. Dumas sat on a dead one, already eviscerated, and cut its head off to collect the jaw. When he tossed the body over the side, the headless shark swam away.

Many of the sharks fought for hours on deck in a stupefying display of vitality. Yet this same creature will often surrender supinely to a hook and, in captivity, is difficult to keep alive. Even though sharks have an incredible musculature, they are physiologically fragile.

During the massacre of the sharks, all their remora passengers left them. A couple of days later, when we had reached port, Kientzy happened to swim under *Calypso*'s hull and found dozens of remoras attached to it. Their head suckers look like venetian blinds.

The following year *Calypso* was in the same spot in the Indian Ocean on the same day of the year and found sperm whales only ten miles from our previous rendezvous. Now there were at least a hundred of them, cruising west in pods at seven or eight knots. They were spread in all quarters around us. There was a new phenomenon present. From time to time, far on the horizon, we saw high geysers of water erupting from the placid ocean. They looked like explosions of depth charges. Some natural cataclysm was taking place, and we could not understand what it was. Then the enigma was revealed. Dumas and Falco saw the thing close from the high observation bridge while I was standing with them watching whales on the opposite side. "There it is!" Dumas shouted. I turned and saw an eruption as large as the Arc de Triomphe a few hundred feet away and heard a loud, splashy boom. "You missed it! It happened so fast," said Didi. They had seen a sixty-foot sperm whale leaping straight up into the air, its tail clearing the water by fifteen feet. It fell back in on its side and sent up the great splash, which was all I saw.

We never saw a whale in the air again, although we continued to see geysers after the whales had fallen back in. Was this the same excitement as that of the porpoises of the Hadramaut? No, it was individualistic; the other whales were quiet. Moreover, it did not seem to be courtship—most of the females were accompanied by calves. I conjectured another possible explanation for the giant leaps.

Sperm whales are known to be the deepest divers among their order. Dead ones have been found entangled with submarine cables that were laid a mile deep. Specialists agree that they can dive at least three thousand feet. Whale stomach dissection usually reveals large squid sections, or entire cephalopods. Dozens of beaks, some of them encysted, are found in the intestines. Prince Albert of Monaco, while whaling off the Azores, harpooned a sperm whale that regurgitated an enormous piece of white flesh which came from a hitherto unknown species of squid with tentacles twenty-seven feet long. The creature to which it belonged was later named *Architeuthis princeps*. Many captured sperm whales carry terrible scars, testifying to merciless fights with giant squids that take place in two or three thousand feet of water. I thought perhaps this was what produced the prodigious leaps out of the water. During a prolonged battle in the dark, a whale might overstay its time in that pressure, break away from the squid and, desperate for air, speed to the surface at twenty or twenty-five knots. The momentum could carry it high into the air where gravity would brake the vertical dash for life. If true, these geysers were merely incidents in the whale's daily feeding ordeal. As I pondered it, I felt that we would have to build deep, fast vehicles to accompany whales on their heroic dives and possibly witness the epic battle with *Architeuthis princeps.*

The behavior of the shark outriders that we always saw near whales remained unpredictable throughout tropical dives. In the Shab Jenab reefs in the Red Sea we had an unusual shark encounter. I was diving with the scholarly trio of Drach, Nesteroff, and Nivelleau, using only masks and fins. We had not ventured far into the beautiful scenery full of bumpfish, groupers, and bonitos when I saw seventy-five feet away at the limit of visibility a moderate-sized *Carcharhinus.* The shark sighted us simultaneously. It paused, then drove directly for me, without wavering, at maximum speed. Why me? I was the least appetizing morsel of the four. I had nothing to defend myself with—but even if I had, the swiftness and precision of the attack would have left me little time to use it. Less than an arm's length from me the shark, at a velocity of at least ten knots, executed an about-face and returned to the open sea. Among all the thousands of timid, inquisitive sharks we had seen, what made this one so quick and bold? And why did it give up just as it had its prey? An interesting aspect of the affair was that the shark unquestionably saw me as far off as I saw him, again testifying to the excellent general vision of the creature, despite the inferior anatomy of its retina. It also whipped into its head-to-tail turn very sharply, so it is wrong to say that sharks have poor maneuverability.

After this brush with *Carcharhinus,* we were prudent about Red Sea sharks. They are more worrisome than their brethren in the Atlantic, although the ones we saw tended to be smaller than those of the big oceans. Most of the specimens were under six feet long. They were abundant in the shallow water along the reefs where we had to work. There was no consistency about their behavior toward divers. Some passed us indifferently, and others hung around insistently. When we tried to get rid of them by hooting they flinched but did not depart. A threatening gesture moved them away, but they came back promptly. If we turned our backs, they came to our legs. If we swam toward them in an aggressive way, which we found the best thing to do, they drifted off and gave us a little time to work; but the tactic had to be repeated. Although we kept scoring on the sharks, it was clearly their game, and sooner or later we had to default by getting out of the water.

When *Calypso* was anchored under the north slope of the black volcano of Djebel Zebair in the Far-Sans, Dumas and Falco took a launch to explore the other side. They dropped the grapnel anchor off a small black beach and nosed down sixty feet. Dumas went down toward a ledge while Falco reconnoitered horizontally above him. The water grew darker, as though shadowed by a passing cloud. For some reason Falco felt uneasy and sharpened his vigilance. Turning his mask here and there, he spotted a shark slanting straight toward him from the deep. It was coming with such speed that Falco had only a moment to act. He jumped into a recess in the lava and hefted his shark billy, a four-foot staff with nail studs in the end. The shark came into the cave. Falco pointed the club ahead and swam toward the shark, ready to thrust the studs into its hide to fend it off. The shark began to turn back. Falco gave it a whack on the flank with the club and the shark departed at full speed.

The diver emerged from the cave and looked down. Dumas was spinning about, keeping his eye on a small shark that was circling insistently closer. Falco started toward him swiftly; there were two more sharks driving at Dumas' feet from below. Falco waved his club at the newcomers and made as much noise as he could. The three sharks moved off apace, and the men got close together and began a cautious ascent, keeping their backs to the cliff. The next stage was the arrival of a dozen sharks, swimming rapidly and weaving closer to the divers. One man watched them, while the other glanced back, picking out recesses in the reef; they lay their upward course along a string of such refuges. The pack was still close when they took their last leap into the boat. The sun was down behind the volcano. The water around them was trembling and splashing. It was evening feeding time.

We felt more secure about sharks deeper in the reefs of the Red Sea. There they were freer and less animated. Once Dumas and Beltran were down at Shab Suleim and some sharks came by patrolling. A yellow triggerfish, a harmless four-pounder, leaped aggressively out of the reef, and the sharks took off into the blue. We had several occasions to watch triggerfish panicking gangs of sharks.

At Mersa Bela, Falco took the launch to reconnoiter a reef. The twenty-five-horsepower Evinrude outboard motor stopped with a jolt. Blood spread behind the boat. A shark had bitten the propeller.

Kientzy and I dived along a slope of fleshy alcyonarians under the Twin Brothers Island one afternoon. We ran into a dozen hammerheads so cowardly that we were unable to approach them. An hour later, when the sun was low and there was little light below, Dumas and Falco went down in the same place with Malle on camera. This time they found the sharks had turned bold and aggressive. As the divers came aboard, the water around the ship became agitated. It was a perfect fury of sharks. Dozens of big *Carcharhinus* roared around crazily, rubbing *Calypso*'s sides and snapping at anything we lowered. Our tuna hooks barely touched the water before sharks gobbled them. Sharks began to pile up on deck, flapping and bending in a gruesome frenzy. Into the scene walked a guest photographer; fins on his feet, Aqua-Lung on his back, flash camera in his hands. He made his way to the diving ladder.

"What are you doing?" I asked, gasping.

"This is the opportunity of my lifetime," he said, starting down the ladder.

"I order you back on deck instantly!" I said. I think it was the only time I have ever issued a direct order on *Calypso*. I actually had to argue with the photographer. He wouldn't speak to me for a day or so. I had spoiled the greatest photographic dive a man could ever want. That was his opinion. Mine was that I had saved him from certain death.

chapter
nine

ISLES

OF

RETURN

Calypso was bound for the Seychelles, which are among the last "unspoiled" tropical islands on earth. They lie far out in the equatorial Indian Ocean. General Chinese Gordon once solemnly declared that Mahé, the main island of the group, was the actual site of the Garden of Eden.

Eight days from Bahrein we raised a fringe of coco-palms on Denys, the northernmost island of the Seychelles. It was a place of South Sea reveries —a copra plantation run by soft-voiced Créoles speaking a swinging French *patois*. The young planter came out to *Calypso* with his beautiful child wife, a dark-eyed creature who did not seem more than fifteen, and his manager, a strapping blond of about thirty. Later we discovered that the planter was forty-one, his manager forty-eight, and the wife twenty-nine years of age. We had come to the isle of abiding youth.

Before we sailed for Mahé, the Denys islanders heaped our deck with coconuts, plantains, green oranges, and a small gray pig that we named Arthur. Bonnard, our Portuguese Diving Dog, was enraptured with Arthur, but the embarrassed pig refused invitations to wrestle and trotted away, trying to elude the romping dog. We saved the pig's dignity by putting him in the antishark cage.

A few miles from Mahé a heavy rain thudded on *Calypso,* so we took showers in it. Then we saw ahead a magic-lantern picture—a tall, green mountain gleaming in the sun and overspanned by a double rainbow. Unlike the typical coral or lava structure of the tropical ocean, Mahé was formed of red-and-black granite peaks thrust from the floor twelve thousand feet below. The lofty monoliths were nobly sculptured by weather and up-holstered with luxurious greenery—vegetation of both the tropical and semitemperate zones. The temperature was an even 75° F. almost all the year round.

As we swung into the long jetty at the little white capital town of Port Victoria, the population poured out. It seemed that the island's thirty-seven thousand inhabitants all wanted to visit *Calypso*. A queue backed down the jetty toward the cast-iron monument to Queen Victoria in the town square. The islanders never miss a pretext for a party, and *Calypso* was an excuse to increase the social rounds. We were fairly carried from one gala to another. My crew took to wearing nineteenth-century straw sailor hats that were still issued to the Mahé harbor patrol. I decided we'd better leave before somebody got married—which was no idle threat, considering the warmth of the feminine reception. Three thousand young men from the Seychelles were away serving in the British Army. We sailed for Aldabra.

The Aldabra Islands are four atolls belonging to the Seychelles although eight hundred miles southwest. They were uninhabited until recent times, due to the foresight of Charles Darwin, who influenced the Crown to refrain from settling them. We understood there was only a small care-taker party on Aldabra. *Calypso* seemed like a time machine, carrying us in imagination back to the age of pterodactyls and *Diplodocuses.*

Long before it was visible above the horizon, Aldabra, the main island of the group, announced itself by a bright green deviation in the blue sky. This was the reflection of a great lagoon. The pterodactyls came out to meet us, flapping their wings. Of course they were only six-foot frigate birds, but they suited our mood. Flocks of boobies flew in from the sea with full bellies, carrying fish in their beaks for the chicks. From aloft the frigate birds swooped on the breadwinners, forcing the boobies to drop the fish, which the predators picked out of the air. The frigates then harassed the boobies until they regurgitated the contents of their stomachs as well.

Aldabra is an irregular oval atoll twenty-two miles long and twelve miles wide, enclosing a lagoon larger than Manhattan Island. The inland sea covered about two hundred square miles. About two-thirds of it drained down to sand at low tide, expelling a tremendous volume of water. The lagoon was the heart of the atoll, pumping salt water in and out instead of blood. The incoming tide was green with spores, plankton, and algae. Going out, it stained the ocean gray with detritus from the battle for life in the lagoon. There were only four narrow channels to exchange the water between ocean and lagoon.

The main channel seemed navigable for *Calypso*. We had been told that it had once been transited by a German cruiser, hiding from pursuers during the First World War, so we entered. The pass was sixty feet deep, but quite narrow. Ahead we saw the great lagoon spreading to the horizon, bordered by watery mangrove jungles topped by pandanus and screw pine on the dry outer rim of the atoll. Strewn across the lagoon were hundreds of dead coral heads looming twenty feet above the surface. I judged the entrance too dangerous and backed out to look at the possibilities of anchoring offshore.

From the outside, the problem was the fringing reef, extending a half-mile from the beach. *Calypso* could not get behind the reef because it was backed by tidal flats that were dry during part of the day. We hove to. A pirogue was coming across the flats from the tiny settlement on West Island. The boat nimbly leaped the reef. In it were four Negroes and a barefoot white man wearing an aluminum-painted sun helmet. He climbed aboard and introduced himself as George Houareau, caretaker of the atoll. I showed him permits from Mahé to land Dr. Cherbonnier's scientific party for a month on Aldabra. Houareau, or "the Guv'nor," as we came to call him with affection, volunteered them three houses. Our launches, piled high with gear, moved off to the fringing reef before the tide went down. Houareau's black pilots took them through a break in the reef, and the boats sped to the beach—a strand of pure white coral sand as fine as confectioner's sugar.

I went down to look at the underpinnings of the reef. I had seen nothing more beautiful since the Red Sea. We had struck diver's gold. *Calypso* echo-ranged along the fringing reef and found a place to anchor.

Our people ashore settled into corrugated metal huts and engaged a tall, smiling matron named Angelina as cook. Delmas concocted *pastis* from medical alcohol and anise flavoring; Camp Calypso, Aldabra, was in business.

Calypso herself was not all that comfortable. She rolled heavily all night. If we stayed in this offshore anchorage, we would lose a lot of efficiency and sleep. Also the chief engineer needed three quiet days to take down one of our main diesels for repair. I decided to try the lagoon again. We entered during next morning's low tide and placed two bower anchors and a stern anchor in one of the wider reaches of Main Channel. The green tide came sluicing in, threatening to pick up *Calypso* and pile her up on the inner shoals. Montupet kept both engines up while Saôut and I maneuvered to keep our hooks in.

We lowered Falco in a launch to inspect the anchors. Wearing a mask and breathing tube, he dropped into the savage current. He hooked one arm through a bight of cable, stuck his head under, and directed the helmsman here and there with his other hand. Falco reported that our three anchors were resting precariously on hard coral bottom, planed smooth by the tides. He bobbed under again and the launch toured around, looking for rough bottom. Nowhere did Falco find anything but slippery floor. Saôut said, "I wonder if there's anything to that story about the German cruiser."

We managed to hold the anchorage through the flow tide. When slack water came, we hauled the hooks, added more cable and chain, and laid the three anchors very wide and tight to get ready for the ebb.

Our fear for the ship had a sort of gaiety to it—winning this fight with the tides was going to earn us a reward. We were excited by our first impressions of Aldabra. What was in that outer reef—in those big gray mushroom heads in the lagoon—in the far-spreading mangroves—in the heights of pandanus? We had already seen enough birds of many varieties to know this place was glutted with wild fowl.

The new anchor placements held through ebb tide, but we had to return on the next flow tide to our turbulent anchorage outside. We put out short-range launch expeditions to the lagoon before nightfall and inspected the big mushroom corals, which ranged in size from haystacks to islets. None of us had ever seen anything like them. They were the undersea pillars of the Far-Sans lifted twenty feet above the surface and then mined away at the base by the dynamic tides. In the gray petrifactions we saw big white staghorn corals in a fossil state. Under the toadstools the tides had fretted out arches and grottoes, floored with white and filled with dancing fish. Forty feet inside one of the tunnels, a pothole let a shaft of sunlight in on a pearl of a beach large enough for a honeymoon couple.

Simone, Dumas, and I took a launch to explore the lagoon from end to end. We entered through a small pass on the east end of Aldabra. At the entrance there was an abandoned palm hut overshadowed by a pile of bleached sea turtle bones twenty feet high. In the lagoon the current pushed us toward a maze of mangrove trees growing in two feet of salt water. We decided to venture inside and stopped the motor to keep from alarming the inhabitants. We poled through waterways arched with leaves. In the green halls there were petrels, boobies, herons, and frigate birds lined up looking at us from branches or perched on the knee roots of the mangroves. Sitting in armistice were birds that would soon be out above the reef fighting over fish. As we glided silently through the mangrove alleys, we saw, a few inches under the birds, the tips of sharks' dorsals. They were lazing in the shade, rolling their bellies on the warm sand. Aldabra was a rest home for sharks as well.

The launch, although drawing only five inches of water, went aground in the lagoon forest, and we were reminded that the afternoon tide was ebbing. The salt-water jungle did not seem the best place to spend a night in an open boat. We retreated blindly from the mangroves, picking out channels on a bearing to Southern Island, the largest segment of the atoll. When we broke out of the woods, Southern was in the offing but was barred by drain-ing shoals. Often the three of us got out into the receding water to push the boat off a mound. At dusk we beached her far out in the lagoon, on a patch of sand whose three stunted palms testified that it remained above water at high tide. We roped the launch to a coconut tree. As Dumas col-lected driftwood for a fire, he swept his arm around the great lagoon, paling into night, and said, "It's a world!"

We warmed ourselves and some rations on the fire, and fell asleep on litters of rustling palm leaves. We were on a mound of sand with three palms—the facsimile of a cartoonist's castaway island.

In the morning green water filled the lagoon, and we sped across the land-locked sea to rejoin *Calypso.*

The sea turtles of the equatorial Indian Ocean swim to Aldabra en masse to mate and deposit their eggs beneath its dunes. A smart, athletic Negro named Michel was the best turtle hunter on the island. He sometimes paddled seven miles out in his dugout canoe to take them. He invited a

Calypsonian to accompany him and his partner on the hunt. Michel's weapon was a harpoon shaft with a short steel barb to which the line was attached. He thrust the lance into a turtle's shell, not deep enough to disable, but enough to engage. The shaft fell away, and he had the turtle on a leash.

He and his comrade hauled in the line that day and lifted aboard turtles weighing up to three hundred pounds. The fishermen placed them on their backs, a position from which a sea turtle cannot regain its feet. Michel captured four big turtles. Then with his dugout almost taking water, he paddled home, flourishing the yellow belly plates in the evening sun, while the turtles shed long, gummy upside-down tears. The canoe leaped the reef and slid across the tidal flat. The islanders butchered two turtles and dumped the others in a shallow pond in an inlet, where two dozen big ones were held in captivity, flushed by clean tides entering through the split bamboo palisade.

After a feast of turtle-and-celery stew our gourmets—Delmas, Besse, and Dugan—asked Angelina about the culinary fate of the turtles swimming in the pond. *"Ah, messieurs,"* she said, "they are waiting for the boat that comes once a year from Mahé. She will take them there alive to become soup in tins. The *potage* will be sent to London, where the only ones who are allowed to drink it are the Queen and the Lord Mayor, Dick Whittington." The Guv'nor modified this legend. He said, "Our turtle soup is sometimes served at the Lord Mayor's banquet in London."

The divers liked to go into the turtle pound and mount the reptiles for a ride. They got on from the rear and grasped the front rim of the shell. The sea turtle has a dangerous beak, which the men were careful to avoid as the reptile struggled to throw them. If they succeeded in getting firmly into the saddle, the turtle would give a thrilling but short ride. It soon sank motionless to the bottom until the rider got off. One of the young assistant scientists, disregarding warnings about the beaks, went into the pond. We heard a scream. The youth scaled the bamboo fence with blood streaming from a turtle bite in his thigh.

We were warming up our electric submarine scooters that looked like stubby military torpedoes with two handles in the back. Each of these diver's tugs contained 24-volt batteries and a one-horsepower motor that gave a 28-pound thrust for two hours. The scooter was ballasted to weigh two pounds underwater. The diver grasped the handlebars; on the right-hand one was the only control, a combined starter and throttle, worked by squeezing the hand. The propeller was under his chest to make a smooth slip stream and avoid prop wash on his mask. To steer the scooter, he angled his body and fins; there was no need for hydrofoils or rudders. One of our scooters had a 35mm motion picture camera shooting through a port in the nose, with the stop-start button on the left handle. The torpedo attained nearly three knots, which is a goodly speed underwater—in fact, one that seems very fast.

Speed was not the only object of the electric tugs. The principal advantages to the diver were range and conservation of energy, the last of which spelled his air out a bit longer. However, the compressed-air diving tables still governed the man on the scooter. When he reached his depth-time limit, he had to surface no matter how much air was left in the bottles.

We took turns going down in scooter teams, alongside the outer reefs, reveling in the frisky chargers that turned easily in three-dimensional flights. We buzzed the floor on long exhilarating sweeps, passing under parasol corals, winding along *couloirs*, and zipping through dark tunnels. We drove at veils of golden fish that dispersed instantly. We got on a giant grouper's tail and chased him. The electric fish gave us the feeling of having turned into powerful and swift predators ourselves.

When we swept over a point of interest, it was fun simply to let go of the scooter and swim to look at the thing, while the machine gently sank into the bottom. When we had finished looking—Tally ho!—we picked up the handles and roared away. Unlike their reaction to Aqua-Lungers, the little fish scuttled into hiding when the scooter came along. The flowering reef seemed to shrink before our eyes.

After a scooter ride with a lot of three-dimensional aquabatics, we would come up with buzzing ears. The rapid pressure changes affected the Eustachian system and perhaps the circulation as well. But we did not think of that when our next turn came. We did not remember the hangover in our lust to have another drink.

When our men encountered sea turtles down in the reefs, they moved in, challenging them to races. These turtles, the rowboats of the sea, could put on spurts and swerves that skidded a man out of the race. Dumas, Falco, and Delmas also rode turtles in the open water. They overtook them by stealth and changed mounts in midwater. Then the scooterman would try to race the turtleman. Falco was able to steer the turtles just about wherever he wanted them to go. However, as air-breathing animals, the turtles were soon exhausted by the game and would surface almost vertically. Falco stayed aboard on several round trips for air, but it was so punishing to his ears that he gave it up.

The most pugnacious of the four arteries of the Aldabra lagoon was Johnny Channel, a narrow, sinuous, and deep gut about five hundred yards long. The tides raced through it at velocities of up to fifteen knots. It was a thriving rendezvous for both reef and pelagic animals. As the flow tide began, thousands of fish gathered by the sea gate, waiting to be picked up by the tide and carried into the lagoon. Johnny Channel was in effect a double reef: the opposing walls, six to ten feet apart, were both flower banks of corals. As we saw the fish borne away in glittering multitudes on a free ride to the lagoon, Falco and I decided to join them. I took a camera and he a shark billy. I asked the launch helmsman to follow us through.

Without moving a muscle, we learned the delights of speed. Ordinarily free divers are sentenced to trudge along at not much more than one knot if they are conserving their leg and lung power. But here we multiplied our speed without effort. The current carried us reeling past lovely corals and around bends. Contact with the walls on either side could strip away flesh at the rate we were going. Man and fish in all sorts of distorted positions were frozen in a spatial relationship in the mass of animals streaming through. Shooting the rapids underwater was an entirely new thrill. Dizzy as rollercoaster riders, we were slammed around corners so fast that crashing into the coral seemed inevitable. Falco and I were swept into a wide bend and found ourselves cushioned in a slowly circulating eddy. We stayed in it to watch the fish go by. From a cave opposite, a big grouper came out and breasted the stream, working his way over to us. Apparently he judged us too big for a meal, for he turned home. A thirteen-foot blue shark came up-tide, magnificently maintaining its equilibrium against the onrush. For the shark, Johnny Channel was the feeding opportunity of the oceans. It swept prey right into his jaws.

Caranxes, barracudas, and exotic reef fish also stemmed the liquid avalanche. Occasionally the water toppled one out of station and bore it away. Falco and I left the refuge and were carried off. We slammed past three shark noses so fast that neither species had time to consider the possibilities of the encounter. Our journey ended with a gradual reduction of speed, a white bottom rising, and an azure vista spreading. We stuck our masks out into the rosy light of the lagoon, and there was the launch sitting placidly by a mushroom islet covered with giant frigate birds.

High-speed Aqua-Lunging became the rage of *Calypso*. We took the launch to the outgoing tidal gate and dropped in two-by-two for the giddy experience. We became addicts of Johnny Channel. In our rapturous rides through this submarine Luna Park we had assumed that its architecture was that of a simple, deep-scored tidal channel. Laban and Dumas found out differently. It was Laban's first descent in the torrent. Instead of following Dumas, he ran alongside the opposite wall. Suddenly the tide thrust Laban into a branching gallery that no one had noticed before. Seeing his fins vanish, Dumas instantly crossed and was carried into the fissure. He seized Laban's ankle, and they were swept pell-mell into a narrowing gut, its walls closing in to mangle them. With his free hand Dumas grabbed a mangrove root. A few feet more and Laban would have been wedged in jagged corals. Inch by inch the two divers pulled each other through the thrashing water until Laban could take hold of the root. They hung on for dear life.

When they did not reach the launch in due time at the end of the channel, the helmsman bucked back into the current. Dumas and Laban were below, clinging to the mangrove, for many nervous minutes before the launch got a safety line to them. Today, if you mention Johnny Channel to a *Calypso* diver, you will hear a spate of reminiscences about the only place where free divers have traveled as fast as fish.

On the outskirts of the settlement we met a remarkable survivor of the ages—thousands upon thousands of giant land tortoises, some with shells five feet long. Aldabra and the Galápagos Islands are the only places where this prehistoric reptile still exists. They were like animated tanks. We got on their backs for short rides before they knelt indignantly and drew their heads and legs into the fortress, leaving us marooned on brown rocks. The tortoises were complete herbivores. They kept the grassy sections cropped like golf greens. They seemed to have no enemies and no voracity for anything save shrubs and grass. The bigger tortoises must have been more than a hundred years old. Apart from disease, there seemed at first to be only one disaster that could befall them—falling on their backs into a pothole of ossified coral and dying of starvation. Ironically, they actually sought out such holes, because they often contained rain pools. Tortoises love a long drink and a good soak.

Then we discovered that they had a terrifying enemy, one likely to annihilate them on Aldabra. We made a land excursion to Southern Island, a twenty-mile bank of dead coral topped by an almost impenetrable bush. A few hundred feet of panting, shoe-slicing, hand-cutting progress in the coral jungle was all we could manage. It would take a bulldozer a month to span this side of the Aldabra atoll. Here we found tortoise skeletons not only in the potholes but in the open. Feral goats had starved them out by cropping the sparse grass and foliage up to three feet. The Aldabra goats were multiplying at a prodigious rate. Riflemen could not keep them down because of the impossible terrain of Southern Island. They were still confined to that segment of the atoll, but the Guv'nor had nightmares in which a male and female goat swam the inlet to his island and sent the place up in slow green flames.

In the morning we found the beaches imprinted with last night's news. The headlines were tractorlike treads from the water to the dunes, where sea turtle mothers had buried their eggs in the sand. There were stories in the crab burrows, and the punctuation marks were sand fleas waiting for sunset to emerge and take our legs off at the ankle. The crossword puzzle consisted of the claw prints of birds that had stalked crabs at night. The typographical case itself was strewn along the high tide mark in fragments of coral knocked off the outer reef and subdivided as they tumbled across the flats. These bits were shaped like every letter of the Latin alphabet, both capital and lower case. Dugan gave the skipper coral fragments that spelled: François Saôut, Master, Calypso, Toulon.

When the tide was out, black herons and white herons came from the lagoon to fish the outer coral flats. During the afternoon low tide we could sit on the laboratory veranda and watch thousands of them, intermingled, stalking on penciled legs, selecting a smorgasbord from dishes of water and coral knobs. The sweep of white and black fowl on the jeweled reef gave a glimpse of what the world must have been before our kind spread over it.

At night, when the beach looked like snow in starlight, the nocturnal breeds came out. Hermit crabs laboriously toted shells three times as heavy as themselves. We found two hermits living in shell trailers parked in the crotch of a pandanus tree nine feet in the air. Charwomen came out at night to clean the beach; they were green ghost crabs. Once a camper threw his burning cigarette butt on the beach and saw it moving away. A ghost crab was carrying the cigarette like a torch.

Another night the shore party saw a spectacle that none knew existed in nature. A racy little thunderhead passed over, distributed its blessing, and puffed on toward Africa. From Asia the full moon leaped into the sky and flashed a lunar rainbow against the cloud. The pale arch was very distinct, and when we squinted, we could see faint colors in it. The moonbow lasted more than a minute.

We tasted these wonders with a growing sadness. The grandeur of Aldabra was doomed and soon would pass. The Seychelles government had put up the Aldabra group for commercial lease and was now urgently seeking bids. The Seychelles economy was precariously held together by family remittances from the three thousand men in the Seychelles Battalion of the British Army Pioneer Corps, stationed in the Suez Canal Zone. The remittances ballasted business and buoyed the low wages of the islands. Now, suddenly, the send-home money was gone; Britain had abolished the battalion, and it was voyaging home to be disbanded.

One prospective lessee wanted to set up a commercial fishery, drying fish and salting sea turtle flesh. Another would raise Chinese ducks in the lagoon. A third would cut down the mangroves for cheap paper pulp, good enough for cartons. There was even wistful talk about establishing a resort on Aldabra. Any of these projects would doom the wildlife of the atoll.

We had grown so attached to the place that it seemed like a threat to our own property. I had an idea: why shouldn't *we* lease Aldabra? We could preserve it as a wildlife sanctuary and invite the scientists of the world to join in founding a tropical research center on an island almost uncontaminated by man. Aldabra would also be an ideal site for a meteorological station for East Africa. I thought of dozens of institutions I could ask to participate.

I sailed to Mahé and laid my plan before the governor, Sir William Addis. He was sympathetic, but explained his pressing need to dispose of the atolls. I drew up a sealed tender for a fifty-year lease, giving my purpose as conservation, tropical research, and the establishment of a meteorological station. When I got back home, I flew to London and pleaded the case for conservation at the Colonial Office. I spoke with Lady Clementine Churchill about it. On B.B.C. television I exhorted the British people to save Aldabra, and I gave newspaper interviews on the subject. The response gave me no illusions that the islands would be spared, but at least I had put up a fight for the coral sanctuary. My bid for Aldabra was rejected in favor of a commercial applicant who intended to cut down the mangroves.

The following year *Calypso* went to Mahé again. Sir William said he had placed a condition on the lessee: Southern Island was not to be touched. It had been declared an inviolable nature preserve. At least something would be saved. It would not protect the tortoises from the goats, but as the largest section of the atoll, Southern Island afforded a chance of survival to other life forms.

Calypso moved on to Aldabra and anchored off the settlement a year after we had first arrived. Through binoculars we saw several dozen people walking on the white beach. It was the hour that the black herons and white herons stalked the tidal pools, but now there were only a few of them. We heard a mess hall dinner gong. Falco and Dumas hung their heads in gloom.

Over the fringing reef came a pirogue with Michel and three other Negroes paddling and, standing in the prow, the mild viking figure of the Guv'nor in his silver helmet. We greeted them warmly. The Guv'nor was downcast. He now had fifty subjects and a hundred woes. The absentee landlord was complaining that the island was not producing enough for him to afford sending a boat sixteen hundred miles with the supplies that the islanders needed. The new residents did not like life without women, movies, cafés, and beer. A dozen of them were usually laid up with sprained ankles, fractures, and coral cuts. The Guv'nor was called out at all hours to rescue boating parties stranded in the big lagoon. The lessee had not been able to build an airstrip or cut a boat channel in the fringing reef. All was despondency.

The more we heard of this melancholy recital, the more our hearts lifted. We were very sorry for Houareau, but it looked as if the island was going to defeat the commercial invasion.

After supping in the gubernatorial mansion, we walked along a familiar piney trail above the white beach among somnolent tortoises. The beach was drenched in moonlight and framed by sighing trees. We came to the cemetery, where lay a dozen workers left there by previous unsuccessful entrepreneurs. The moon picked out their weathered crosses and stones inscribed in Chinese and Arabic. On the graves were empty bottles and glasses that once held flowers. Birds, turtles, and land crabs rustled on the needle matting of the tombs.

THE
TRUCIAL
REEF

chapter ten

Luis Marden and I were gamming on the after-deck as *Calypso* ranged south on a soft night in the Indian Ocean. He was anxious to dive on tropical reefs and photograph as many species of fish as possible. I pointed to a streak in the water and said, "A flying fish. In a day or so, you'll be able to shoot thousands of them without getting wet. We're coming to the big girdle of flying fish wrapped around the Equator. They'll come big as mackerels and land on board as high as the spar deck."

The *National Geographic* correspondent said, "You're kidding. They can't fly more than two feet off the surface. I've seen plenty of them in the Caribbean."

Marden staggered back from a blow on the head. A half-pound flying fish lay flapping on deck. I led Luis to a mirror and showed him fish scales sticking to a red bruise on his forehead. Hardly had the laughter at his discomfort ended than we heard nightmare cries from Malle's cabin. A flying fish had entered his open port and fallen, struggling, on his sleeping face. In the morning we picked up ten pounds of them for breakfast.

A newly stranded flying fish looks rather ordinary except for its distinctive asymmetrical tail. Unfold its pectorals and you will see the long, gauzy, metallic blue wings that sometimes glint with iridescent orange patterns. By day, flying fish rarely collide with a vessel, but skitter away from it. Their flight seems always to be motivated by the threat of a predator. In *Calypso*'s underwater observatory we had a pursuer's view of flying fish. They swam just beneath the surface, their white bellies blending into the shiny ceiling. When alarmed, they picked up speed and steered sharply up through the surface.

We could follow the rest from the deck. Breaking water, they immediately spread their wings and warped them to increase the lift. The long lower tail lobe remained in the water, sculling rapidly to drive the fish to take-off speed. They flew into the wind close to the water where ground effect assisted flight. The flying fish does not beat its wings like a bird. It is a glider with an "outboard motor" that it dips into the water several times during a flight. Many times we saw flying fish traveling out of the water for more than six hundred feet. The animal used its last spurt of propulsive energy to deceive the pursuer about the point of re-entry. After flying a long straight course, it veered off into cross-winds or even doubled back downwind until it had to go below again.

The gliding fish thrives despite constant attacks by swift enemies like jacks and dorados by day and jet-propelled squids by night. The very act of flight also exposes it to sea fowl, which gather hungrily when the underwater beaters send up flying fish. This is a species that succeeds in life despite continuous aggression underfoot and overhead.

During the winter of 1955 *Calypso* was making a battered, uneasy passage from Diego Suarez, Madagascar, to Aldabra in the southeast trades. I decided to take shelter for three or four hours at Assumption, the southernmost island of the Aldabras, to wash the salt cake off the ship and give the hard-working men some rest before we bucked on to the big atoll, where we could only expect the same state of constant alert we had experienced on our first visit to that ship-hating island. The chart showed that the west coast of Assumption was protected from the trades by a bay in the scimitar-shaped land. And the depths were good for anchoring. As we approached in white water, we saw the high filao trees on the island bending their tops in the wind. *Calypso* descended from rolling crags into calm water where mild zephyrs played around our subsiding decks. Across the bay there was a crescent of alabaster sand. Falco, who was leaning over the forepeak, called back, "The water is crystal clear." I heard mechanical hissing on the afterdeck. Already Jean Delmas was filling the triple-tank blocks. I dropped anchor in sixty feet of water close to shore and got word around that we would have a look at the place and sail for Aldabra in the afternoon.

Delmas treated himself to the first dive. He went head down through the looking glass into the most enormous vistas he had ever scanned in the underwater world. The sea was transparent for two hundred feet in any direction. Delmas had been with *Calypso* in the Red Sea reefs, at Antiky-thera, and at Aldabra, but had not seen anything approaching the scenes that Assumption Reef offered to the human eye. The corals were richer. The fish were thicker and had no fear. They came to Delmas in a multitude, wearing all the colors that can be imagined. He stumbled back on deck under his heavy gear and said to me earnestly, "Let's stay here instead of going to Aldabra. This is the place to make friends with fish. You must tell all the divers never to carry a gun, never to swim fast or use menacing gestures, never to set off a dynamite cap. Let's take food down to them. You'll see something."

Before I could reply, the newly beatified St. Francis of the Fish left me for the galley and began dicing lunch leftovers to take to them. Marden returned with the second relay of divers, and he too preached Assumption. "Jacques," said he, "it is incredible down there. It is the ocean turned inside out. When I tried to take close-ups of the fish, they came too near to stay in focus. When I backed off, they came with me."

The third pair underwater—the veteran, objective men, Dumas and Falco—came out babbling. I couldn't get a sober report from any of them. I hefted an Aqua-Lung onto my back.

Underwater, while I still had a hand on the ladder, I was enslaved by Assumption Reef. I climbed back and announced that we were going to stay there as long as our fresh water lasted. Somebody said, "Let's start rationing it now, so we can stay longer." The first divers at Assumption Island were Albert Falco, Frédéric Dumas, Émile Robert, Luis Marden, Henri Plé, Octave Léandri, Jean-Louis Teicher, Louis Malle, Pierre Goupil, Edmond Sechan, Dr. Denis Martin-Laval, Simone, Delmas, and myself.

The structure of the island was classical. A shallow fringing reef, sparkling with sunshine and dancing color, extended two to three hundred feet from the white beach. It dropped off rather abruptly into a chaos of standing coral and grottoes for about two hundred feet, where a gray sedimental plain faded away into the ocean. Every foot of the slope was a model of extravagance, with the richest cocktails of coral that you could expect to find in the reefs of the world. Along the bank, mixing in friendly anarchy, were most of the species of fish we had met in a thousand other places and a quantity of new ones we had never seen before—as well as some kinds that no one had ever seen. Among the animals there prevailed a spirit of mutual interest and confidence. It was almost as though the struggle for life was suspended and the Peaceable Kingdom had been translated into the bosom of the waters.

During the next forty days our thirteen divers spent so much time with the fish that we became lean and haggard, hardly able to drag ourselves up the ladder to eat and sleep, but at the same time impatient for the next descent. Our skins became blotched with unhealed wounds. We developed unbearable itches from coral burns and the stings of invisible siphonophores. Delmas, whom we called "Tonton," had an attack of fever. He would shake and rattle his teeth for several hours and then dive again. The surgeon could not identify the illness—it had no relation to malaria. We called it "Tontonitis." Before long, one after another, we were stricken with Tontonitis, which seemed to be a marine allergy.

Here and there on the deep floor were cones of sand from six to twelve inches high which occasionally erupted like miniature volcanoes, presumably from the spout of a hidden animal. Again and again, Marden tried to photograph an eruption. As he lay on his stomach with his camera trained on a cone, all about him the other volcanoes spouted, but Marden's always remained dormant. After several days of this I went down to see what was keeping him busy. He was flat on the floor, looking with disgust at a non-performing volcano. I pointed my forefinger at one nearby and flipped my thumb like a trigger. It erupted. On board, Luis begged for my secret. I said, "I just had the fantastic luck to point at the thing when it was about to squirt." After many more patient hours Marden got his shot. We excavated several of the mounds to find the animal that was producing the jets, but we could not find one. It probably retreated into subterranean galleries deeper than we could dig with our hands.

Emile Robert, a stout Marseilles pastry cook turned professional diver, was Marden's assistant, bodyguard, and timekeeper. Once Robert came up from a session on the lower reef and described a small fish he had seen that had disappeared before Marden had a chance to photograph it. The fish was covered by a perfect grid of tile-red and white squares, for all the world like a checkerboard. Robert's "checkerboard fish" story drew pointed remarks about rapture of the deep. He was infuriated by our disbelief and, when below, dragged others to the haunt of the checkerboard fish. He could not produce it and the kidding got worse.

One day I was setting up a movie sequence around a deep black gorgonian, using the big flood lamps. All the divers were working on the shot. There came a loud hoot from Robert, who was giving off bubble balloons like a figure in a comic strip. He jabbed his finger at a branch of the black tree. There sat a fish three inches long with a body pattern of perfect squares like a tiled floor. After that, I think I would have believed a man who came out of the reef and told me he had seen an octopus wearing a derby hat and smoking a cigar. We have described the checkerboard fish to marine biologists; none have heard of anything like it.

During her protracted anchorage at Assumption Reef, *Calypso* became a sort of satellite island and attracted her own finny populace. At dusk each day, schools of two-foot-long milkfish arrived and spiraled around the ship in geometric formations, holding their heads out of the water. The slightest human interference—a shout, a spotlight, or a diver's fin off the ladder— dispersed this timid assemblage of eyes and tiny, upraised mouths.

During our dreary decompression stops ten feet under *Calypso,* we noted a lone barracuda, about four feet long, that skulked on the outskirts, never coming near us. We also saw three dozen remoras that had clamped themselves on the stern quarters two thousand miles back when we killed their shark hosts. The suckerfish had apparently been living on *Calypso's* garbage. We inventoried the remoras during stage decompression and learned that one or two of them left the ship each day. We wondered why. When a dozen suckerfish were left, Falco started diving at dawn to see why the remoras were leaving. His prowl was rewarded by something none of us had seen in thousands of hours underwater.

Falco came dripping to the breakfast table. "I saw the barracuda take a remora," he said. "I was a hundred feet away. The barracuda dashed to the stern and picked it off. I went in quickly. The barracuda had cut it in two and swallowed half. It had the other half crosswise in its mouth as it swam away." There it was: *Calypso* was providing bed and breakfast for a barracuda. We broke our truce on killing in the Aldabras. "Get your *arbalete*," I told Falco. He dived with his spear gun and executed the barracuda with a single shot.

There are three disturbing aspects of barracudas—their evil, threatening faces, their disagreeable habit of swimming close to your feet, and their gaudy reputation as man-eaters. The latter is merely an assumption based on the first attribute. Still . . . early in our work at Assumption, I was sixty feet down in the reef, filming close-ups of the guests in a fancy coral hotel. When the reel ran out, I gave the camera to my assistant to carry up while I used the rest of my air on a sightseeing ramble.

I turned away from him and looked at a wall of middle-sized barracudas. I looked up and down and to the sides through my diving mask, which limits vision like horse blinders. The bulkhead of barracudas extended from the ocean's floor to the surface. Alone and barehanded, I could not suppress a tremor of panic. We had never paid attention to barracudas, and I had dismissed them in print as being of no danger to divers. Now, in this confrontation, I was not so sure. They might have a mob psychology that would produce a sudden, irreparable act at any moment.

I told myself to stop being frightened and take refuge on the reef. I wheeled. A curtain of barracudas obscured the reef. With a hammering heart, I turned full around. I was encircled by wild animals, revolving deliberately around me, three or four fish thick. I could not see through them. There was no way out. I sank motionless to the bottom of the well, conserving the remainder of my air. The great silver cylinder turned evenly on the axis of my exhalations several times and then unrolled in a curtain of tail fins stroking west in the ocean.

On his first dive at Assumption, Marden encountered a grouper of about sixty pounds with a brownish coat and a pale marbled pattern that changed from time to time. The big fish strolled up to Marden, and he prepared to take its portrait. The grouper nudged the flashbulb bag with its nose. Luis backed away to get proper focus. The fish followed, showing interest in the shiny parts of the camera. By a series of retreats, Marden finally shot it in focus and swam away to find other fish. The grouper tagged along, nuzzling the photographer and his glittering gadgetry. As Luis lined up on another subject, the big fish interposed itself in the camera field. The diver dodged aside and made his shot. As he detached the used bulb from the reflector, the fish tried to eat it.

After Marden brought up this tale, Delmas and Dumas went down into the grouper's territory with a canvas bag full of chopped meat. The big fish came to them. The divers released some food in the water and the cavernous mouth opened. Giving the appearance of a flock of birds entering a tunnel, the meat scraps vanished into its belly. The underwatermen experimented cautiously with hand feeding, and the big fish plucked meat off their fingertips without harming them. In that first session Dumas and Delmas, using food rewards in various acrobatic situations, taught the grouper several tricks. They named the clever beast Ulysses.

Ulysses became our inseparable friend. He followed us everywhere, sometimes nibbling our fins. After deep dives, when we were decompressing thirty feet down on a weighted and measured cable, the boredom was enlivened by Ulysses' horsing around with us until we went to the ladder. Afterward he would hang around just under the surface, sitting on his tail, like a boy sadly watching his playmates being called in to supper. Ulysses quickly got on to our diving schedule and would be found early in the morning waiting under the ladder for the day's first sortie. He would go bounding down with us for a round of clumsy mischief and meals from the canvas bag.

Ulysses was a close cousin of the *merous* we knew in the Mediterranean. However, after twenty-five years of underwater hunting the *merous* had been conditioned to distrust man. In the first Aqua-Lung days they had come close and stared at us as Ulysses did, but in our home sea spears had ruined the possibility of an intimate association such as this. We had previously met at Aldabra another innocent grouper that could have been Ulysses' twin. It lived in a large black coral tree that we were attempting to remove as a specimen. The fish watched our labor. We got a sling on the tree and heaved it out with *Calypso*'s biggest winch. The grouper nervously accompanied his tree as it slowly ascended. Several times he dropped back to look at where it had been and then climbed up to where it was presently. As his home left the sea, the fish looked more down-in-the-mouth than usual.

Ulysses had refined his home life to a greater degree. We located his apartment, a deep crevice in the coral, which was hardly big enough to contain him but had the security factor of two entrances. The lair was thirty feet down, opening onto a terrace of white sand. The entries were bare and polished from his comings and goings. The place might as well have had his name plate on the door.

When in a good mood—and his emotions were by no means uniform—Ulysses would let any of us caress him and scratch his head. Dumas, partially concealing the meat bag in his hand, stood in midwater and turned at a slow, three-step tempo. Following the bait around, Ulysses joined the dance. When Dumas spun the other way, the fish followed right on the beat. It was done so lightly and rhythmically that we were able to film it as a waltz.

But Ulysses had a temper, too. Sometimes he bungled into camera setups of Marden's or Malle's, and they shoved him away impatiently. Then he would leave, slamming the door behind him. As a matter of fact, when he flounced off, his first tail stroke was so powerful that it made an audible boom, probably caused by cavitation. He also resented us when we forgot to bring the meat bag. When angry, he would hang thirty feet off, keeping to that distance whether we went toward him or away from him. However, next morning he would be waiting under the diving ladder, his grievances forgotten.

Delmas observed a certain cautious etiquette about feeding Ulysses, for as soon as one lump of meat was out of the bag, that huge gaping mouth flew at it. A grouper has no real teeth, but his mouth and throat have rows of grinders that would not improve the use of your arm if you placed it inside. One morning, Ulysses made a sly and rapid dash for the sack, tore it out of Delmas' hand, and swallowed it whole. He marched brazenly away, well aware that there was no more food forthcoming.

The next morning there was no Ulysses under the ladder. Down in our studio he did not appear. In the afternoon divers spread out to look for him. We found him lying on the sand in front of his den. His gills were pulsing at an unreasonable rate like the panting of a sick man. He had no interest in us. On the following morning he was still in bed with a severe case of indigestion caused by the stolen bag. I consulted Dr. Martin-Laval, who said Ulysses was in danger of a fatal intestinal obstruction. He advised us to keep him under observation. On the third day, we found the fish fallen flat on his side, seemingly critically ill. I went up and asked the doctor to do something. Martin-Laval was confronted with his most unusual case. Since he could not bring the fish to his surgery, he prepared to operate in the patient's bedroom. He gathered anesthetics, knives, surgical clips, and catgut and needle to suture the opening after he had removed the bag from Ulysses' tortured interior. The surgeon briefed three divers to act as his assistants. It was sundown before the preparations were in hand, and we went to sleep hoping that Ulysses would last through the night.

At first light, a reconnaissance team plunged. Ulysses was gone from his veranda. The divers roamed about, looking for him. Falco felt somebody pulling at his back harness. It was Ulysses, announcing that everything was okay. He was gay and hungry. He had managed to eliminate the meat sack.

Reluctantly we decided that *Calypso* could not postpone her trip to

Aldabra forever, so we took four days off to journey to the big atoll. Moving out of the bay, we came upon a boat containing one of the four inhabitants of Assumption Island. He held up an enormous grouper. It was a sixty-pounder, undoubtedly Ulysses. Our passage to Aldabra was full of mourning and disgust. We said a lot at table about the disastrous influence of man on nature. Our species was cursed! Ulysses would never have grown so large had he not had an instinctive aversion to hooks, but we had accustomed him to association with man—we had baited him with finger morsels and led him to bite the fatal hook.

We returned to Assumption in a different mood from the joyful day of discovery. With Ulysses gone, the reef wonderland would not be the same. While I was maneuvering *Calypso* toward the anchorage, Falco could not contain his impatience. He jumped overboard with mask and fins and swam toward the fabled reef. Then his fins shot into the air and down he went. He popped back, leaping out of the water like a hysterical porpoise. "Ulysses is alive!" Falco bellowed. As soon as the diving ladder was down, our friend was there waiting for the fun to resume.

Although Ulysses was a loner, there were two slightly smaller groupers living a hundred feet from him on either side. They were much less interested in men. As we came to know the region, we observed that none of the three would venture into each other's territory. They were chieftains of three principalities. When we swam into the flanking domains, Ulysses would stop at the border and accompany us no further. Just across the invisible boundary the other lord would be on patrol. We never witnessed a border fight but sensed that they occurred. Observance of property rights was relaxed for two other smaller groupers that traveled freely across the frontiers. Their attitude toward divers was unpredictable. They were usually aggressive, but at other times seemed timid. We were fairly sure that they were females. Once we found them close to Ulysses, weaving in a suggestive way, all three fishes turned completely white.

We experimented with feeding other denizens of the reef, and all responded heartily. We swam along, distributing chopped meat from a bag in the manner of a peasant sowing grain. This attracted fish by the thousands —especially pretty yellow snappers, which swept along at our heels pecking the manna from heaven. Watching us feed them put Ulysses in a towering rage. He would crash into the sack, bite our fins, tug on our bathing trunks, and whip his big tail to scatter the little ones.

We wanted to film this golden host following a manfish across the reef, but Ulysses kept breaking it up. He would not get out of the scene and often bumped the camera or the flood lamps. Falco thought of a way to get rid of him without banging his snout and injuring his *amour-propre*. We assembled the antishark cage and dropped it to the bottom. Ulysses supervised the placing of the yellow cage and the opening of the door. Delmas waved his feeding arm toward the opening and the fish swam in. The door clanked shut, and Ulysses was in protective custody.

As a sort of object lesson, Delmas fed a rally of snappers just outside the bars while Ulysses glowered. But the caterer did not have the heart to torture his friend more and decided that Ulysses should have a special treat while he was in jail. This was the same day that Falco killed the barracuda that had been feeding on the remoras. We wondered whether Ulysses would care for a twenty-pound barracuda, which was as long as he was, although sticklike by comparison. We took the still-bleeding marauder down to the cage and poked the head of the long fish through the bars. Without hesitation Ulysses gulped in more than half the barracuda's body, leaving the tail sticking from his mouth. The grouper seemed to regard this as nothing out of the ordinary and remained for hours with the barracuda protruding from his mouth. When we left for the night, there was still about a third of the barracuda visible. In the morning it was gone. We were puzzled over how Ulysses managed it. The barracuda was stiff as a broomstick and certainly could not have been doubled up in the stomach. The head must have been jammed right into the pit of Ulysses' gut. Apparently the grouper simply turned on his gastric juices to melt away the front end, bones and all, and ingested the rest when he had made room for it.

Ulysses was caged for three days while we completed the film. When we opened the jail door, the grouper watched with interest but made no move to depart. In vain did Delmas wave his magic arm. Apparently our friend, considering the abundant food provided in the cage, preferred to stay there. Falco went in with him and pushed him through the door. Ulysses swam off in a sulk, at a much slower pace than usual. He was fat and out of shape.

After five weeks at the reef, cook Hanen warned me that we were running low on food. He refused to let Delmas and Dumas have any more meat to feed the fishes, so they turned to bootlegging Ulysses' daily fare. The twosome stretched this out by diving for tridacnas and mincing the clam meat in with the kitchen scraps. There were some curious looks from hungry deckhands who passed the kitchen and saw two madmen chopping up delicious protein to give to fish. The divers were exhausted and wobbling with reef fever, but nobody wanted to leave. We still had a week's rationed supply of fresh water.

Six days afterward, Hanen told me he had no meat left. Since we were about to leave, I decided we should make a decent final meal. I asked Delmas to go down and spear a fat grouper, and I accompanied him. So did Ulysses. It was like hunting with a retriever dog. Delmas selected a black grouper and triggered his spear gun. What happened then came so fast that it took a moment to sort it out. Virtually synchronized with the flight of the spear, Ulysses hit the fish, and then we saw its tail and the four-foot harpoon protruding from his mouth. Delmas placed his foot against Ulysses' head and heaved hard to extract the spear. This gave the grouper more room to accommodate the catch, and he swallowed it all except the tip of the tail.

We returned to *Calypso* and told the hungry mob that our pet had eaten their dinner. Delmas and I were much impressed by Ulysses' reflexes. For weeks he had followed us about at a lumbering gait, with only a hint of his power and speed when he cracked his tail whip or when he stole the meat bag. Now he had showed us how sharp he was the first time another creature got into trouble along the reef. This pointed out one of the main laws of our jungle. To catch a healthy fish in a three-dimensional world was a difficult task, but there was no mercy for any kind of disabled individual.

By the close of our sixth week at Assumption Reef, we were a bunch of rickety scarecrows, breaking into teeth-chattering bouts of Tontonitis, and covered with pious sores. The eye still came alight with pleasure at the thought of the next dive, but there was a glint of dementia in it. The game was up. We had to leave. "Let's take Ulysses with us," said Delmas.

The idea was met with enthusiasm. The bosun planned a tarpaulin-lined pool on the afterdeck. However, I had to oppose the notion. In France, Ulysses either would face life imprisonment in an aquarium or would have to be liberated in the sea. He was probably not adapted for colder water. On top of that he was so friendly that the first spearman he met would have an easy kill. As the capstan rattled, we dived for the last time and waved good-by to our friend.

Four years later, after Ulysses had become a movie star in our film *The Silent World,* a boat sailing around the world made a special call at Assumption Bay and sent divers down to look for the tame grouper. The circumnavigators reported, "Ulysses is doing fine. He was easy to recognize.

He swam up immediately to the divers." Perhaps we will go back someday and see him again. He's a fish worth going halfway round the earth to meet.

The sea floor around Assumption was littered with sea cucumbers. We saw many of the species, which is fished commercially and dried for human consumption in the Orient, where it is considered a great delicacy. This creature grows to be two feet long. It has a thick brown mufflike body covered with blunt white spicules. Robert brought one aboard *Calypso* and was holding it up for a photograph when the sea cucumber emptied itself. The organs fell out and with them two slender living fish about a foot long, which wriggled desperately on deck. They showed no injury from gastric acid. They had not been eaten by the sea cucumber, but were its associates, called pearl fish, who find hospitality in the intestine of the cucumber. Most of the holothurians we examined had at least one tenant.

On the sea floor we observed the curious method by which a frightened pearl fish retreats inside the cucumber. It does not enter the mouth. The pearl fish places its tail in the anus of the host and wiggles in backwards. The sea cucumber gets its food by sucking in sand and filtering out minute organisms. This thin gruel did not seem adequate to feed one or two active fish as well. We thought that the pearl fish must spend most of the day in the cucumber and go out at night to make its living.

Falco has seen uncommon doings among Mediterranean sea cucumbers, which are smaller than the Indian Ocean variety. On a certain day in April each year the big diver would go out in the morning to the green posidonie grass prairies at Sormiou to witness an annual rite that he discovered. The rest of the year the holothurians lie about like so many abandoned sections of pipe, but on this spring day around noon a single sea cucumber raises its body vertically, stretches itself out thin, and begins swaying back and forth like a cobra undulating to the music of a fakir. Then all the cucumbers in the meadow arise and take up the movement. They gather in pairs, stretching themselves higher and thinner still. Suddenly milky liquid jets from their higher extremities, spreads and dissolves in the water. The holothurians fall back. Ninety seconds later they arise again and repeat the dance and the white spout. It goes on for over an hour until apparently the fluid is exhausted. It is surely a love ceremony. During the following week the Sormiou holothurians are very active, feeding heavily on weeds, crushed shells, and sand. Then they fall into their usual torpor until the magic April noon comes around again.

Falco came across another surprising phenomenon while diving with Philippe Cousteau off the rocky coast of Madeira. They were crossing a dark sand flat a hundred feet down when they sighted a large patch of brown, pencil-thin stalks eighteen inches high and curved at the top like question marks. There were about twenty growths to a square yard. At first they appeared to be weeds, but on closer inspection they moved in an animal fashion that indicated they were worms.

As the divers closed in, the creatures retracted into the sand. Falco and Philippe loitered above, and some of the animals reared back from the floor. Falco noted that they had tiny eyes and mouths. The rest erected themselves and bent into the prevailing current.

Günther Maul, curator of the Madeira museum, could not identify the animal from Falco's description and asked us to bring him specimens. When we tried to dig them out by hand, they burrowed faster than we could. Reluctantly we exploded an ounce of dynamite and got some. Maul exclaimed, "It's an eel, *Heteroconger longissimus!* In my twenty-five years here, I've seen only two caught on the surface."

"There's a million of them downstairs," Philippe said.

Edgerton's camera cables have furnished us with social introductions to a number of interesting animals. Once in the Tyrrhenian Sea *Calypso* was adrift with a camera down, and we went mask swimming. We could see more than a hundred feet down the wire on which the camera was clicking away, six thousand feet below. We saw a whitish shape coming up the wire. It materialized into a young wreckfish, *Polyprion cernium,* with large, grieving lips and lively eyes. The species makes surprising vertical migrations. Divers have speared them a hundred feet deep, and Commandant Houot photographed one from the bathyscaph 2300 feet down. Sailors named them wreckfish because they often shelter under floating crates and dunnage.

This wreckfish, all alone, came steadily up the wire, which was an event in its life, a trail worth following. It went to Falco, who held out his hand. The wreckfish nibbled roguishly at his fingers, never quite touching them. The traveler from the deep played around with us for a half-hour and then followed us to the ladder.

Now, substitute a floating palm frond or egg crate for Falco, and the wreckfish was merely following its custom of surfacing under flotsam. But why did it come all the way up from great depths? We gathered some information on the problem in the mid-Atlantic. *Calypso* was working her various remote instruments on a sea mount that reached to within six hundred feet of the surface. Several large manta rays were circling on the surface in the area. The mantas appeared to have curious appendages swinging from their bodies. We manned the bow chamber and nosed closer to the black flying carpets. The underwater observers saw that the thing underneath each manta was a half-grown wreckfish of the same white hue as the ray's belly and swimming with it in perfect unison. The reason for the wreckfish's vertical migration seemed revealed. It came up to patrol for food under the manta's wings. Since the ray eats only plankton, the fish had no reason to avoid it. Thus, innocent prey was delivered to the camou-flaged wreckfish. What the manta got out of the symbiosis, we could not determine. It seems possible that young wreckfish escort other large marine animals in this fashion, but we have yet to witness that. For the moment we only know that they like to team up with flotsam, mantas, and Falco. However, we have never seen a mature wreckfish ascend in this fashion.

The wreckfish was not the only creature that arrived in our ken along the deep instrument cable, an Ariadne's thread from their maze to ours. On a Mediterranean station Octave Léandri was leaning over the rail, lazily watching the top of the wire on a deep-water sampler. From the depths he saw a long shining shape arrive along the line. It cast blue and brownish reflections on the surface. Léandri called to Falco, a man ever ready to examine strange things in the water. Falco had his fins on in an instant and was molding his mask to his face as he hurdled the rail. Down along the wire he looked at one of the most beautiful creatures of the abyssal sea: the *Regalecus*, king of the ribbonfish. It was about six feet long and an inch thick, seemingly constructed of silver foil overlaid with a few orange and vibrant blue patterns. Its flat forehead sprouted orange antennae.

Some writers see in *Regalecus* the source of sea serpent legends. Here it was alive, three feet from Falco's mask, standing head up along the wire in the sun after an inexplicable climb from the abyss. Swift undulations of the ribbony body carried it upward. Then the ribbonfish reversed the undula-tions and went down just as efficiently by its tail. As the animal slid up and down like an elevator, Falco surfaced and called for Léandri to toss him a spear gun. This was the first ribbonfish the diver had seen, and a valuable specimen.

Falco shot. There was a fiery flash, and the *Regalecus* exploded in a shower of silver dust. As Falco reeled in his spear line, he saw shining fragments sinking into the blue. This was the most fragile fish he had ever encountered. Through the falling remains another ribbonfish climbed the cable toward him. It repeated the up-and-down rippling motion along the top of the cable. Falco exchanged his powerful gun for a hand spear. He pierced the newcomer very gently and carried an intact specimen aboard. The tinsel serpent expired quickly, its nonesuch gleam turning gray and the vivid orange designs fading into blue polka dots.

Several times since then and always in the same spring season, ribbonfish have climbed *Calypso*'s deeply-stretched instrument wires. At such times we like to snorkel around the cable and watch the dazzling fish arrive. No longer do we kill them. We address them with a mute aspiration: you have come all this way to meet us in the light; one day we shall return the visit to your home in the space without sun.

chapter
eleven

GOLDEN
SNAKES

By 1954 the unforeseen financial demands of Port
Calypso and the new O.F.R.S. undersea research center were driving me
close to despair. I plunged my literary, film, and lecture income into pay-
rolls. My petitions to the Ministry of National Education for support had
gotten as far as the budget estimates when the government fell. I started
from the beginning again with successive cabinets, but they all went out of
office with my applications in their dead files.

The turning point of our fortunes, when our outfit was facing com-
pulsory dissolution, came on a dank drizzling afternoon in Marseilles. I
was ashore, looking for help, when a man in a tight Savile Row suit, de-
tachable collar, and black umbrella came aboard *Calypso* and said to
Simone, "I say, Madame, would Captain Cousteau be interested in con-
ducting a submarine prospection for the British Petroleum Company?"

She said, "Please come in out of the rain," and gave the angel a whiskey and soda. "I have heard of British Petroleum," said Simone. "My cousin, Basil Jackson, is the head of it."

"Yes, rather," the supernatural visitor replied. "However, Sir Basil does not know of my call. I represent the D'Arcy Exploration Company, a subsidiary of B.P. My chief read your husband's book and thinks he could do a good job of looking into our offshore concession at Abu Dhabi."

"Where is Abu Dhabi?" Simone inquired.

The angel said, "A sheikhdom on the Trucial Oman Coast of the Persian Gulf, formerly known as the Pirate Coast." Simone offered a toast to pirates. He asked, "And how are you related to Sir Basil, Madame?"

She said, "Through an Irish grandmother."

When I came gloomily back aboard, I found my wife laughing with the stranger. That is how D'Arcy Exploration saved *Calypso*. Our fee was a fraction of the cost of the customary sea-exploring rig, but I calculated that we could do the oil survey in four months and have enough left over to buy equipment we were longing for.

In the Hormuz Strait, gateway to the gulf, I broke the voyage to penetrate the Elphinstone Inlet, reputedly "the hottest place on earth." It is a steep, narrow fjord slicing through naked limestone mountains in the Arabian peninsula. At the entrance we made a snap underwater reconnaissance, and the men came up with baskets of concreted oysters, which they cracked open and ate without bothering about edibility or season. Laban proffered me one on the tip of his knife. It was as fine an oyster as I have ever tasted. Later we met nobody in the Persian Gulf who knew that edible oysters existed there.

The "hottest place" was suffocatingly hot, even in February. *Calypso* went into its deepest recess and anchored off a sand bar under a thousand-foot cliff. There lay Sibi, a village of mud huts with slate roofs—surely the most hellish habitation on earth. It consisted of a hundred puny, desiccated people. We went ashore at twilight. No women or children were in sight. A few dark wraithlike men squatted on the sand. They did not answer salutations, although *Calypso*'s call may have been the event of the century in Sibi.

There was not one leaf of vegetation in the whole Elphinstone Inlet and no sign of fresh water. There were no domestic animals, not even a starved dog. Not until we called in Bahrain did we learn how the people of Sibi lived. In winter the women weaved goat-hair carpets and the men seined small fish which they dried on the burning beaches to sell as cattle food in

Bahrain. In the summer, when even they could not survive the heat, the entire populace scaled the thousand-foot cliff and trekked to oases in the Hadramaut to harvest dates and collect goat hair.

Next morning at anchor we heard harsh chants coming through the thick mists of the fjord. Out of the fog came Sibi boats, their men begging water. We gave them all we could spare against our running time to Bahrain. The boatmen drew their fingernails across their throats. I thought it just as well that we had confined the interchange to our respective vessels. Saôut and the bosun took up boat hooks. Just then, Malle said, "Hold it. They are asking for razor blades." We gave them some.

A Sibi skipper began a harangue, pointing to a large bundle of black rags in his boat. Thinking we might be able to use the rags to wipe the motors, we began finger bargaining with him. He wanted the equivalent of fifty dollars in Marie Theresa silver thalers, the only coin trusted in Arabia. The bundle of black rags moved slightly. We gestured that we would like to see what was inside. He was opposed in principle but finally lifted a corner of the cloth. We saw four kohled women's eyes, burning with anxiety. One pair seemed that of a child. We fell silent with loathing before the ancient infamy of our race. The skipper was trying to sell us two girls for fifty dollars. "Let's haul anchor!" I said. The Sibi boats faded behind, the men shaking their fists at *Calypso*.

To our minds the Persian Gulf meant pearl diving, an industry that was rapidly dying out. We put Louis Malle ashore to film one of the last pearling sambuks on a cruise out of Dubeh. The divers were elderly, wretched-looking men. On the pearl grounds they donned nose clips made of shark's vertebrae, laced hooks on two fingers of each hand, and took up a collecting basket weighted with stones. One pulled on a suit of black underwear, which the *nakouda,* or pearling captain, said protected him from shark attack.

Malle followed them to the bottom, where their naked eyes were nearly blind, but their hands moved rapidly and surely, tossing oysters into the basket. In the hundreds of shells they brought up, there was not a single pearl. Working away from the regular grounds, *Calypso* divers found a lonely, lopsided pearl that we kept to make a ring for the fiancée of bosun Raud, who was to be married when we got home.

The Persian Gulf was often swept by unannounced shamals, a severe gale that lasted about twelve hours. Saôut anticipated busy days holding anchorages and recovering divers when the shamal pounced. Between blows the sea was usually without swell or breeze; the blue-gray expanse looked like a sheet of lead. In this state, on moonless nights, it was the most phosphorescent water we had ever seen. On such a night, I was standing in the bow with Dugan and Allen Russell, an Australian geologist with D'Arcy Exploration. The top one-inch layer of water was like a radiant glass panel that came alight at the touch of a switch. *Calypso* moved in an aureole of glowing plankton. Out in the dark an incandescent sea turtle paddled along. The pressure waves of our propellers churned up a silver maelstrom that rolled several hundred feet in our wake. The bioluminescence, however, was not entirely caused by our intrusion. Considerably below the surface panel there were explosions of light that we called "flash bulbs," thousands of which fired at random. We netted the creature that caused them—a jelly barrel, shaped not unlike a flash bulb. Russell said, "You know, sailing on board *Calypso* is so interesting you lose track of time. One morning you could wake up an old man." I thought he touched on what we received as compensation for the dire struggles ashore. We were wresting weeks of timelessness from the sea.

British Petroleum had assigned us a survey area as large as four French departments, in which we were to make detailed maps of gravity variations on the sea floor and take samples of the bottom. We used a marine gravimeter, a large bell-like contraption on a traveling crane that ran on rails on *Calypso*'s deck. We would roll the gravimeter out over the side and lower it to the floor, where it adjusted itself to perfect level and transmitted gravity readings to receivers on board. If it struck an anomaly in the earth's gravity level, there might be an oil dome below. The bottom samples also gave helpful information on oil-bearing pockets. If an anomaly coincided with the presence of certain Eocene fossils, the geologists would mark the spot as promising for test drilling later. We were pledged to carry out this procedure in at least two hundred stations in the Abu Dhabi marine concession.

When *Calypso* arrived in the potential oil field, she was buzzed by a Shell Company aircraft, defending the invisible dotted line between Shell and B.P. concessions. The Shell expedition consisted of hundreds of men in launches, barges, and an air-conditioned dormitory ship, *Shell Quest,* which was a former passenger liner. Some months before, the liner had arrived rather light on a high tide and anchored in very shallow water. As she sank under the weight of men, fuel oil, and stores, the *Shell Quest* became trapped in a sandy bathtub. Since then the empties her inhabitants tossed overboard had raised the rim of the tub. The "bottle reef," as they called it, was mounting steadily in obedience to Darwin's Law of reef building. The

Shell Quest seemed destined to become a lagoon of rust in a glass atoll.

Dumas and I visited her by launch and were most amiably received. The Shell people said we could calibrate our gravimeter on their buoy, which was placed at a point where absolute gravity had been accurately measured, close to a desert island called Halul where they had a Decca station. Later *Calypso* called at Halul after dark. We saw a light and went ashore. We stumbled across rugged terrain to a window and looked in. A young man with fair hair reaching his shoulders sat engrossed in a book. Dumas knocked. The young man opened the door and gasped. He pointed to Didi and said, "You're Frédéric Dumas!" He showed us his book, opened to the place where we had interrupted him. There was a photo of Didi. The book was *The Silent World.*

"I'm Tony Mould," he said. "Please come in." We entered the hermit's air-conditioned lair. "In summer," he said, "we get 130 degrees and ninety percent humidity."

Dumas said, "It must get monotonous for you."

Mould replied, "Busy time here a few weeks back. The shamal was blowing, and a pilgrim sambuk from Persia beached here in sinking condition— two hundred people who hadn't eaten for five days. I radioed for relief, but no ship would come out in the storm. Had to thin out my stores to feed women and kiddies. The men didn't like it. They were bloody well shocked to see food passing over the head of the house. Had 'em here eight days before a ship came."

We took the Decca hermit with us to dinner on *Calypso,* and Laban gave him a haircut. The divers gathered around the barber chair and asked Mould about underwater conditions. "Don't happen to be one of you diving johnnies," said he. "But the pearling boats bury their divers on my island. Come by and I'll show you their graveyard. Twenty-two blokes there. Two of them taken by sharks, I'm told. The rest by sea snakes."

Before we took up Station One of the survey, I went to Bahrain to arrange for supplies and find out about sea snakes. The French consul and several physicians told me that the lethal marine serpent of the Persian Gulf was no myth. There were untold numbers of them in several species growing as long as cobras, and they dealt a venom for which no antidote was available. "However," said an expert, "even a seven-footer has such a tiny mouth that it cannot bite the major planes of a human body. It has to strike a small fold of skin, such as the soft tendon between the thumb and forefinger." I wondered why nature had made a killer with such a poor applicator and returned to *Calypso* apprehensively pinching a certain tendon.

At our first geological station we rigged the drop corer to obtain bottom samples. The corer was a bomb-shaped steel device that weighed a third of a ton. Fitted in its nose was a tempered steel coring pipe. We dropped the bomb in forty-five feet of water. When we hauled it in, the coring pipe was missing. Divers went down and found it lying on a flat sand bottom, bent into an S. The cutting mouth was crumpled like a paper napkin. The divers scooped into the sand. An inch below was rock like armor plate. In previous tests the coring pipe had bitten several inches into limestone. What sort of rock was this?

We fitted another pipe and bombed the floor again. The pipe came up attached but bent into a Z, and the cutting edge was smashed. Two of our four coring pipes were ruined on the first station. Another team went down with a crowbar, stuck it in a mollusk hole, and pried off a few chips, but there were not enough for the geologists. Dumas went after a bigger sample with a pneumatic chisel. He inserted it in a mussel boring and turned on the compressed air. He bounced ten feet off the bottom. Each time he tried to dent the rock, the stabbing chisel sent him flying.

Dumas surfaced and added weights to his belt. We also lowered the anti-shark cage for him to cling to for leverage. He obtained a few inadequate rock fragments. Short of a prolonged and expensive blasting attack, the armored floor seemed to be resisting all methods of sampling.

However, we tried again, sending down one man with a cold chisel and another with a big maul. One held the chisel and the other pounded it, as if driving a tent stake. It is an extraordinary physical feat to swing a hammer through a medium at least eight hundred times heavier than air, and without a purchase on the ground. Yet our men did it. They chiseled out acceptable samples on 150 stations. We continued working in this sea-in-a-desert through squalls and sandstorms. While the water was as cold as that of the Mediterranean in winter, we baked on deck. The only diversion on days off was to watch camel races in the primitive village of Abu Dhabi.

We used the antishark cage as an elevator to take the divers to and from their labors. On the floor it also served as an emergency refuge. However, its bars, spaced eight inches apart, would not exclude sea snakes. During the first week's work we saw no snakes. Then, passing to a new station, we came to a flat sea covered with writhing white-and-yellow-barred ribbons.

The snakes looked as unreal as the articulated wooden ones that pop out of Hindu trick boxes. Some dived away from *Calypso,* while others drifted past quite close. It would have been easy to scoop some of them up with a spoon net, but nobody dared to do it. To our relief, the next geological station lay beyond the big snake patch.

I took a movie camera and joined Dumas and Kientzy in the cage. Visibility was poor below—fifteen or twenty feet. When the elevator reached bottom, Dumas fanned away the thin layer of dust on the hard rock, looking for a crack into which he could insert a chisel, while Kientzy and I wandered about inspecting the paltry life forms on the floor. Around scrubby little gorgonians there were colorless reef fishes—nothing worth filming. Then, materializing from the fog, came our first sea snake. It undulated along close to the bottom. Its head was ridiculously small and its mouth was unimpressive. It passed us without curiosity and faded into the turbid sea. A second and bigger one arrived. It was about seven feet long. The snake circled around us languidly. The eyes in its incredible pinhead were so small we could not tell whether or not it was interested in us. I maneuvered for a camera position in front of it and motioned for Kientzy to swim into the lens field. He misunderstood and swung his hammer, trying to batter the snake's head into the floor. It was pretty ludicrous to see a man trying to hit an animal almost as fluid as water itself. Yet Kientzy succeeded with a terrible blow near the head. The snake swam nervously away despite the mortal wound. I asked the divers not to attack the snakes.

Several days passed before we saw another sea snake. In fact, it was a rare occurrence, and they never molested us in thousands of dives in the Persian Gulf. I think they are just one more creature defamed as a monster.

We left the gulf with "Station 400" proudly chalked on the blackboard. We had completed twice as many gravimetric readings as were required. Several areas of the concession showed anomalies, substantiated by Eocene rock samples. British Petroleum was sufficiently encouraged to send a seismic refraction expedition and later a test drilling platform. In July, 1962, the first tanker load of petroleum from the "*Calypso* grounds" left the offshore terminal at Abu Dhabi. The marine field was already producing forty thousand barrels a day.

Our oil search ended with an unexpected augury of good days ahead: a radiogram announced that the National Centre for Scientific Research and the Ministry of National Education had agreed to help finance Calypso

Oceanographic Expeditions. We would receive about two-thirds of our annual operating costs in return for carrying scientific missions nine months a year. We had waited four years for a minister to last long enough to fulfill this pledge of government support.

Since their novitiate in undersea petroleum work, *Calypso* and the O.F.R.S. have been involved with other industrial operations. We decline chores that could and should be handled by regular commercial helmet-diving or Aqua-Lung teams and pick new and challenging jobs. We test submerged devices and have helped lay electrical cables in the Gulf of Lions. One of our strangest jobs was hunting water underwater.

Like many communities today, the sea town of Cassis east of Marseilles faced a water shortage. Yet fishermen and divers knew that a large volume of fresh water was pouring into the sea under a white limestone headland at nearby Port-Miou. The phenomenon had been recorded as early as 1725. To investigate the submarine resurgence for the town, the O.F.R.S. took the *Espadon* and thirty-five divers and technicians to Port-Miou.

The subterranean river opened to the sea about forty feet below the surface. Eight two-man diving teams worked in relays to penetrate the hidden river, stringing electric lights along the ceiling as they leapfrogged forward. A hundred and fifty feet inside, they hit a pocket of daylight and surfaced in a pothole whose dry walls rose fifty feet above the water. They shortened the length of the flare path by moving the generators up to the top of the pothole and letting the power lines into the water there.

The long cave continued on a horizontal axis with a water depth of about fifty feet. It proved to be a split-level river. On the bottom, salty warm water flowed into the cave, while on top, cold brackish water moved out. The interface between the opposing streams was a very distinct tissue that looked like glycerine. If a diver popped his head up through it, he was tugged between north and south and warm and cold. However, the split-level river was a natural commuting system for the explorers. They went in on the bottom and out on the top.

Three hundred feet inside there was a small air pocket in the ceiling. Beyond, there was nothing but solid, rock-walled water. The salinometers never indicated pure fresh water, but there were many instances of very low salt content that indicated a fresh-water source further away. The O.F.R.S. men reached a point 975 feet from the cave entrance, where the bottom of the river fell away to a water depth of 95 feet and the roof slanted down to 50 feet. It was impossible to penetrate further because of the distance. However, a geological analysis of the less saline currents led us to recommend to the Cassis authorities places where they might in the future strike fresh water with rock drills.

Another unusual industrial experiment was called Project Red Mud. The aluminum plant at Gardanne, near Marseilles, was virtually burying the countryside in piles of red waste. The disposal engineers, as is always the case when they have to dump excess waste, thought of turning to the sea. They proposed to dilute the stuff and pipe-line it into the Mediterranean shelf. Fishermen and marine biologists protested that the red muck would kill everything on the bottom, and I agreed with them. However, I told the aluminum people that I would help them find a marine solution, if one existed.

First, we would have to see the actual effect of dumping on the shallow floor. Would the mud settle, scatter, or be diffused by currents? I borrowed a lighthouse tender, loaded it with mud, and moved out to clear blue water at Morgiou where, fifteen feet down, there was a typical Marseillaise bottom of sand and posidonie grass pasturage. We put a color cinematographer on the floor under the discharge pipe, and the ship started pumping. A dark column jetted down. In midwater it spread rapidly in scrolling waves, followed by a hail of red gravel that thudded into the sand. Fish fled in all directions. Soon it looked like an inverted atomic bomb explosion as the fallout rolled away and slowly settled. Divers were obscured by red fog. The trial proved that this kind of disposal would finish the fishing grounds on the Continental Shelf.

But suppose the aluminum wastes were released from a deep pipe mouth into a natural container such as a submarine canyon? We selected a six-thousand-foot-deep mud canyon four miles off Cassis, which was too deep to be exploited for food but deep enough to hold all the red muck on hand as well as all that the plant could make in a hundred years. We made a detailed sonar survey off the canyon and outlined a deep pipe line that would discharge into the canyon at a depth of a thousand feet. The mud would roll down to the bottom, well below the trawling range. The deep outflow handed us an unexpected scientific bonus. The regular and measurable artificial sedimentation could be kept under observation to tell us how turbidity currents behave and how far the mud spreads on the abyssal plain.

Calypso's largest industrial job came in 1958, after drillers in the Sahara had brought in natural gas wells at Hassi R'Mel that contained reserves unprecedented in Europe or Africa. Unlike the United States with its wealth of natural gas, Europe relies on expensive gas made from coal. Hassi R'Mel could fulfill the enormous consumption potential of Europe, which was calculated to reach at least 750 billion cubic feet a year. One way to bring the Sahara gas to cookstoves in Stockholm and factories in Trieste was to have it piped to the Mediterranean, liquefied in plants, carried in tankers to European ports, evaporated again, and piped to consumers. However, this enormous investment in plant and ships could not begin to cope with the natural production or the need.

M. Jacques de la Ruelle, inspector general of the French national company, Gaz de France, came up with the exceedingly bold idea of piping the desert gas right across the Mediterranean floor, thus eliminating liquefying and evaporating plants and tanker fleets. The sea line would have to be laid more than eight thousand feet down at the shallowest cross section of the western Mediterranean, and the shortest distance would be 115 nautical miles. De la Ruelle was not so much concerned about the depth as he was about laying pipe on the steep, broken continental slopes of Africa and Spain. He asked *Calypso* to survey a wide area around the proposed crossing to find the best pipe bedding. We resigned scientific grants for six months and went to work for the gas company.

The job called on every art of bottom exploration that we knew—and some that we had to develop. The pipe-liners wanted to know exact depths within a three-foot margin of error and to have geographical positions with an accuracy of fifty feet. In the prodigious slice of vertical data we had to account for current velocities at all levels, obtain a close series of bottom samples all the way, determine the microbiological and oxygen content of the samples, run corrosion tests, and take stereo and motion pictures of the route along the bottom.

For her precision survey *Calypso* was fitted with a sixty-foot radio-navigation antenna on the afterdeck. It transmitted waves bounced from two shore stations in Algeria and Spain. We installed precision sonar and a hydrographic charting table, where shifts of draftsmen correlated the Decca fixes and sonar profiles to make charts as accurate as the largest GHQ military map sections.

At the end of five months I was able to give de la Ruelle a three-dimensional scale model of the ideal pipe-line route between Mostaganem and Cartagena, along with a truckload of supporting evidence, classified mud and rock samples, a sheaf of charts, stacks of data and interpretations, and thousands of photos and film reels keyed to chart references; whereupon the inspector general sailed out and laid several miles of test pipe in various sections of the route.

The first intercontinental pipe line may be as important to the peoples of Africa and Europe as were the first transoceanic telegraph cables a hundred years ago. I share de la Ruelle's firm belief that it will be successfully laid and that it can be inspected and maintained by submarine vehicles.

BOTTOM

chapter twelve

OF

THE SEA

My father, Daniel Cousteau, was having a precautionary talk with an inspector in the customs office at Cannes, to persuade him to pass promptly some unique and nondutiable scientific apparatus arriving that day. From a liner offshore, Harold Edgerton came in on a lighter with boxes of the devices in question. The inspector dutifully pointed to one and asked to see what was in it. Papa Flash blushed and opened it. Inside were jars of peanut butter, without which U.S. Calypsonians seemed unable to carry on.

The *douanier* pointed to another case at random. His eyebrows rose as he gazed at a pack of red M.I.T. freshman caps. Edgerton scooped up the hats, with which he had wadded his new undersea invention, the Pinger. In order to convince the inspector that here was a real scientific device, he tripped a mercury switch and the Pinger began to ping. Suspecting that he might be dealing with a bomb, the inspector detained the two for six hours before they could get the gear released.

The Pinger was Edgerton's attempt to overcome the frustrations of the summer before when we had first tried to photograph deep bottoms with his electronic flash camera. We would focus the camera for eight or ten feet from the bottom and set it to take a picture every twelve seconds. The trouble was that when we lowered it, we did not know how far it was from the floor. We reeled the camera down, guessed when it hit, and bounced it, hoping for some clear shots. The lens often came back encased in a lump of mud of interest only to sedimentologists.

In the middle of this feckless campaign we repaired to the Naval Arsenal at Toulon and scrounged a magnetostrictive sonar transducer, the device that is fixed to ships' hulls to send and receive echo sounds. Edgerton coupled it with a waterproof oscillator to make an audible ping each second. Then he hitched the rig to the electronic flash camera rack and attached a mercury switch to an eight-foot tripline beneath the assembly. We focused for eight feet and lowered away, while I listened to the sonar pings on earphones. When they ceased, I yelled "*Stoppez!*" to the winchman and had him haul the camera up a few feet until the pings started again. The camera was now placed eight feet from the floor.

But our difficulties did not end there. *Calypso* drifted the depth rig across irregular terrain in which it bumped obstacles or went out of focus. The pings stopped and started unpredictably, and the winchman could not adjust the camera quickly enough. Edgerton tackled this problem by aiming the sound source attached to the camera downward, bouncing echoes off the floor, as well as signaling directly to the surface. Now on shipboard we could read the distance from the bottom. This improvisation, born on *Calypso*, became the Pinger with which oceanographic vessels now deploy instruments within a foot from a deep floor.

Calypso trailed the Pinger over miles of abyssal landscape in the Atlantic, Mediterranean and Indian oceans. The apparatus, pointed down like an aerial survey camera, took up to eight hundred shots on a single lowering in depths ranging from a half-mile to three miles. Our film cans piled up. However, in the thousands of photographs showing floors riddled with craters, cones, and serpentine burrows, not a single picture showed an animal that could be definitely associated with the building of these bottom structures.

Papa Flash had built the most sophisticated depth camera in existence, and instead of giving us answers, it merely raised more questions about life in the dark reaches. "Robot oceanography is getting nowhere," I said to him. He grinned. Edgerton is the sort who will throw his life's work out of the window if he can envisage a better technique. We both knew what that better technique was: the unaided human eye plunged into the dark mystery.

Only the watchful eye, not the random probe of lowered instruments, could reveal the identities of the dwellers beneath the floor. Professor Jean-Marie Pérès came nearer than any of us to discovering an abyssal underground creature. He went down ten thousand feet in *F.N.R.S.-3* off Portugal and asked Commandant Georges Houot, the master of the bathyscaph, to park on a mud floor. Under the droplights, a hidden creature took off underground, raising a winding mound like a big mole track. It passed into darkness without emerging.

In 1954 we took Papa Flash's camera to explore the haunts of the famous "living fossil" fish, the coelacanth, around the Comoros Islands in the Mozambique Channel. This vigorous fish is the world's oldest known unchanged fish species, with a physique identical to fossil coelacanths in rocks laid down sixty million years ago. *Latimeria chalumnae smith* is its scientific name. The Comoros Islanders refer to it eloquently as *"le poisson,"* *"The* fish." This fantastic throwback that no one imagined could still exist was identified in 1938 from a decayed specimen by the South African ichthyologist, Professor J. L. B. Smith, a discovery hailed as "the most amazing event of the century in the realm of natural history."

Not until 1952 was a second coelacanth hooked in the Comoros. Professor James Millot of the Paris Museum of Natural History posted a $280 reward for each further specimen—a sum equal to two years' income for a Comorian fisherman. The reward was double for a living specimen. The island fleet had stopped baiting for food fish in order to go after *the* fish by the time we took Millot in *Calypso* to study the habitat of the coelacanth.

The half-dozen specimens ranged in weight from 64 to 127 pounds and were caught by hook and line in depths varying from five hundred to thirteen hundred feet by frail islanders in outrigged pirogues too narrow for a person to sit inboard. The men hooked and fought the mighty animal at night. We met Houmadi Hassani, captor of the third coelacanth, which weighed only twenty pounds less than himself. Using a 3/32-inch cotton line and a crude iron hook baited with catfish, Hassani had pulled his specimen out of a depth of 650 feet in a half-hour struggle.

The fish is a powerful carnivore with hard scales and curious limblike fins, which Millot said "shed fresh light on the all-important anatomical problem of how the fins of primitive fish were able to develop into the limbs of the terrestrial vertebrate, of which the human arm is one derivative." Professor Smith held that it "is the closest living relative of the long-extinct fish that is accepted as the ancestor of all land animals. The coelacanth was almost in the direct line of man's ancestry."

Since the specimens were caught fairly close to shore, *Calypso* rounded the islands, making the first precision sonar survey of their steep black lava foundations. When we lowered cameras, the islanders assumed that we were trying to photograph *the* fish. We knew that chance would be one in a million. We were, instead, photographing the environment of the coelacanth. We obtained scenes of its volcanic haunts and took temperature readings, showing that it lived in water colder by $47°$ F. than the surface layer.

One night two fishermen, Zema ben Said Mohamed and Madi Bacari, were sitting in their pirogue a mile offshore with catfish baits hanging 840 feet below. The moon came up and they felt a violent strike—from *le poisson*, Zema believed. He and his partner decided to try for the $560 Millot had offered for a fish brought in alive.

The men strained to bring the fish to the surface. It was five feet long, and it was a coelacanth. They hauled the fighting giant alongside the pirogue, and Zema ran his hand along the line into the fish's mouth. His hook was lodged firmly in the palate. He thought they needed more control, so he reached into the mouth again and passed another line through the gill slit. With the coelacanth close-reined, Zema and Madi took up their paddles—wooden disks lashed to staves—and dug hard to bring the thrashing captive ashore. As often as not, the fish towed the slender boat.

The little fishermen won. On the beach they placed the live fish in a whaleboat full of water, and the populace got out of bed and danced and sang all night around *le poisson*. They stretched a net over the boat, but the coelacanth seemed to accept captivity. It swam slowly by strange rotating movements of its pectoral fins, using the second dorsal and anal fins as a rudder. The people lined the gunwales of the boat, looking in with awe at the glowing greenish-yellow eyes that seemed to cast light rather than reflect it.

When the sun came up, the fish huddled in the darkest parts of the whaleboat. It seemed physically hurt by light, so the villagers put a tent over the boat. Professor Millot arrived at noon, entered the tent, and stared in rapture at his first living coelacanth. It was losing strength and swimming with increasing feebleness. In midafternoon *the* fish rolled on its back, vibrated its fins convulsively, and died. Millot sadly concluded that it had been killed by photophobia, or sensitivity to light, perhaps with the drastic change of temperature as a contributing cause. He paid Zema and Madi the double reward, and two more wealthy fishermen joined the local coelacanth aristocracy.

Edgerton's Pinger cameras gave *Calypso* scientists big surprises, such as the one that befell Professor Pérès during a biological study of the submarine shelf between Sicily and Tunisia. The divers collected specimens as far down as they could go, then Pérès went deeper with a conventional dredge. From two thousand feet we hauled a load of sticky yellow mud into which Pérès plunged his forearms, palmating it for signs of life. He smelled it and tasted it on the tip of his tongue, while we grimaced. "Seems to be nothing here," said he, plopping a handful into a specimen jar. He dictated to an assistant, "Station ten, yellow mud. Azoic bottom—no life here."

I had been sceptical of dredges for a long time. I said to Pérès, "Mind if I check the bottom with a camera?"

He said, "Of course not, but you ought to move away from this dead spot to a place where you might hit something."

Without moving, we shot Edgerton's camera right into the "azoic" floor. It brought back several of the most picturesque, varied, and populous scenes of bottom life we had ever obtained.

Pérès immediately made double demands on winch time. He wanted to send a camera down on every dredge station. *Calypso* seamen-divers turned out cheerfully day and night for monotonous hours of winch and cable work. Handling oceanographic gear bores the average seaman, who works on caste-ridden ships where the scientists dine and discuss things separately from the men. But *Calypso* scientists mess with the crew, who ask them what they are trying to do. After a decade with scientists, many Calypsonians are fair journeymen biologists and know more than a little about submarine geology.

The divers assured the scientists of thorough collections in the upper two-hundred-foot zone, but we joined them in a common miserable struggle with the pendant gadgets we were forced to use for the deeper layers. Oceanographers, bless them, are blind beggars, tottering about on crutches of cables. All we divers and seamen can do is to throw an occasional idea their way. We, too, limp blindly through this *Cour des Miracles*.

For twenty years I have been trying to get rid of cables in undersea research. The Aqua-Lung had dispensed with the air hose, lifeline, and signal cord of compressed-air diving. *Calypso* was fitted as a platform for free diving. I had also championed independent bathyscaphs to replace dangling bathyspheres. To oceanographers I preached free-sinking instruments that automatically returned with depth data.

When I took over *Calypso,* she had only an anchor winch and a small hand-reel for sounding with piano wire. I had to take on another winch to haul archaeological baskets and cargo and to assist in moorings. It was a treacherous, secondhand, one-cylinder diesel that we called Lombardini after the maker. To start it, we thrust burning cigarettes into the cylinder and ran away while two heroes heaved a hand crank. Lombardini would belch a choking cloud of greasy black smoke and drive the men off several times before starting. Then scientists came aboard with their dredges and other pendant gadgetry and demanded more winch power. We scrapped Lombardini in favor of a heavier electrical winch. On top of this, the hydrologists needed a special winch of their own. During each winter lay-up the bulk of winches and stowed cable increased, and so did *Calypso*'s draft. I was insidiously transformed from a foe of cables to their foremost slave. Harold Edgerton was the main offender. Each winter he would build deeper and subtler electronic depth cameras that I could not resist.

One summer he turned up aboard with bales of shiny white rope, three miles long, less than a quarter of an inch thick, and made of braided nylon. "I figure it will be better than steel wire," he said. "Nylon is almost weightless underwater; in fact, this wax-coated line is slightly buoyant. It has a breaking point of fifteen hundred pounds and an elasticity of about twenty percent." At Cape Matapan, Greece, not only did the synthetic braid work for depth cameras, but we anchored a launch with nylon in fourteen thousand feet of water. This led to a daring speculation: could we use nylon to anchor *Calypso* in great depth? If so, we could stabilize a camera near the floor and record happenings in a single area in hundreds of flash photos, maybe even spying out the creatures living under the bottom.

We calculated the strength, thickness, and resilience of a nylon anchoring cable six miles long. A New England ropework turned out the record-breaking skein, dyeing 1600-yard sections of it in different colors to indicate how much line was down. This led to the most ignominious moment in my war on cables. I stood on the dockside at Abidjan on the Ivory Coast of Africa and looked at a grotesque transformation of my lithe, white *Calypso*.

Fore and aft she was a cat's cradle of pulleys, wires, and leather belts, spinning a multicolored six-mile rope onto massive reels on the afterdeck. She looked like a thread mill contrived by a maniac. We were spooling nylon for the deepest anchorage ever attempted.

We sailed for the Romanche Trench, the lowest hole in the Equatorial Atlantic, a twenty-five-thousand-foot depression discovered by line soundings from the French survey ship *La Romanche* in 1883. The trench was eight hundred miles from Africa and only a few miles wide. The chart position could be erroneous because the equatorial cloud belt often hampers astronomical fixes in these latitudes. We were approaching the trench on a parallel axis and could expect to spend days echo-groping for it.

Two and a half days out, we steamed into the trench area on easy swells from the southeast trades. I turned out at 0430 and went to the bridge. Saôut reported that overcast had kept him from taking star shots at twilight. I stepped back into the chartroom. Laban was on the sounder with his nose to the stylus, sniffing for the first appreciable change in depth. Simone and Philippe hung over his shoulders. I gathered up the yards of echotape that had gone through the machine. We had left the monotonous thirteen-thousand-foot flats of the Eastern Abyssal Plain and were running over the rugged foothills of the Atlantic Ridge nine thousand feet below.

"*Tiens!*" said Laban. "She's going down."

"Is it the trench?" asked Philippe.

"Too soon to tell," said the precision engineer. "It would be tremendous luck. Look, she's going down steadily." Below in the abysmal dark, the bottom was falling: 11,000 feet . . . 15,000 . . . on down. The bottom stabilized at 24,000 feet. Saôut had threaded the needle on the first pass after two days without a fix. We followed the valley for six hours and took several transverse sonar cuts, which showed we had hit the center.

Now it was time to try something no seaman had ever attempted—to anchor in nearly five miles of water. Thirty years before, the German oceanographic ship *Meteor* had achieved an anchorage with wire in eighteen thousand feet. We were going to try it a mile deeper with nylon. We chose the synthetic material because a steel cable of such length would have to be tapered to a great thickness at the top mainly to support the weight of wire below. Nylon was weightless—but that virtue in turn posed a new problem. If anchor flukes are to dig in and hold, they must be dragged by horizontal force across the floor until they bite in. The weight of conventional chain, looping down to the horizontal on the floor, usually aligns the anchor flukes. Nylon, on the contrary, would hang straight, and the anchor would not engage.

However, since we were reverting to fiber, we could use a lesson of ancient seamanship learned in the wine wreck at Grand Congloué. The sailors of old overcame the similar light weight of their hemp lines by putting a heavy leaden stock at the top of their wooden anchor, which toppled it into position for the flukes to dig in. *Calypso* humbly adapted the old wisdom. Next to our 200-pound standard metal anchor we attached a hundred feet of chain, a 350-pound ingot of pig iron, and a hundred feet of steel cable before the six-mile nylon thread began. These weights would provide the horizontal pull.

We had improvised a two-stage take-up system to offset the elasticity of nylon. Had we simply run it off a drum, when we hauled it back under tension, the many windings of line would build a contractive force that could crush the strongest drum. To recover the line, we planned to relieve the tension by a huge block attached to the main winch shaft. The nylon would shrink to normal before it was wound on a large light drum made by native blacksmiths on the Ivory Coast.

I took a place by the African drum with the wizard of Edgertronics. *Calypso* kept her stern to the wind. The sonarman called on the loudspeaker, "Twenty-four thousand, six hundred feet!" and we began. Saôut shinnied up the stern crane, passed the end of nylon through a block, and spliced it to the steel leader cable. Into the water went the anchor and weights. Octave Léandri at the winch brake paid out nylon. The changing colors of the braid passed into the blue ocean. His job became progressively easier as the friction of the water against the nylon retarded the sinking weights. When the anchor assembly was two miles down, it had a hard time just pulling the line through the water.

By intercom I called off instructions to the bridge. *Calypso* maneuvered with both engines in a strong current and a fifteen-knot wind to keep the anchor falling vertically. Two-and-a-half hours after it went in, the dynamometer went dead, and we knew the anchor was on the floor. Although we were still far from being anchored, nylon was doing a fine job.

We reeled out additional slack line to drag the anchor and hook it in. As it went over, I got the ship under way, trying to guess what sort of pull she was giving the line in the wind and current. After four hours the dynamometer needle came to life. *"Stoppez les moteurs!"* I called to Saôut. We seemed to be hooked in. And high time. There was only 500 feet of

© National Geographic Society

Free diving for science. Climbing *Calypso*'s diving ladder is an Aqua-Lunger returning from one of the sorties we make to observe, collect and photograph submarine phenomena.

© *National Geographic Society*

THE RESEARCH SHIP *CALYPSO*

From the ship's galley, Henri Goiran goes down the wet diving well passing through *Calypso*'s hull amidships. We use the well when rough seas make it dangerous to go over the stern.

Louis Malle in *Calypso*'s underwater observation chamber at the bow, eight feet below the water line. It is entered through a twenty-five-foot tube bolted to the stempost.

Simone Cousteau with a trophy of black coral from the Red Sea. To wrest the tough black bush from the floor, Albert Falco and François Saôut used winch and cable.

Plunge to ancient history. A divers' briefing before we go down to excavate a Greek wine freighter sunk in the third century B.C. Left to right: Falco, André Laban, Armand Davso, Cousteau, Raymond Kientzy.

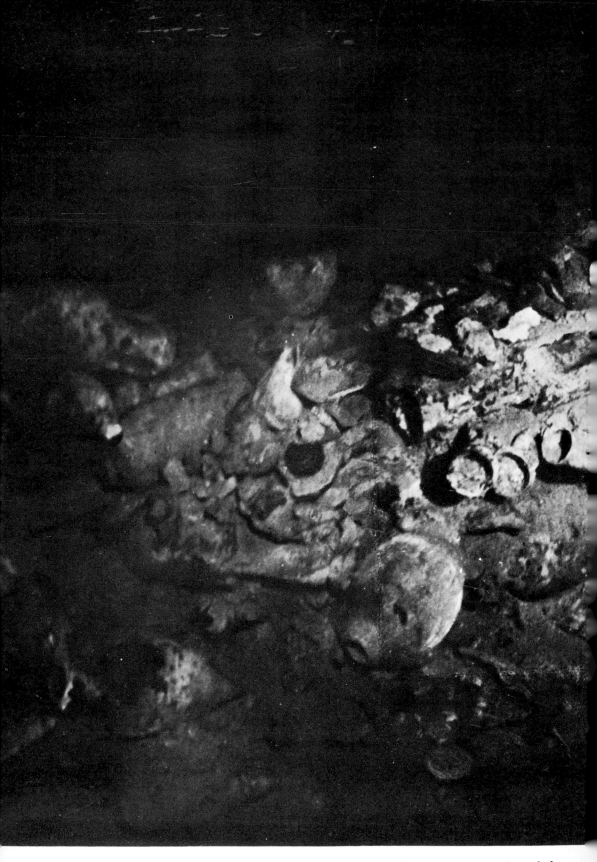

Inside the third-century-B.C. wine ship. A twenty-five-foot transverse section of the excavation, 135 feet from the surface. Elongated jars are Roman, fuller-bellied ones are

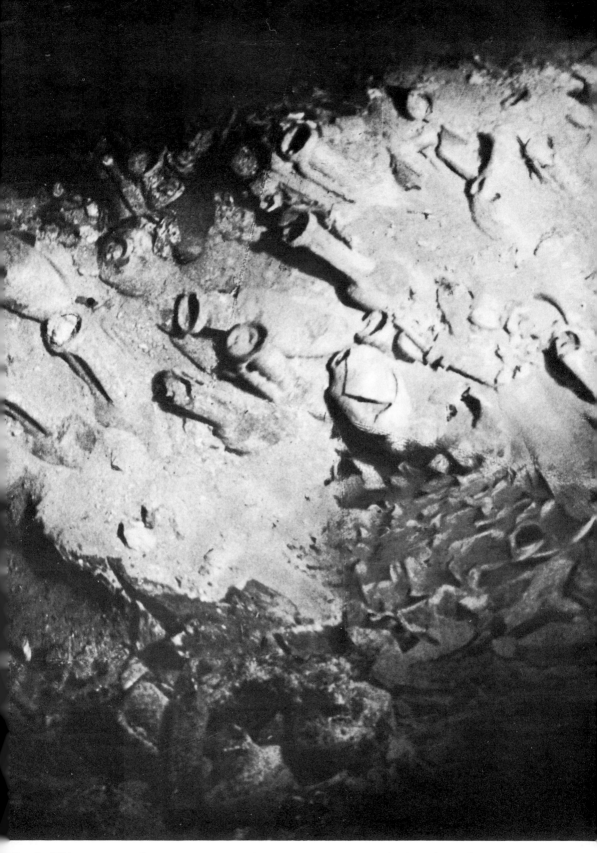

Greek. This was a ten-thousand-amphora ship, a super-tanker of antiquity. She sank at Grand Congloué Island, ten miles from Marseilles.

Flying the amphorae to the surface with compressed air was one method we used in the marine archaeological project. (A composite photo.)

After cold dives in the wine ship, Frédéric Dumas and I used to shiver our way back to normal. Then we adopted a better way of building caloric energy before and after a dive: Kientzy warms up by a brief infrared-ray exposure.

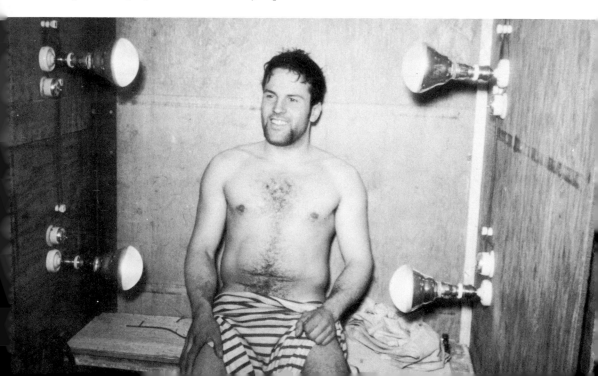

Chief archaeologist Prof. Fernand Benoît examines Campanian potteries recovered from the wine ship. Below, a diver rides the bucking suction pipe we used to dig out the old wreck.

© National Geographic Society

At Port Calypso, the island archaeological station, divers Davso, Kientzy (rear) and Jean Delmas study fossil-encrusted dinnerware from the top layer of the wreck mound. Below, Goiran and Falco bring the leaden anchor stock of the wreck to Marseilles.

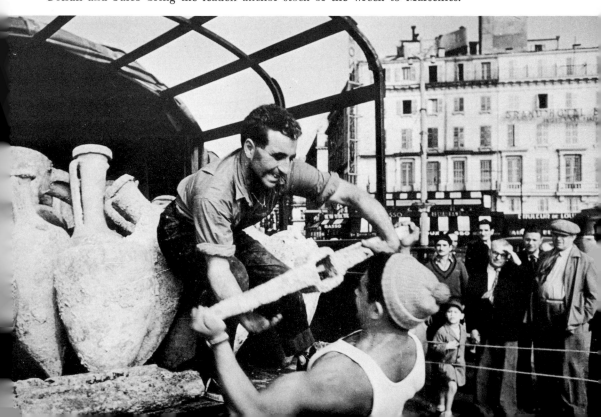

The big blow. For five years archaeological divers at Port Calypso fought the autumn and winter mistrals. A storm swept away the original engine house, but the men successfully defended the big boom that carried the suction pipe out over the excavation.

Kientzy and his diving comrade, Jean-Pierre Serventi, who was lost at Grand Congloué. His memorial is fixed to the cliff above the ancient wreck.

A LA MÉMOIRE DE
JEAN-PIERRE SERVENTI
MORT EN PLONGÉE
LE 6 NOVEMBRE 1952
SES CAMARADES DE LA CALYPSO

© National Geographic Society

Amphorae from the wine ship bore the initials "SES" and a trident symbol. At Delos, Greece, where the shipowner, Markos (SES)tios, lived, we found a villa with a trident mosaic. The tines and the "S" brackets suggested the cipher "SES."

© National Geographic Society

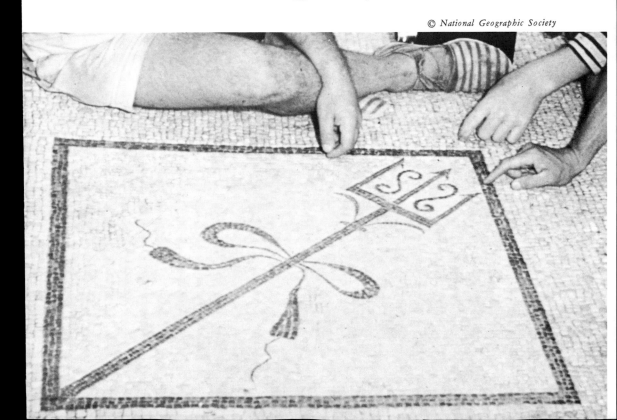

In 1953, a new freighter, *Donatello D*, crashed and sank on the island next to the one that took Sestios' ship more than two thousand years before. Our archaeological divers rescued the crew, guarded the wreckage and dived on the sunken ship.

Two modes in wrecks. Top, Goiran visits the freshly sunk *Donatello D,* and below, he and Kientzy sit on the boiler and engine of an eroded steamer on an Indian Ocean reef.

Frédéric Dumas swims along the port promenade deck of the sunken liner *Andrea Doria*.

From a 35-m.m. motion picture by Louis Malle.

© *National Geographic Society*

S.S. *Thistlegorm* at the bottom of the Red Sea. Sunk by German bombers during World War II, she carried military equipment, including motorcycles in poor working order.

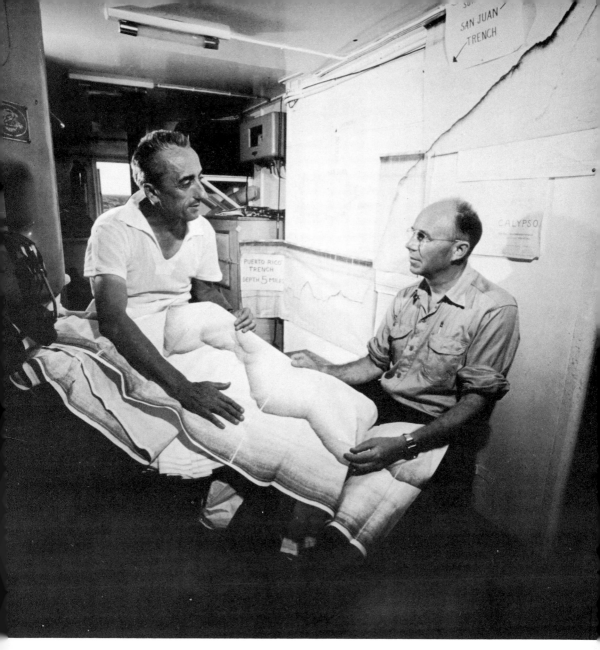

When *Calypso* studied the **Puerto Rico Trench**, Harold Edgerton and I pinned sonar profiles of the deep on the chartroom wall.

As Edgerton's depth camera went down it was tracked by sonar. Bottom left, Jean Delmas, James Dugan and I examine a sonar graph that shows the thin slanting line of the camera disappearing in the Deep Scattering Layer at my fingertip. Bottom right, our midwater glider with movie camera mounted.

© National Geographic Society

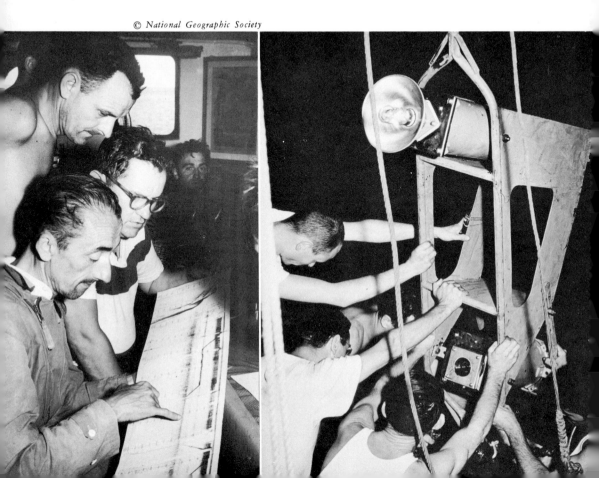

© *National Geographic Society*

The bottom that came to life. After oceanographic dredges brought totally lifeless sediments up from the submarine plateau between Sicily and Africa, we lowered an Edgerton camera to the same spot and found these living sea fans.

© National Geographic Society

© National Geographic Soc

Creatures of abyssal night. *Calypso*'s electronic cameras flashed these deep drifters. Above, a stringy colony of siphonophores about thirty inches long. Below, a medusa (*Solmaris leucostyla*) pulsating in the dark.

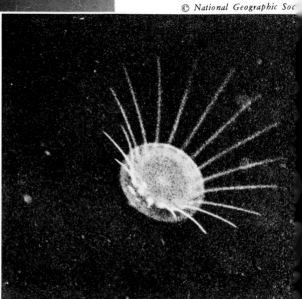

Calypso's high observation bridge reveals many exciting things on the ocean. The wide crow's nest permits several observers to scan the entire horizon.

A dolphin entertains *Calypso* in the Sea of Oman.

The living reef. Frolicking dolphins splashed up what we thought was a rocky reef off the Arabian Hadramaut. Below, from the underwater chamber, we saw them swim, dive and rocket into the air.

The Arabian Sea dolphins averaged six feet long.
Estimate for yourself how high they leaped.

From *Calypso*'s underwater chamber, men witnessed for the first time marine mammals racing under the open sea. Above is a pair of sporting dolphins.

Opposite page, top, sixty-foot sperm whales march along in front of the submarine observatory in the Indian Ocean. They often swam upside down or on their sides, like the top one shown here. Below, right, blood streams from a baby whale that accidentally collided with *Calypso*'s propeller.

© National Geographic Society

Beneath the Indian Ocean, sharks come to the whale, upper left, injured by our propeller. Below, after we execute the whale, the sharks move in.

Aqua-Lungers in *Calypso*'s antishark cage film the predators surrounding the whale. Below, Albert Raud and Saôut get down on the diving platform to heave sharks aboard.

A moment of adventure frozen in time. At Ila do Lobos off Punta del Este, Uruguay, we attempt to net an Atlantic sea lion.

© National Geographic Society

Aldabra, a paradise we earned. Everyone struggled to save *Calypso* in the racing tides of the lagoon channel. Left to right, Goiran, Dumas, Maurice Léandri and Falco. Below we hit the beach at Aldabra after negotiating the fringing reef.

On Aldabra Island, Simone and the rest of us took rides on giant land tortoises that have survived there by the scores of thousands.

Exploring the mangrove forest in Aldabra's lagoon are Jean-Marie Basso, Goiran and Tony Besse. Below, when land exploration was stopped by jungle and potholes, Malle (top), Besse and Goiran put the best face on it.

© National Geographic Society

Under Aldabra Reef, Falco rides a sea turtle, chased by Dumas with a Submarine Scooter. Below, after work the divers hitched scooter rides home to *Calypso*.

© National Geographic Society

The peaceable kingdom of the Aldabras. Black surgeonfish and snappers throng around Étienne Puig's bag of food scraps. Here we did not spear fish and gained the trust of the entire population.

Reef motif at Aldabra. Two *Heniochus acuminatus* sail by a scrawly white virgularian, a form of gorgonian. Below, Maurice Léandri plays host to a remora.

© National Geographic Society

The patient photographer. Pierre Goupil, top, delivers a lead-ballasted bag of flash bulbs to Luis Marden, middle picture, who is anchored by an assistant in a vigil to photograph the eruption of a sand cone. After three days, Marden finally got this picture.

Dumas waltzes with Ulysses, the grouper that practically took charge of us. His friendly but clumsy interference with our work obliged us (below) to imprison Ulysses in the anti-shark cage.

© National Geographic Society

Ulysses, right, glowers in jail as we feed fish outside. When not in jail (below) he usually accompanied us aloft for stage decompression on the anchor chain.

This Persian Gulf pearl diver wears no mask, is nearly blind below, although six hundred years ago his forebears used tortoise-shell diving goggles.

Calypso explores the "hottest place on earth," the Elphinstone Inlet

© National Geographic Society

in the Hormuz Strait. At lower right is the sinister village of Sibi.

© National Geographic Society

Prospecting for oil, Persian Gulf.
After mechanical means failed to
obtain samples from the armorlike
floor, *Calypso* divers chipped rock by
hand among poisonous sea snakes,
below.

In the Aegean our men visited sponge divers in traditional helmet suits. Such demonstrations are winning them over to free diving. Below, we show that industrial wastes dumped at random destroy large living areas of the sea floor.

In mid-Atlantic we lower the Deep-sea Camera Sled. A stereo camera is mounted on the left and an electronic flash tube on the right.

When she arrived in New York for the International Oceanographic Congress, *Calypso* received the classic welcoming parade.

Calypso's Deepsea Camera Sled traveled many miles in this deep fissure in the mid-Atlantic Ridge. Among thousands of haunting photographs taken in a ten-thousand-foot depth range

ATLANTIC RIFT VALLEY

was the one at left of powder-sprinkled rocks with four discernible species of fixed fauna. On the right-hand page are eruptions of pillow lava from recent geologic times.

The Deepsea Camera Sled records a mysterious eruption eighteen inches high on the deep Mediterranean floor. It was probably set off by the approach of the sled. The craters in the foreground are presumably inhabited.

© National Geographic Soc

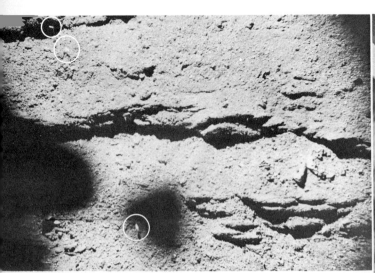

© National Geographic Society

Edgerton's vertical bottom shot, taken 24,600 feet down in the Romanche Trench, shows living creatures (en-circled) in about nine square feet of terrain. After this exposure the camera port cracked.

Through the silken arras of the waves, divers leave for night exploration of the Forest of Albaron (below), a jungle of twenty-five-foot seaweeds of the laminarian family.

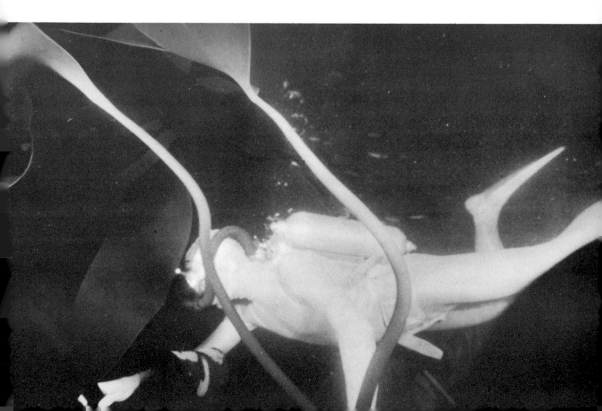

Closing the entry hatch on my first bathyscaph dive. Below, *F.N.R.S.3* sinks into the blue. Conning tower contains oil-filled electric connection boxes.

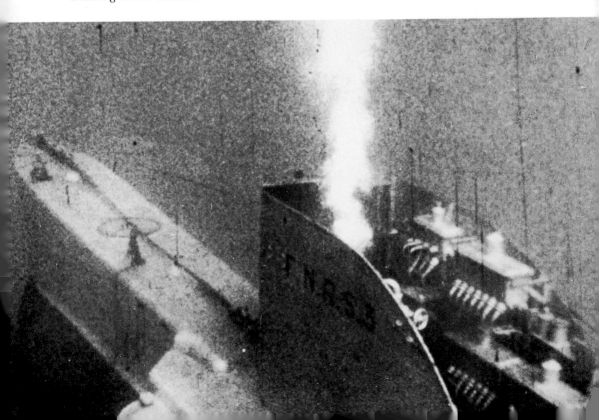

The diving saucer *DS-2* in her afterhold garage on *Calypso*. Fiberglas fairings are removed, showing plastic pipes curled around the hull to the forward hydrojets.

© National Geographic Society

Diving saucer in the Caribbean. I hand *DS-2*'s chief engineer, Jean Mollard, a pitcher of ballast water while Edgerton watches at right. Below, *Calypso*'s Yumbo crane launches and recovers *DS-2*. The divers and boatmen handle lifting tackle.

© National Geographic Society

The Diving Saucer jets past with her movie flood-lamp spar extended. Note conical white jet nozzles at either side of the bow and three optical viewing ports on top. Below, I film Falco putting *DS-2* through her tricks in the Caribbean.

The countries of Western Europe saw these sprouting divers on a direct undersea telecast we made for Eurovision. Below, divers of the Oceanographic Museum at Monaco plant fish houses in the Marine Biotron.

Albert Falco collects live Red Sea fish without harming them. Fish come out of the coral head, get stuck in gill net, and are carried off in plastic bags of water. The fish never leave the water on the air journey to the Monaco aquarium.

Continental shelf station. Falco and Claude Wesly, center, are given a psychotechnical test in front of their undersea billet, by physicians Xavier Fructus, left, and Jacques Chouteau.

I dine with Wesly and Falco in Conshelf One on the sea bed. Below, greeting Falco as he and Wesly (center) surface after living and working 169 hours on the bottom.

nylon left on the drum. We had 29,500 feet out, which was now stretched to an actual length of 31,860 feet—more than six miles.

In the silence we heard waves slapping against the sides. The sea was flowing past like a river. *Calypso* was an island. The sonar graph settled into an unwavering flat line at 24,600 feet. We were at anchor in four-and-one-half miles of water in the middle of the ocean and the middle of the earth.

Everyone came running aft to lean over the fantail and look at the thin red cord slanting down stiffly from the shackle. Edgerton passed out M.I.T. caps. We sang *Calypso*'s ribald anthem, accompanied on the guitar by Bates Littlehales of the *National Geographic* and by African zithers and tom toms. Bates swung into "Home on the Range" and blinked when we sang it as *Un Chant de la Plaine.*

I am a deep sleeper, but I was awakened several times during the night by boisterous cries on deck. The Calypsonians were jigging big red squids that had come from the deep to feed on flying fish. The loudest was Philippe, who had the prize catch, a four-footer.

In the morning *Calypso* was still firmly at anchor, a stationary point in the ceaseless flux of the Atlantic Ocean. We ballasted bits of cork with lead and dropped them over the stern quarters. The corks flowed by under the surface and were clocked at the bow. The current was moving north at 1.2 knots. Past the quiet ship it carried a belt line of brilliant blue nudibranches, dilating jellyfish, plankton, and lazy fish. Biologist Christian Carpine hung over the rail cooing at this specimen parade while Edgerton made ready for the first photos of the Romanche Trench.

His latest synchroflash camera was encased in two tempered stainless-steel cylinders rated to withstand a pressure of five-and-one-half tons per square inch. It was mounted on a rack with a new powerful Pinger that would permit us to focus the camera nine feet from the bottom. Papa Flash set the delayed-action camera button to begin in two hours, closed the case, and lowered the unit.

In the sonar headset I listened to the tick-tocks as it journeyed down. At a depth of three miles the clock faded out. "Harold! We're blind. Should we haul out?" I asked.

He pondered over some mental arithmetic and said, "No. It would cost us about seven hours to bring it up, check it, and send it back. We'll have to gamble. Keep the winch rolling."

We sent the camera deeper without depth control until the nylon line went slack at the winch. The camera had encountered the bottom. For three hours we bounced it up and down, hoping that some exposures would occur at nine feet and bring back the first impressions of the deep floor.

It was dusk before we had the camera back on deck. "Hey," said Harold, "look at the lens port." This glass, one-and-a-half inches thick, had a star-shaped crack in the middle. Whether it came from pressure or collision we could not determine. Edgerton unscrewed the porthole and drew the camera mechanism out. "Dry as a bone," he said. When the precious film was processed, there were two pictures taken before the lens port cracked. We had added a half-mile to the previous record for depth photography.

Romanche photograph No. 1 showed about nine square feet of the bottom, scored by little ridges and fissures that had a fresh-looking appearance. The terrain was granular, with some pebbly material strewn on it. In three places in the picture there were tiny pale fish shapes, casting shadows beneath them. One animal had a suggestion of feelers. It proved that mobile species lived nearly two miles deeper than had been previously observed by Houot and Willm in the bathyscaph.

Romanche photograph No. 2 showed a fairly level bottom with a litter of varicolored, clean-looking pebbles and rocky fragments. There were nine minuscule life forms and what seemed to be a living brittle starfish about four inches in diameter. The two photographs indicated that aquatic organisms may live in the most stupendous pressures. The absence of a general overlay of sediments surprised geologists.

On the third morning we began a precision sonar survey of the structure of the Romanche Trench as a whole. The deep anchorage was a vital part of the survey. We had determined by many sun and star shots that *Calypso* lay at 0° 10′ South by 18° 21′ West. We erected a radar target in one of the launches, and Saôut transferred the anchor line to the boat. Now we had a fixed beacon to use as a radar reference as *Calypso* went pinging up and down the trench and made transverse sonar sweeps. Edgerton and I were in the chartroom, entering positions and courses on the unreeling sonar profiles and transferring depths to large-scale charts. The floor of the trench was from two to five miles wide. The walls were a series of giant steps on a slope of twenty-five degrees on the north side and thirty degrees on the south. Carpine and Laban worked our data into a three-dimensional plaster cast of the trench. The ship's doctor entered and said to them huffily, "If either of you types breaks a leg, it will serve you right." They had pinched his surgical plaster to make the model.

The radioman drew me out of the chartroom and gave me a personal message from Nantucket, Massachusetts: Bill Edgerton had been lost in an accident with an experimental diving device. It was my bitter duty to tell his father. Numb with grief, but ever the scientist, Harold did not want to spoil the expedition. I took him below to Simone and went to the radioman. "Send a message to the Commandant, French Navy Base, Dakar," I said. "Request special aircraft at Konakry for compassionate reasons to fly Professor Edgerton and myself to quickest connection with trunk airline to New York."

I said to Saôut, "Pick up the launch. Get the nylon cable on the winch and haul up everything."

The skipper took the winch controls and began reeling in the six-mile line. He said, "I'm getting more than normal strain. If I pull harder, I think the line will part."

"Haul away," I said. "We have no time to play games." Saôut gave more power. I saw the colored braid distending near the drum. Crack! The nylon broke with a report like an elephant gun. The rope whipped off the stern and our deep anchoring gear was gone. I said, "Take her to Konakry, full ahead."

After several *Calypso* campaigns that yielded scores of thousands of excellent bottom photos, Edgerton and I had to admit that the results did not quite meet our expectations. We saw sea mounds and excavations until our eyes were dizzy, but never an animal that could have made them. Equally disappointing was that we rarely snapped a swimming animal despite bathyscaph observations of many mobile creatures on the bottom. We knew that the flash-scatter kept them away from the small camera field and that the long camera cable acted as a sea anchor for the *Calypso* so that we covered only short stretches of terrain. We needed a new photographic approach to the bottom.

I said to Papa Flash, "Would you mind losing a camera?"

"No more than my right arm," he replied. "What's on your mind?"

I said, "Let's work up a sort of sled and drag the camera across the floor."

"Shoot the works," Edgerton said.

We took a portable diving ladder whose handrails curled at the end like a nineteenth-century child's sled. Edgerton lashed his camera and flash tubes to the treads, Saôut added a plank as a hydrofoil, Raud hung a chain as vertical ballast, Simone put the National Geographic Society flag on it,

Girault affixed artificial flowers, Dugan tacked on an R.I.P. sign, and Dumas pronounced the last rites.

We lowered the first crazy "deepsea camera sled" into a submarine plain off eastern Tunisia and dragged it slowly for two hours. There was little resistance on the cable, and we thought the sled had torn away. As we winched in, Saôut felt the wire and grinned, "I think she's still there." And so she was. The contraption came aboard intact, flag, flowers, and all. The photographs were exciting. The bottom was paved with brittle stars waving their tentacles. The diving ladder had ploughed through them for three miles, and the shots overlapped, giving the first continuous strip picture of the sea bottom.

At the O.F.R.S., Alinat and Laban cunningly designed a professional Deepsea Camera Sled to surmount obstacles and right itself when tipped over. The tubular frame was twelve feet long and five feet wide with a roll-over bar six feet high. It traveled slightly crabwise so that mud stirred up by the runners would not flood the camera field. Moreover, the sled extricated itself when fouled on an insurmountable barrier. We attached the wire tow cable to the after end of a runner, then bent it for'd to the bow, where it was made fast by thin rope lashings. Thus the sled was pulled forward until it butted against an obstacle it could not climb; then the increased towing strain ripped away the bow lashings and the cable lifted the structure clear by the tail.

We put all our know-how into the Deepsea Camera Sled. We were able to afford seven sleds, three with cinécameras. Knowing we would lose some of them, we designed for expendability, with rough, cheap welding and mass-produced tubing on the camera and flash cylinders.

Sled hauling took a blend of seamanship and diving experience. Sufficient cable had to be paid out to account for depth and slope. To haul it at a steady one- or two-knot pace, the bridge officer had to take surface currents into equation. He was linked by intercom to a seasoned man on the fantail who kept a bare foot on the towing cable and reported the faint shocks from below that proved the sled was on the ground and not flying. A dynamometer showed when the sled was blocked. When that happened, *Calypso* stopped, paid out more cable, and maneuvered to disengage the vehicle. It always seemed a miracle when the sled came back, gaily spraying water from the tube framing.

The Deepsea Camera Sled's first major mission was our intercontinental pipe-line survey in 1959. Keyed to precision soundings and radio navigation, the sleds brought up stills and motion pictures of an uncluttered 115-mile route across the Mediterranean. No other camera system could have done it. The movies gave one the thrilling sensation of actually traveling along the floor at two miles an hour. The sled was the poor man's bathyscaph.

As is always the case with a successful new device for studying the sea, the sled discovered more mysteries than it did explanations. On test runs at two thousand feet the pictures showed ditches in the bottom, some lightly scored, others a foot deep. The tracks resembled those made by the runners on commercial drag nets, but nobody drags as deep as this in the Mediterranean. The furrows were always oriented across the slopes, exactly like contour lines. After many hauls a movie sled caught an undersea ploughman in the act. A fish about a foot long, half-buried in virgin mud, wriggled its tail energetically to cut a straight line in the floor. But what tiller of the bottom made the deep ditches? The sled has not yet told us.

Nor has it explained a phenomenon in sled films taken in depths of from two to four thousand feet—freshly dug craters three to six feet in diameter and as much as four feet deep. Seeing these excavations, I could not help imagining large animals burrowing into the floor to nest, hibernate, or retire from battle. Again, photographic evidence was prodding us toward building new vehicles to go deep into the cratered lands and stay long enough to see the fabulous diggers at work.

Somehow, I thought, the big craters might be connected with basking sharks. In April the great basking shark flies its sluggish dorsal sail on the surface of the Mediterranean. This exceptionally large shark has a cavernous mouth and appreciable teeth that it does not use. It feeds on plankton, which it sorts out with a filtering mechanism in the gill silts. After some weeks of feeding on the rich spring plankton, basking sharks disappear from the surface on a given day in late May. Obviously all these half-comatose swimmers could not clear the Gibraltar sill into the Atlantic so suddenly. I incline to believe that they retire to the abyss and perhaps dig into the floor, for long periods at least, during their ten months' absence from the surface.

Encouragement for this hypothesis came from a startling basking shark discovery made in the North Sea by Dr. H. W. Parker and M. Boeseman. During the winter they caught basking sharks that had lost their gill rakers. The two investigators concluded that after fattening up on plankton in the spring and summer, the sharks returned to the bottom and underwent "a resting, nonfeeding, demersal stage," during which a new set of gill filters were developed for the spring explosion of plankton.

Our camera sleds made some fascinating journeys in the Atlantic during a *Calypso* crossing from the Canaries to New York. We hauled a sled on the Great Meteor Sea Mount, a flat-topped cone 15,000 feet high that terminates 430 feet from the surface. Great Meteor and other Atlantic sea mounts appear to have been islands long ago; they were planed off by erosion and then subsided into the water. Bermuda is such an exposed sea mount and may in the distant future sink as its submerged sister peak, the Challenger Bank, is thought to have done.

The sled came up from crossing the top of Great Meteor with views of a flat plateau with a dense low growth of siliceous sponges, shells, and dwarfed corals. Another mount nearby was the same depth as Great Meteor, which reinforced the theory of subsidence. When we pulled the sled across the summit of Hyères Sea Mount, we found it eroded to bare rock. The sled came upon fissures in the rock that were piled with good-sized fish. However, to assume that this was typical of the whole mountain would be quite false. When we sent the sled, backed by dredges, down the slopes, we found life and variety. On the eastern and western flanks there were fields of white or yellow siliceous sponges growing on white sand that often bore ripple marks. Moreover, between the flanks the southern slope was composed of black volcanic slag like the refuse of a steel mill. A few tall gorgonians appeared in this macabre desolation. The overall surprise of the sled operations was the radical contrast of geological and living environments within a fairly short span of submarine terrain.

Our main sled target in the Atlantic was the longest mountain chain on earth, the Atlantic Ridge, which stretches virtually from pole to pole and divides the ocean into two basins. The ridge winds about halfway between Eurafrica and the Americas, roughly in contour with their coasts, supporting the old, controversial, but still challenging theory of continental drift advanced by Penck and Wegener. Peaks of the Atlantic Ridge cleave the air at the Azores, St. Paul's Rocks, and Ascension Island.

The sinuous summit of the ridge is deeply split by an almost continuous crack called the Atlantic Rift Valley, which may contain the epicenters of that ocean's earthquakes. I wanted to risk a sled in this tantalizing ravine.

Calypso's sonar picked up the buttresses of the Atlantic Ridge, which arose on the graph exactly as they had been described by the outstanding U.S. Atlantic explorers Maurice Ewing and Bruce Heezen. As we sailed toward the summit, the peaks climbed to an altitude of minus five thousand feet. Then came a dramatic fall ten thousand feet into the Rift Valley. Sailing on the flat sea, it was hard to realize we were on top of a staggering system of peaks and valleys drowned in eternal night.

Before committing the sleds to this untidy playground, we had to chart the valley floor from a fixed point in the center. We dropped a grapnel on eleven thousand feet of thin nylon fishing line with a breaking strength of only sixty pounds. It took the grapnel an hour to reach the floor. We tied the line off on a very small, free-floating, plastic buoy. On the afterdeck the men inflated a large balloon with hydrogen. This was a "kytoon," resembling a barrage balloon covered with aluminum foil to increase its radar echo. Seamen towed the balloon by rubber boat and made it fast to the plastic buoy, flying the kytoon 150 feet in the air. Now the abyss and the lower atmosphere were hooked up to assist our sleighing party.

Calypso ran a ten-mile-square sonar survey off the fixed kytoon and discovered that the Rift Valley was amazingly narrow. We would never have retrieved the sled from this crevasse without the sonar map that the balloon rig had made possible.

The first sled was equipped with a stereo color camera. We dragged it cautiously, Maurice Léandri's bare foot feeling for shocks on the taut wire stretched four miles into the rift. Five hours later, the sled came squirting into the air. It was surprisingly transformed. The yellow paint had been removed from the frame, and it was dented by many collisions. Yet Edgerton's camera and flash tube were undamaged.

The stereo pairs were awesome. The camera had come upon scenes of suddenly shifting and bewildering variety, as though riffling through a catalogue of geology. One shot would show a jumble of lava blocks, cut as sharp as taffy, and the next would carry you across a miniature Sahara, followed by the gray bedrock of the Alps powdered with a thin snow of sediment. Within a small compass the scenes were as suggestive of enormity as the creation of a cunning Japanese garden architect.

The sled roamed over flats in which the first stretch would be pure white sediments that build at the rate of about three feet in ten thousand years, whereas the back stretch would be littered with volcanic cinders that seemed laid down by contemporary eruptions.

The bottom water was marvelously clear, and the pictures had readable details as far as fifty feet away. Some shots showed the narrow, steep valley walls, which were lined with basalt boulders that had recently rolled off the peaks. In two places the photos depicted barrel-shaped blocks of pillow lava, ribbed with concentric patterns, which appeared to have just cooled from yesterday's fiery extrusion. The pillows were so similar in size and configuration that a heap of them might be thought parts of a fallen temple column in mythical Atlantis.

We rigged a movie sled to cross the Rift Valley floor and made three more hauls, but each was negated by malfunction of the camera or flash tube. While we were at work, a German passenger liner came over the empty horizon and changed course to look at the silver kytoon hanging above the ocean. Perhaps we started another flying saucer story.

At Bermuda we took aboard a diving scientist and sailed south to the Challenger Bank, the plateau of a sea mount reaching to minus 150 feet. Our guest said no one had yet dived on the bank, so we invited him to accompany Falco and Davso on the "first." We dropped anchor out of sight of land in the ocean at its wildest. I sent the trio down in the antishark cage, instructing them not to swim out of sight of the refuge. A few feet from the bottom, Falco rang the buzzer, and we suspended the cage there.

The water was transparent to a radius of a hundred feet. Everywhere they could see, the Challenger Bank was paved with pebbly concretions, varying in size from a plum to an orange. There was only one differing feature: a shiny object near *Calypso*'s anchor. Davso swam toward it. The scientist made urgent noises of distress in his mouthpiece. Leaving Falco to deal with whatever this was, Davso continued toward the bright object. The scientist pointed to it and then to his air tanks. Falco began hooting, and Davso returned. They entered the cage and buzzed to be lifted. On deck the scientist tore the grip from his mouth and cried, "That was a brand-new live torpedo with a magnetic warhead! My tanks are steel. If they had triggered it, we'd have gone up and the ship too."

I said, "Well, I have a steel anchor down there." I questioned them on the lay of the anchor and the torpedo. We eased the *Calypso* about and hauled anchor away from the explosive. We started to run as soon as the anchor left the floor. I said, "Davso, the sea is big; but there are too many damned man-made objects in it."

Calypso moved on to attempt sled hauls at the lowest point in the Atlantic Ocean, the Puerto Rico Trench, which is nearly 28,000 feet deep. We took station north of San Juan and late in the day set the grapnel and kytoon system on 30,000 feet of nylon, in a wind blowing at fresh gale strength. During the night the kytoon vanished from the radarscope. In the morning our oceanographic planet was nowhere to be seen. We anchored another balloon. Soon it began to drift, towing the buoy behind. We caught up with the rig and reeled in the nylon line. It had parted a thousand feet under the buoy. We put the clean-looking break under a microscope. It had been sliced on a bevel from both sides.

Falco said, "It looks as if the tool was a beak rather than teeth."

I said, "There seem to be squids around here that don't care for oceanography."

Now in addition to the high winds we had the fish against us in the Puerto Rico Trench. I decided to lower the camera sled without giving them another balloon to play with. Our new winch, the largest of these impediments that poor *Calypso* had had to lug about, was especially designed for the Puerto Rico deep, but it had not been tested at such depth. Since we could not drag a sled on resilient nylon, we used conic steel cable. We put a sled on the bottom on seven miles of tapered wire and dragged it with difficulty. When we reeled in cable, the tension threatened to demolish the big winch drum. Weldings cracked, and the drum flanges bent outwards. The wind swept hard. But we managed to get the sled aboard after hours of struggle. The film was entirely blank; the camera and flash were out of synchronization. One must be prepared for many such bitter outcomes when trying to learn a little about the ocean.

We went into San Juan, where the U.S. Navy raised our morale with a quick repair and reinforcement job on the big winch drum. The second attack on the trench was made in the same nasty weather. We put the sled on the floor and began the tedious drag of seven tons of wire and a ton of camera sled. I could barely keep the ship's head up. Then the wind veered from northwest to west, furnishing more opposition. I computed true bottom speed against these handicaps. We were not moving at all. *Calypso* was, in effect, anchored by the sled. We persisted for an hour without avail. "Hoist her in!" I called to the fantail. It was a relief to get the sled back. Edgerton took the film to the darkroom. This time the lens and flash were coordinated. We had made the deepest photographs in the sea as of that date—27,885 feet down.

The Puerto Rico Trench photographs revealed a flat sedimental bottom without the holes, burrows, or craters we customarily found in the deep places. In several frames there appeared a pair of fish about a foot long, swimming close to the floor. They had crossed the camera field several times.

As my men fought on the tossing work deck to recover the last sled, I stood on the port bridge wing, squinting into the falling sun, the gale whistling in my ears, and reviewed our tribulations. In ten days' battle for a few photos, I had burst a winch drum, towed a camera that didn't work, got myself anchored involuntarily, spent hours paying out and hauling cables, lost a balloon and 59,000 feet of nylon, and been prevented from setting a radar target by a silly squid. I swore in the teeth of the west wind that I was going to cut my way out of this web of cables and abandon the tormenting surface of the sea. I was more certain than ever that exploration of the deep was the job of men in scientific submarines.

chapter
thirteen

DOWN

IN

THE DARK

Under a work light on the afterdeck the divers talked in hushed voices as they shook powder on their bodies in order to slip more easily into their tight suits. There was no moon. *Calypso* was blacked out except for wreck lights atop the mainmast. Above us a feeble window glowed from Port Calypso, and late-flying seagulls cawed in the night. In the tranquil sea the usually menacing rock was a meek shadow standing in a wrinkle of surf. Near the port rail the long archaeological boom let the suction pipe down into a burble of black water.

Under the work light lay a thick yellow cylinder and two glass bubbles with cables attached—our new television camera and floodlights. The iconoscope had a much higher resolution than the one used in commercial TV and many more scanning lines. It was fitted with a correcting lens to extend the field and overcome underwater aberrations. Its daytime results had been exceptionally good, and at night we would be rid of haze produced by the scattering of ambient sunlight on suspended particles.

Kientzy, Goiran, Etraud, and Davso sucked their mouthpieces to test the flow of compressed air and went into the sea. Octave Léandri and Paul Martin lowered the hundred-pound camera and lamps and paid out the thick black coaxial cables strung with glass floats. I asked Martin to turn on the submarine lights. There was a flash, and *Calypso* sat like a flaw in an emerald. The sea light washed over the white cliff and seemed to pull it toward us. The gulls screamed and fled Port Calypso.

I leaned over the fantail and watched the men descend into transparent night. In the saucery wave patterns their silhouettes expanded and contracted. The flood of light turned into shattered *gemmail* of blue and green, and the men dissolved. They were nearing the bottom. I went to my quarters, where Simone and the technicians were watching the ancient ship excavation, the amphorae cemented in the pit side, and the suction pipe waiting like a sleeping boa. Davso swam into the scene and took the pipe nozzle. He turned on the air cock, and the pipe sprang to life. He rode it across the trench to our front line.

I was interested not in seeing Davso carve out more amphorae but rather in judging the quality of TV transmission. I took the microphone connected to the speaker in the camera housing and said, "Kientzy, move out of the hole and give us some distant shots." The cameraman heaved the barrel out on the slope and sent up images from the outer bounds. Satisfied with the twelve-minute test, I said, "Okay, Kientzy, bring the team up." We turned off the camera and left the floods on to aid their return. From the stern I watched the light sharpen as they climbed to take three minutes' stage decompression ten feet from the top. But they halted deeper and overstayed. After five minutes they had me puzzled. Obviously nobody was in trouble, or the others would have brought him out of it. Something interesting was going on. I wished that I had dealt myself in on the dive instead of playing critic on the surface.

Not until they had dried out their air bottles did the team break water. They climbed aboard, whooping and laughing. Little Goiran's big baritone rang off the cliff. Hopping with excitement, he yelled, "Commandant, you can't imagine! We ran into a mass of *séverots* [horse mackerel] about ten inches long. They crowded into the lights completely out of control, swimming crazily in all directions. It was incredible. There were thousands of them. So many we couldn't see each other. A hundred of them would be hitting your body at the same time. You felt like a piece of paper in a typewriter."

Davso said, "Every time I closed my hand, I caught one or two of them."

Goiran's jig got wilder, and he slapped himself. "Help!" he shouted. "Get my suit off quick." We skinned his tunic over his head. Out fell a flapping *séverot,* a silvery fish that looked like a large sardine. It must have entered Goiran's suit through the collar.

We opened a bottle of cognac for the chilled heroes of the fish panic. During a hilarious session in the mess we evolved a plan for another dive with the lights only, after the quartet had rested for three hours. I was going along, and I had an idea that I kept to myself.

After midnight five of us slowly descended the pipe, beaming the lights around to signal the *séverots.* Thirty feet down the first ones arrived, closely followed by the army. My friends had not exaggerated their behavior. The finny myriad had lost all sense of direction. Abandoned was the law of schooling that oriented each fish in a common direction. It was a Bastille Day parade turned into a street riot. Tiny snouts pattered over my body. My companions were concealed by a living barrier of shuttling fish. Looking straight into a six-thousand-watt lamp five feet from my eyes, I saw nothing but a pink glow of translucent flesh, sliding, weaving, and crossing, always solid, never letting a wink of direct light through.

To swim was like crawling on your stomach across animated pebbles. I moved through this can of berserk sardines and took the lamp from an invisible comrade. I felt for the suction pipe and followed it down, directing the lamp upward—a Pied Piper luring fish to an unknown destination. They all followed. I set the lamp down near the nozzle of the pipe and turned on the compressed air. Every fish within a foot of the opening went swiftly up the pipe. As they pressed toward the fatal lamp, some fish were brought out of the trance by their instinctive reflex to swim against the current. As they hung on the edge of the danger zone, they were tumbled into the pipe by the frantic, jostling crowd behind. After five minutes I turned off the air. There seemed to be no fewer *séverots* than before.

We ascended through frantic fish. I stuck my head out of the water and heard a cacophony of gulls. In the sea light they filled the sky, almost as excited as the fish below. I dressed and climbed onto the island. The archaeological filter basket was brimming with fish. Hundreds had spilled over, slid down the rock, and were floating dead on the sea. The birds plunged raucously into this unexpected midnight supper.

The next night we went to Port Calypso again to film the *séverots'* frenzy. Thirty feet down the pipe we played the lights about. No fish approached.

We descended to a hundred feet. The host arrived, packed almost as tightly as the night before. But they remained in an orderly schooled formation. They did not turn to the lights. Three or four individuals fell out and drove toward us, but the mass remained aloof. We could not break the disciplined array. I have no explanation for this change of behavior between two successive nights at the same place and time. I felt sympathy for commercial fishermen, whose fortunes are made and broken by such anomalies.

Fishing with lights is no novelty in the Mediterranean. We had only added a submerged light and a suction pipe to the ancient art of *lamparo* fishing. Every night in good weather thousands of sixty-foot boats towing smaller ones go out from Mediterranean ports to attract sardines into nets with brilliant electric or acetylene lamps. A *lamparo* fleet on a sea station is brighter than many a city. Sardine boats from Almeria and Malaga go far out to a Spanish islet called Alboran, the first island lighthouse east of the Gibraltar Strait. It is the crest of a rocky sea mount rising 8250 feet from the abyssal plain. Fishermen call its waters the Sea of Alboran.

Calypso made a biological survey of the Alboran Sea with Philippe Cousteau aboard. Between dives the youngster glued himself to the sonar, intrigued by pictures of the passing floor. One day he saw a very curious bottom 150 feet down. The line was dense and flat. Six feet above it there was another heavy black line, following the one below as straight as though drawn by a parallel rule. The boy ducked out to find Falco, whom he regarded as the quidnunc of undersea puzzles. Falco looked at the parallel lines marching across the paper roll.

"Can it be fish?" asked Philippe. "I never heard of a thick layer of fish stretched out evenly across the bottom."

Falco said, "I don't know what it is, but we ought to go down and see." Saôut and the senior scientist agreed to turn back and put Falco and Philippe down. Falco swung off the ladder to feel his buoyancy and quickly grabbed back for the ladder. The Gibraltar current was running too strong to swim against. The two followed the anchor cable hand-under-hand.

A hundred feet deep they saw a uniform yellow-green bottom, above which a long shark, tunas, and several large leer fish were swimming. Further down they discovered that the bed was a mat of colossal leaves, some twenty-five feet long. Thousands of them streamed flat from slender stalks. The divers parted the leaves and passed beneath them. They found themselves in still, dim water, in a thicket of seaweed stalks planted in almost regular rows two feet apart. Each stem was exactly six feet tall. While the green roof rippled in a permanent gale of two or three knots—the Atlantic rushing into the Mediterranean with a freight of oceanic predators and pelagic wealth—underneath, in the becalmed glade, there was a prosperous, settled way of life. The very soil was plastered with vivid animal accretions. Big groupers lumbered about. Short-spined sea urchins, lobsters, starfish, and scorpion fish seemed well adjusted to life in the submarine storm cellar.

Philippe grabbed his big friend and pointed to a large pink scorpion fish wearing its familiar mock coral masquerade. Attached to its head was an additional bit of camouflage, a ramified hydroid. This was a place where a fish could keep its hat on. The divers skirted a moray waiting for a meal with its tail twined around a stalk and its head swaying in the current.

Passing through the stalks took careful work. The plants fouled the air bottles. It was well that Philippe was with Falco, whom he respected too much to stray from. Six-foot leer fish came down through the green canopy to look them over. The silver nomads were probably inquisitive about air bubbles erupting from the forest of Alboran. The divers unsheathed knives to dig a specimen of the great weed instead of cutting into the inch-thick stalk.

When Philippe and Falco appeared on deck with a brown seaweed thirty feet long from root to tip, their companions gathered in amazement. The scientists identified it as a laminarian, a species not previously reported in the Alboran Sea. In fact, marine botanists had never heard of a laminarian more than six feet long in the Mediterranean.

When Falco and Philippe told me of their adventure, I took the *Espadon* on a full-scale exploration of the forest of Alboran. We arrived on a quiet day, but since seasonal storms were due, we decided to dive day and night. In the submarine gale I regained the thrill of anchor cable diving. We went down on the lee side, our bodies streaming in the current, our hands picking secure holds. If we slipped off the cable, we might be carried hundreds of yards away before we could surface. We covered our diving suits and fins with silver paint to be more easily spotted by the *Espadon*'s searchlight if we fell off the wire at night.

On my first night visit to the sunken arbor I passed down the wire through an eerie black world filled with flashing metallic forms. Goiran and Kientzy, the leer fish and schools of sardines, all wore the same glaucous livery. We parted the green roof and slipped into the glade. Kientzy held the flood lamp while I filmed Goiran. Suddenly Goiran blacked out. Preoccupied with the camera, I did not realize what had happened. But Kientzy did, and he acted fast. He dropped the lamp, which went out. Then he put Goiran under one arm and hauled him up the wire with the other, also managing to keep the unconscious man's mouthpiece in place. Confused by this whirl of events and left in total darkness, I stuck my head and shoulders up through the leaves. The current wrapped a long laminarian around me like a constricting snake. I struggled in the dark to free myself without stirring other leaves up into the current to add to my predicament. I tore loose and sank into the stillness. I paused to make sure I remembered which way the anchor lay. Groping along, butting into stalks, and backing out when they snagged my tanks, I finally put my hand on the *Espadon*'s cable.

Kientzy's prompt action and his stalwart one-handed haul while carrying a man were well done, but we did not care to repeat it. Goiran, who had regained consciousness on the way up, joined in the planning of a better road to the forest. We decided to accept the Gibraltar current and make it work for us. We took the *Espadon* west to the edge of the seaweed jungle and hung pig-irons on wires down to within three feet of the tree tops. Divers, lights, and cameras went down these firemen's poles as the *Espadon* drifted across the forest. Securely embraced by the current instead of fighting against it, we buzzed the rippling fronds like free balloonists riding the wind. It was relatively safe to plunge ahead of the traveling perch, pass under the leaves for a short distance, then come back through them and reach for the cable. At the eastern end of the weeds there was an inclining desert of white sand, the signal to climb the pole for stage decompression before regaining the *Espadon* and taking her up-current for another glide.

Hanging under the drifting boat to pass off nitrogen was an education in marine biology. We rode in a subway jam of Atlantic plankton, long transparent Venus girdles, and lower animal forms. We could examine them intimately by flashlight as divers and drifters passed east together. Some of our neighbors resembled soft crystals with iridescent facets. We were among thousands of five-inch salps, which we had first seen illuminating the Persian Gulf. Here they looked like tumblers of water. They joined into trains, sometimes a hundred feet long, that looped in the Gibraltar current like the bandoliers of a giant gunman.

One night as we drifted under the *Espadon*, I trained a floodlight on Falco in his silver suit. Smiling inside the glass visor, he took a spectral chain of salps and wound it round himself, an undersea knight entangled with a gelatinous dragon eighty feet long. Moving amidst nightmares of planktonic globs in this submarine dungeon, we were reassured to glimpse something that looked like the sea again—a nervous flying fish taking off or a brave, blushing squid.

Our *raison d'être* for night diving stemmed from the advantages of water clarity and animal psychology, but its most fruitful use came about quite accidentally. A technician at the O.F.R.S. built an inexpensive, improved divers' hand lamp with a large, highly-polished reflector and stronger batteries. We tested the prototype in daylight two hundred feet down and liked it very much, without suspecting the surprise it had in store.

While Falco was witnessing the reproductive season of the sea cucumbers of Sormiou, he took the new torch on its first nocturnal expedition. Our previous floodlights, depending on power cables to the surface, were too cumbersome for his sorties, although they lighted a sizable area of the bottom, creating a local piece of daylight. Falco was disappointed with the new flashlight. It had a useless narrow beam. Although it pierced the darkness in a long brilliant shaft, the spot it stamped out was too small. He had to discover the cucumbers one by one, wasting time. He decided to cut his dive short and abandon the new tool.

The stiletto beam alighted on a fish. It was a middle-sized white bream, a shy animal quick to run into slits in the rock when a diver approaches. This one remained frozen in place. Falco held the beam in its eyes and slowly swam to the motionless fish. He touched the bream. It snapped out of hypnosis and sped away. Falco stabbed the light at more fish and arrested several species in the same way. When he reported the discovery, I said, "There's something new here. Of course, the light should never be used for spear fishing. It would amount to poaching. But you may have hit on a good way to take live specimens for the aquarium." I helped Falco and Claude Wesly organize nocturnal missions in the *Physalie,* the catch boat of the Oceanographic Museum of Monaco.

They went down a cliff wall turned into water spirits by glowing plankton, Falco's light beaming around and Wesly's spoon net a silver web. Along the reef sardines gleamed like the facets of a dark mirror. When Falco cast his spell on a fish, Wesly deftly drew the net mouth over its head. At the first touch of the meshes the fish sprang to the bottom of the net, and the diver folded the bag over it. Falco blinded a red mullet walking on the bottom with its restless feelers. Wesly placed the bag in front, and the mullet marched right in. They picked fish out of the water as fast as they could locate them. They caught a repertory of common Mediterranean fish—sea bass, mullets, saupes, white bream, cardinal fish. Only one species did not fall for the light—the verada, a handsome green wrasse. It turned tail on the paralyzing light and briskly departed.

The best sport was catching large rock bass. This species does not go out at night but sits in its cave facing the entrance. Falco shone the magic ray in its eyes while his partner held the net open in front of the niche. Then, as Falco describes it, "Just reach in, tickle the tail, pull the light away, and almost lose your arm as the rock bass jumps into the net." The rock bass fought violently. To keep it from ripping the bag apart, Falco put the bass back to sleep with the light and held it in the trance while taking it up to the catch boat. At the end of the sortie Falco and Wesly stood on the *Physalie*'s fantail smiling at a menagerie of 150 fish in a floating pond behind the boat. The captives were in fine shape. Mullets leaped out of the moving pool. The divers roofed it with a seine net.

Ashore we found a number of dead rock bass floating in the pond on their sides or backs. We reasoned that while being held in photohypnosis on their way to the surface, they had not been able to adjust their swim bladders to the pressure change and had died of decompression. In fact, the divers too felt out of sorts from swimming up and down to put the fish in the pool. I was concerned about this: they might be inviting complex effects from pressure changes as a price for the night's fun.

Falco had the answer. The next night that he went out to mesmerize fish, he took down an armload of transparent plastic bags, filled them with water, and placed his captives in them. He tied the bags to a line from the *Physalie* and took them all up in one trip. He ascended very slowly. All the fish lived through it, including the furious rock bass.

chapter
fourteen

UNDERSEA
AVALANCHE

At sea off Toulon I stood on the bridge of the navy research ship, the *Élie Monnier*, talking with Commander Georges Houot and Engineer-Lieutenant Pierre-Henri Willm of the bathyscaph *F.N.R.S.-3*. The bathyscaph, bobbing in our wake on a long tow, was designed to take two men to the average depth of the oceans—13,200 feet. I was feeling good; today I was to make my first dive in the bathyscaph, for which I had campaigned since 1948 when Dumas, Tailliez, and I had taken part in the unsuccessful trials of the first one, *F.N.R.S.-2* The initials stood for a Belgian government trust, *Fonds National de la Recherche Scientifique,* which had financed the first deep-boat of Professor Auguste Piccard and participated with the French Navy in the building of this one.

A bathyscaph is an undersea dirigible with a metal envelope containing gasoline as a buoyant medium and a pressure-resistant observation car. The first model had taken well to the deep, but her poorly designed envelope was destroyed by surface swells. Nonetheless Claude Francis-Beouf and I believed in the principle and worked to revive it in a new version. We managed a treaty between the French Navy and the Belgian fund by which the original two-man sphere was incorporated in a shipshape hull designed by a naval architect, André Gempp. Dumas contributed a valuable improvement over the original bathyscaph. The 1948 boat could be entered and left only while on the deck of a mothership. Dumas suggested an entry tube descending through the envelope to the observation car, so that the crew could get in and out while the *F.N.R.S.-3* was afloat. The tube could be flooded during a dive and evacuated by compressed air when she surfaced.

The new boat was not yet broken in. Recently Houot and Willm had taken her down to 6890 feet, but failure of the echo sounder had made them decide against trying a landing on the floor. We had heard that Professor Piccard's bathyscaph *Trieste,* which he had built concurrently with the *F.N.R.S.-3,* had hit the mud on a dive and partially buried her observation car.

My first dive with Houot was planned for 4500 feet, where we would make contact with the floor by our dangling guide rope and cruise along using two electric motors atop the envelope. Five miles out, the *Élie Monnier* stopped over an appropriate depth in the Toulon Canyon, which had been charted by Professor Jacques Bourcart. The three of us went to the bathyscaph in a rubber boat, Willm long in the face. For the first time he was yielding his place in the submarine to another.

Houot and I boarded the deep-boat and opened the entry hatch. He pointed to Mt. Coudon rising majestically over Toulon. "We're going deeper than that," said he. We went down the tube, and Houot locked us in the sphere by tightening sixteen hatch bolts. The interior was six feet, six inches in diameter. The walls were cluttered with instruments. I dropped my camera gear on the square yard of floorboard and knelt at the forward window like a Moslem prostrating himself toward Mecca. Outside, Aqua-Lungers were making us ready to dive. Their all-important task was to remove seven clamps from the electromagnets that held the external batteries, the heavy guide chain, and the ballast to the bathyscaph. When we were below, any sort of electrical failure would cut the magnets and drop these weights for emergency ascent. To be doubly sure that the clamps had been removed, the divers showed me all seven at the window and checked them with Willm on the surface.

Houot switched on the oxygen regenerating system, and the vital gas hissed softly into the gondola. He pushed a control and flooded the entry tube. That weight of water was enough to send us down, but the *F.N.R.S.-3* hesitated while pockets of air emptied from the top hamper. As she trembled on the brink, the loud voice of the *Élie Monnier*'s commander, Georges Ortolan, rumbled from our loud-speaker. "You are over a depth of—" Ortolan was cut off. Our antenna was submerged. The pitching stopped. A calm silence prevailed. We had cut all ties and belonged to another medium. In the cathedral stillness Houot and I said little—and that in low voices. The small noises of machinery took on great importance. I looked out eagerly for my first glimpse of scenes beyond the free-diving range. I asked Houot to descend as slowly as possible so I could take a long look at the midwater populations.

The pellucid sea darkened quickly from nile green to blue. "Three hundred and twenty-eight feet," whispered Houot. I was already deeper than I had ever been before. I turned on No. 2 droplight out on the hull, which sent a dazzling ray straight down.

At 525 feet we entered a snowstorm of tiny organisms glaring out of the darkness. "This is what Edgerton and I have been photographing blindly," I said. Houot pressed the button to an outside electromagnet, and iron pellets from a ballast silo drummed against our car. This delicate discharge slowed the *F.N.R.S.-3* almost to a stop.

Above my porthole on the outside hung one of Papa Flash's electronic flash units housed in a Pyrex tube. A cable passed through the hull to my hand-held camera inside. The glass tube had been tested to withstand mile-deep pressure, which had limited the distance of our dive. If the glass imploded, the shock would be equal to a small TNT charge and could damage the envelope or electrical circuits. I began flashing pictures of the white specks. Most of them were stationary, the rest moving spasmodically. "Oh, Houot! A superb siphonophore." Outside, there was a living transparent organism with filaments two feet long. Houot noted it in his log.

At 850 feet the bathyscaph slowed almost to a standstill without any manipulation from us. Apparently she had entered a cold layer that, in effect, took several hundred pounds off her weight. Houot resorted to the opposite pole of the bathyscaph's ballast system: he valved away a small volume of gasoline from the envelope, and our submarine resumed her vertical voyage.

At 1200 feet I switched off the droplight and acclimated my eyes to the dark. There was still a tinge of blue in the water. I made out faint shrimps, blobs of organisms, and little jellyfish pumping slowly. The first hatchet fish appeared, miniature grotesques with scabrous silver flanks, glassy tails, and eyes starting out of their heads. Some tiny fish looked like anchovies. Eel-like creatures made vertical bounds of three to six feet.

At 1500 feet we passed beyond the sun. We were falling in inner space. The snow flakes grew larger. Houot maneuvered his long legs in the steel cocoon, keeping our logs and trimming ballast with fastidious flicks of his fingers while at the same time avoiding stepping on me. "This ship gives you confidence," he said.

"She's marvelous," said I, "and so are you. I feel you are the absolute master of the vertical. Suppose we start the motors."

"Here they go," he said. I heard the purr of the electric motors immersed in oil baths on top of the envelope.

"But we aren't moving," I said.

Houot chuckled, "What's your hurry?" he asked. "She's heavy and takes a little time to pick up speed."

The *F.N.R.S.-3* got under way horizontally. "All the little animals are rushing toward us," I reported. "Let's cut the motors and go on down. Cruising will be more fun on the bottom." The boat sailed on momentum for a bit and sank again.

When we reached 3300 feet, the particles became thicker. Among them were what seemed to be red-and-white fish about five inches long. I switched the light on and recognized shrimps with bodies completely stretched out, their multiple legs jerking. Then I received a reward for my labors to advance bathyscaphy—the sighting of a creature never reported before. Entering my field of vision from the left was a fish twenty inches long and shaped exactly like a draftsman's triangle. It was the shade and thinness of aluminum foil with a ridiculous little tail. This thrilling animal had scarcely crossed my threshold before I began seeing flashes—the wakes of creatures moving at great speed.

With the surprise of legerdemain, one of the disturbances turned into a beautiful red squid that halted in the light for a split second. Its spade-shaped anterior and ten arms were engraved on my inner eye. It was about eighteen inches long. The squid vanished, and in its place I saw a puff of ink. The ink was white.

It is a well-known fact that squids and octopuses produce brown ink. I cried to Houot, "A squid making white ink!"

"Come, come," said he. "You have strained your eyes. Take a rest from that window."

Another squid jumped into life and out of it, leaving a white cloud. I turned off the light. The ink glowed phosphorescently in the dark. "Swish! Another luminous puff!"

Houot said, "Let me have a look." I yielded the port. The skipper cried, "One of them just left a white burst that practically covers the window!" I reclaimed my place. I didn't want to lose a second of the show.

"Four thousand feet," said Houot. My pulse rate increased. We were nearing the bottom. I peered down the sovereign shaft of light to where it melted into darkness. Deeper still there was a faint, diffused glow—our light reflecting from the floor. For the first time the *F.N.R.S.-3* was about to land. The bottom materialized 150 feet away, clean and bare, rising toward me. The hanging guide chain touched ground and relieved just enough weight to stop our fall. There was no jolt. The *F.N.R.S.-3* was trimmed off sweetly ten feet above the sea floor at a depth of 4240 feet.

"A shark!" I sang out.

Houot said, "First case of nitrogen narcosis I've ever heard of in atmospheric pressure."

I called, "Another shark!"

He said, "The case seems serious." I moved my head and let him have half the window. We saw an unusual little shark about three feet long. It nosed up close to the Plexiglas port, sniffed, and sauntered off stage, its low mental equipment apparently overtaxed by this cyclopean creature.

Larger sharks, eight to ten feet long, arrived in the arena of light. Unlike their familiar cousins in the heights of the ocean, they had broad, flat heads and distended, opaque, greenish-white eyes. They turned sleepily, casting shadows larger than themselves on the pale mud floor.

Why did these sharks have eyes at all, since they lived in eternal darkness? Possibly to detect the phosphorescence of their prey? My speculation broke off at something I noticed on the bottom. I pointed it out to Houot. A legible newspaper lay spread on the floor. The other world was still with us.

"Shall we try to lower the ball right to the mud?" I inquired.

"Okay," said Houot, turning the valve that bled off gasoline. He was extremely frugal about it; gasoline was precious. It was like losing your own blood. She settled gently. From my porthole, now three feet from the bottom, I had a close-up of creatures much smaller than sharks. I saw shrimps kicking along. The floor was not barren. It was blistered with mounds two feet high, each with a terminal hole like the burrow of a marmot. An unknown species, or a number of them, was living under the floor.

The bathyscaph had brought me within a few feet of the mysterious warrens we had photographed so many times without seeing what manner of creature had made them. We had four hours of bottom time ahead, and I pressed my nose to the window for the long-anticipated first sight of deep subsea creatures. My cameras were ready for them. The shovel-nosed sharks kept up their weaving saraband. As many as four at a time cast their baroque shadows under the droplight.

Houot broke the silence with a macabre remark in a low voice: "If we had an accident and could not go up, we could be satisfied to know that the bathyscaph had stood the test and the idea will not be dropped."

I said, "If it's all right with you, I'd just as soon take that satisfaction when we get back to the surf—"

There was a loud rumble. We looked at each other. "We've only lost the guide chain," murmured Houot matter-of-factly.

I told him, "The outside lights have gone out. The batteries must have fallen off."

After a while my companion said, "If so, we should be going up."

In the blank darkness outside, it was impossible to tell if we were moving. I looked at the pressure gauge, which was just above my head. The hand did not move. I gave it a rap. "The pressure gauge says we're still on the bottom," I reported.

It was a fearful and puzzling moment. We began checking for the cause. The lights were still on in our sphere; their batteries were inside with us. All sorts of thoughts assailed our minds. Houot said, "What about the vertical speed indicator?" We practically banged heads, looking at it. It showed maximum ascending speed. "We are going up!" said Houot. "And we're going up fast!" I looked back at the pressure gauge. The needle gave a tick and then swung into conformity with the speed indicator. The pressure index had simply been slow to respond.

Houot shrugged and got food and a bottle of wine from his brief case. We had scarcely washed down a sandwich before the *F.N.R.S.-3* broke through the green surface chop. I had never seen the sun so bright before.

Apparently a minor electrical failure had cut out all magnets, jettisoning everything clinging to the boat. As we came out of the entry tube, the *Élie Monnier*'s divers were joking about the missing batteries and empty silos.

"This ship is too safe," said Houot on the radio phone to the tender. The *F.N.R.S.-3* had left quite a mound of metal down there for the blank-eyed sharks to sniff.

It was the last dive before the bathyscaph went to her climactic rendezvous, a dive to the design depth of two-and-one-half miles. As they left, I wished Houot luck and felicitated the jubilant Willm on regaining his place in the gondola.

On February 17, 1954, 160 miles southwest of Dakar, my friends took the deep-boat 13,287 feet down, then the record descent of man into the sea and the first triumph of bathyscaphic navigation. On that far bottom they saw a six-foot shark with blank protruding eyes, and a beautiful garden of sea anemones.

That summer I took a month off from *Calypso* to work with Houot on applying advanced Edgertronics to deep-boat photography. At M.I.T. Papa Flash had built improved abyssal cameras, and he and his son were at Toulon fitting the bathyscaph with two external cameras coupled with two flashes provided by our indulgent uncles of the Research and Exploration Committee of the National Geographic Society. For my second dive I showed up with two hand-held movie cameras and two still cameras to use inside. The traffic jam between Houot and myself was aggravated by a plaster cast on my right foot. I had broken it playing tennis with my son Jean-Michel after a twenty-year layoff. Kneeling before the window I found that the cast relieved the customary cramp in the foot. "You ought to put casts on both feet of your passengers," I suggested to Houot.

Again the *Élie Monnier* placed the *F.N.R.S.-3* over Professor Bourcart's canyon on a sonar reading of 5300 feet, and Houot phoned the topman, "Is the tow rope free?" . . . *"Oui, Commandant."* . . . "Have them show Commandant Cousteau seven clamps from the electromagnets." So it went, as Houot religiously read off the golden rules of bathyscaphy: a list of twenty precautions against twenty ways not to come back. Among the black-suited navy divers working outside my window, I saw Edgerton *fils et père,* in bathing trunks, making sure of their camera. Harold swam toward me and held up his finger eighty inches from the window—the exact distance for me to catch fish in focus. I clicked the first test shot: father and son as menfish. From the *Élie Monnier* came a radio voice: " 'Allo, bathyscaph! The topmen are off in the rubber boat. They are recovering *les* Edgerton."

The sea smothered the *bon voyages* from the tender. We sank into green silence. It was almost night at a thousand feet. In the droplights I saw the snow falling upwards. Otherwise there was no sensation of motion. I seemed to be in a calm room in the Alps at night. Again the mass of organisms increased in density in the 2000-3300-foot stratum; again the red squids appeared subliminally and left their ghosts of phosphorescent ink. I touched off the camera often, hoping to capture one of them at the focal point, although aware of the long odds against it. The real photographic mission would come on the bottom.

Houot stooped over me and reached around, handling the controls. I looked up at the pressure gauge—4500 feet—and asked, "Could you slow her down?" He produced a shower of pellets and reduced our falling speed to a few inches a second.

He read the sonar graph: "The bottom is about two hundred feet below." That was odd. The down-directed sonar beam was recording bottom far short of Bourcart's most carefully corrected hydrographic survey of the Toulon Canyon.

Beyond the droplights I saw, just under our bow, an amorphous yellow shape. "Mud," said I. "A cloud of mud directly ahead. We're down already."

The master replied, "That's absurd. The echogram is still showing two hundred feet of clear water under us. It can't be wrong."

I was an equally devout believer in vertical echo-sounding. I said, "If it isn't the bottom, what am I looking at—a squid giving off a yellow cloud as big as a house? Or . . . or did we touch the side of the canyon with our bow?"

The droplights were still stabbing down through clear black water, with the dull yellowish presence as a backdrop. The lights picked up a vague reflection below. "It's getting brighter," I announced. "I can see our two forward lights overlapping on the ground maybe eighty feet below."

Houot retorted, "The gauges show four thousand, eight hundred feet. Is it really the bottom? We're short, aren't we?"

Descending, I saw five sharks and a big rayfish that shook its wings and flew away. The guide rope touched. Its clanking dispersed the sharks, and unquestionably the *F.N.R.S.-3* had landed in 4920 feet of water.

But we were 380 feet higher than the place we should have hit. Had we drifted during the descent? I looked out and reported, "We are on a wavy mud shelf at the edge of a vertical cliff." Houot could not believe it. "Look for yourself," I said, letting him lean over me. He gazed for some time and got off my back with a perplexed expression.

"It's a shelf all right," he declared.

I said, "And believe it or not, the yellow cloud I saw came from a mud wall we hit on the way down."

The water outside was unsullied, so we sat on our tiny deck and talked things over. The survey echo-sounder used to chart the canyon was at the root of the anomaly. Its beam expanded with depth and was unable to detect such steps as we had landed on. Instead, it averaged them, giving the false impression of a smooth decline. We decided to turn the ship ninety degrees to port and take off for the canyon floor.

While we were reaching this decision, the bathyscaph had settled, coiling her long heavy guide chain into the mud until the gondola itself touched earth. Houot dumped some shot ballast and lifted the boat. He put the starboard motor ahead and the other astern to swing our bow toward the sea. But owing to the embedded chain, the *F.N.R.S.-3* would lift only five feet. Houot ran both motors full ahead to pull her out of the mud. The boat tugged hard but made no progress. Here was a dismal sort of anchorage.

Then things began to happen. The bathyscaph took off. Through my window I saw an enormous hunk of hard mud tumbling off the ledge below. It dislodged more mud that sank in a slow-motion explosion. The droplights rebounded from a blooming, spreading, climbing yellow boil.

"Houot, we've started an avalanche!" We laughed nervously. An uncomfortable thought came to mind. Suppose we had triggered a turbidity current? Some oceanographers are convinced that high-speed mud currents scour the sea floor following land slides at the head of a submarine canyon. The avalanche is thought to pick up velocity when cramped in the bottom of a canyon and, by a Venturi Effect, bursts at great speed out of the canyon to roll hundreds of miles before it slows down and settles. If the *F.N.R.S.-3* was caught in anything like that, we were in for a pretty bad ride.

"I think we'd better keep both motors going and get away from here," I said—a sentiment readily approved by the skipper. For twenty minutes we cruised slowly over immense mud clouds that churned higher toward the bathyscaph. We thought we might find an undisturbed area by crossing the canyon on a compass bearing, even though it meant sailing through the cloud tops.

It was a mad crossing. We passed through alternating black space and ocher billows that blanked out my window as though cardboard had been pasted over it. In the open stretches I could see yellow-strato-cumulus peaks ahead to the limit of sight. "How could one hunk of mud fill a canyon?" I wondered as I watched particles streaming into the glass. Suddenly they stopped. I looked again. The particles were stationary. Yet our motors were whirring smoothly. "Stop the motors," I said to Houot. "We are not moving." Had we collided with the other side of the Toulon Canyon?

In the solemn silence we heard only the gentle sigh of the oxygen system. Houot looked out of the after port. "Nothing but cardboard," said he.

I said off-handedly, "Let's wait for the current to wash the stuff away." The master had nothing to say. In the heavy stillness within and without, we looked out of our respective windows with our backs to each other, each unwilling to voice the thought that possessed us: we had unloosed a mud cascade from the other canyon wall, and the bathyscaph was entombed. I looked at the depth gauge: the needle seemed cemented to the dial. "You know, Houot," I said, "somebody had better make a narrow-beam sonar. Bourcart charted a gradual slope on the other side, and we found that it stepped down almost vertically."

"Yes," he said, "and with overhangs as well."

"There could be overhangs here, too," I said.

Houot replied, "Let's just relax and wait for the mud to settle."

We had twenty-two hours of oxygen left in our rebreathing system. We sat down and arranged our long legs and gear on the tiny deck and talked in low voices, two perplexed men a mile under the sea. A foot outside my window we had fastened an iron bracket with a baited fish hook. I kept looking for the hook as a sign that the mud was thinning out. The window remained entirely opaque. We had the sea to ourselves.

An hour passed in a desultory fashion. I cleared my throat to overcome the possibility that my voice might crack and said, "Well, the dive is lost for photography. What say we surface, *mon vieux*?" Houot got up and pressed his fingers into both shot buttons like a skyscraper tenant impatient for an elevator. He held the magnets open until hundreds of pounds of ballast had fallen from the silos.

I watched the pressure gauge and vertical speed indicator. They did not budge.

Through my porthole no mud particles moved.

We remained outwardly cool and technical while hot, antitechnical thoughts raced through our brains.

The vertical speed indicator was the most sensitive recorder of motion aboard. We both watched it. Only one little flicker of the needle was all we wanted from the bottom of our hearts. The dial remained as still as a photograph.

We had dropped enough weight to be soaring at a good speed, but the *F.N.R.S.-3* remained dead as a fly in amber.

"We must have forgotten something," I said. We began reviewing everything we knew about bathyscaphs—a syllabus of physics and a litany of operation. The answer was most simple. During the hour we had been waiting in the deep, the gasoline in the envelope had cooled enough to offset the weight of shot pellets Houot had just dropped. He squirted pellets again. "We're climbing!" I announced. Mud specks skidded down my window. We were enclosed by them for the first eight hundred feet of ascent, but there was definitely no turbidity current at work. We felt no pull of current on the deep-boat. We broke into clear black water, and I watched the yellow thunderheads until they faded from the droplight and the sun commenced faintly to tinge the sea.

The next time I met Jacques Bourcart, I said, "Remember that canyon off Toulon that you charted so carefully? You'll have to do it again. Houot and I have just wrecked it."

chapter
fifteen

DIVING
SAUCER

On the diving deck the center of activity was a big yellow steel depth bubble. Inside it Jean Mollard and André Laban strapped strain gauges on various diameters to see how it would be deformed under pressure, while Saôut rigged four tons of weights to send it down. *Calypso* was standing off Cassis in 1957 preparing to test Hull No. 1 of the depth machine I had pledged to build six years before. The O.F.R.S. had been working on its design and construction since that undersea laboratory was founded.

The hull was six feet and seven inches in diameter and five feet high with two windows and a top hatch. Today we were lowering the unoccupied shell to two thousand feet, midway in a progressively deeper series of trials, hoping it would survive an immersion of three thousand feet, the crushing depth calculated by Émile Gagnan. If it did, we would assign an operating depth of one thousand feet, giving the little exploring submarine a safety factor of three.

278

The hull and weights went in smoothly, and Maurice Léandri winched out two thousand feet of wire. We soaked the hull for fifteen minutes and began hauling. Laban leaned over the fantail and reported, "It's in sight a hundred feet down." He frowned; there was a whiff of mistral in the air and a running swell that he could sense in variations of speed in the winch motor. "Slower, Léandri," he called. He dropped his arm. "Stop. She's within fifteen feet." Falco went down the diving ladder with a cable and hook upon which to transfer the hanging ballast to relieve the hull for swinging it aboard.

A violent swell lifted *Calypso*'s stern. As she dropped back into the trough, the lift cable slacked and jumped out of the block. The ship came up, and the cable snapped like a violin string. The end lashed back at the winchman. Falco plunged into the sea and saw our precious yellow egg disappearing. The depth was 3300 feet.

Fortunately, Léandri was only superficially cut by the backlash. Henri Plé switched on the radar and took three shore bearings to mark the spot. The downcast Calypsonians sailed home minus our prototype depth vehicle and an expensive set of strain gauges. In Marseilles the O.F.R.S. was already fitting out a sister hull in the confidence that the first one would pass the pressure test. Now we could hardly go ahead with Hull Two unless we spent a lot more than its replacement cost to dredge up the crushed remains and find out which part had given way first. I accepted this punishing price of two ships and a special cable dredge, but first sent Laban in *Calypso* to give the sweepers a precision sonar survey of ten square miles centered on the point of loss.

When he brought in the echograms, I noticed a distinctive trace on all tapes that bisected Plé's radar fix. It was a heavy black spot thirty feet above the floor. The ballast cable on Hull One was thirty feet long. The prototype was intact, floating at anchor nearly 3300 feet down! It had exceeded a safety factor of three. We could go ahead with Hull Two without dredging. Pointing to the black spot, I said to Laban, "*Chef,* someday with an even deeper boat we'll visit this unlucky baby." Many times since then *Calypso* has echo-ranged over Hull One. She was still afloat when this report was written.

Mollard, the constructor, and his O.F.R.S. team labored long and late for eighteen months to complete Hull Two and realize the demands I had made on them for a scientific submarine capable of exploring the entire continental shelf—today the most important area of the oceans. The shelf is the submerged fringe of a continent extending as far out and down as the drop-off line of the continental slope, where the true oceanic environment begins. This coastal escarpment extends generally to a depth of a hundred fathoms (600 feet) and comprises about eight percent of the oceanic surface of the globe, equal to the area of Asia. The continental shelf is already the theater for the dragging fishery, the seaweed biochemical industry, and petroleum, natural gas, sulphur, and diamond mining. In effect, it is another continent.

The offshore realm has been claimed by various governments but never occupied by man. Once upon a time, in order to annex territory for your country, you had to set foot on it and plant your flag. Today, politicians do it with a pen stroke. But even this could not be followed up by occupation and exploitation: hermetic military submarines were of no use, and because of the relatively shallow depth of the shelf, bathyscaphs would be wasted on it.

In talking about a continental-shelf vehicle during its period of conception, I recommended to Laban, "Put all you can of the power plant and auxiliary systems outside the hull; that's the main lesson we have from the bathyscaph. Pay no attention to speed. It isn't needed in an exploring submarine. We want agility, perfect trim, tight turns, and hovering ability. Let the men look out with their eyes and make them more comfortable than the awkward kneeling attitude in the bathyscaph. Put them on their bellies on a mattress. Give them a new kind of ship's log: still and movie cameras with lighting systems, a voice recorder, and a claw to pick up things outside. Throw the classic idea of submarines out of the window and start with what *we* need."

Laban and Mollard infected the O.F.R.S. with their enthusiasm. Jacques Roux and Armand Davso made wooden scale models of various hull forms and tested them for dynamic stability in wind tunnels. The O.F.R.S. chose hydrojets instead of screw propulsion, although jets had never been proved on an underwater vehicle. After they had selected a flattened spheroid hull form, Alexis Sivirine constructed a full-scale papier-mâché dummy of the jet submarine, so that we could work out how to place the power plant and instruments. Looking at the mock-up, we had a uniform reaction: "It looks just like a flying saucer in a comic book!" That is why, for better or worse, we called it *la soucoupe plongeante,* the "Diving Saucer," or *DS-2*.

When the *DS-2* was finished, it had tractor jets flanking the bow—a "front wheel drive." Together or individually the jet nozzles turned on a vertical axis, affording all angles of climb and dive as well as backing. The jet pump on the stern ejaculated water streams through flexible plastic pipes. The pilot could clamp either pipe, diminishing the flow to make turns. By reversing one jet he could spin the saucer on her axis. He could tilt the submarine up or down by pumping mercury ballast between fore-and-aft trimming tanks. Electrical controls were kept to a minimum, and we employed a central hydraulic plant for servo-mechanisms.

The engineers placed the power and hydraulic systems in a flooded outside girdle, covered by Fiberglas fairings that assisted her hydrodynamic qualities and made her more snag-proof. On the starboard bow we fitted an Edgerton depth camera, synchronized with a flash tube on the other side. For convenience in changing film the movie camera was inside the hull, trained through a small port between the two crew windows. The movie flood lamp was outside on a retractable hydraulic spar. Another hydraulic limb with an elbow and thumb-and-finger joints could be extended to cut and pluck specimens and tuck them into a collecting basket through a spring-hinged lid.

The Diving Saucer had ten eyes. Three consisted of hemispheric optical ports in the dome to see what was overhead. Passenger and pilot each had one looking forward, and two were photographic. The other three were the sonar transducers beamed up, down, and forward, which related the pilot to things he could not see himself. He lay within an encircling instrument panel, showing indexes of inside air pressure, oil pressure, sonar, depth gauge, voltage, gyrocompass, oxygen pressure, and carbon-dioxide percentage, as well as the stop-start buttons for the cameras, lights, and tape recorder.

The oxygen rebreathing system supplied two men for twenty-four hours. We deliberately put hand-powered controls on the safety system so they would work in a total power failure. Hand levers released two 55-pound pig-irons and the 450-pound emergency weight hanging under the hull. The precision-trimming ballast with which the submarine attained neutral buoyancy consisted of a twelve-gallon tank between the two crewmen, to which they could add water when the DS-2 was light or subtract it when she was heavy.

Mollard drove himself in vain to finish the construction in time for Calypso's 1959 Atlantic cruise, "Mission Sea Mount." He made a pierhead jump in order to work on the DS-2 on the way across. At sea, while the rest of us were concerned with lowering instruments or chartroom computations, four half-suffocated individuals—Mollard, Laban, Jacques Roux, and our radio engineer Bernard Marcellin—toiled day and night in the after-hold around the strange yellow bubble with the big silver eyes. They still had not finished by the time we arrived in New York for the International Oceanographic Congress.

In the big city the Empire State Underwater Council relieved my men for shore leave by furnishing guides to show American divers over *Calypso*. I stood behind a crowd gathered around the Diving Saucer and listened to the guide, an off-duty New York police officer, explaining how the thing worked a thousand feet down. I shivered and sincerely hoped he was right. The *DS-2* had not yet been a foot under water.

I remained in suspense through a round of courtesy calls in the States. At the Woods Hole Oceanographic Institution *Calypso* tied up outside the legendary research ship *Atlantis*. As we crossed her to the quay, I said, "Saôut, we are on the deck of an oceanographer that has made more miles and more stations than any other in history. We'll be a long time catching up with the A-boat." When *Calypso* went to Washington as a guest of the National Geographic Society, a photo of the Diving Saucer appeared on the front pages; I became an uncomfortable party to ballyhoo over an untried device. It was nobody's fault. We could not conceal the saucer.

Free at last, we carried the *DS-2* to the shallow Puerto Rican shelf, where we found the sea rough and the water murky. But we had waited long enough. In a fairly calm spot off the west end of the island, the *DS-2* made her first dive in eighty feet of water. It was a cautious fifteen-minute lowering on a cable with the vehicle overweighted to check hull integrity, oxygen renewal, carbon dioxide absorption, and the workings of controls and power. If anything went wrong, the depth permitted free escape to Falco and Mollard and we could easily retrieve the vessel. We got her back, and they came out of the hatch grinning like devils. Mollard said, "I never knew it would be like that."

I asked, "Like what?"

He said, "It's the first time I've ever been underwater."

The second dive took the *DS-2* a hundred feet down. Falco and I were not quite ready to give the Diving Saucer complete freedom. A false, obsolete sense of security led us to attach her to a surface buoy by a 330-foot slack nylon cable. The dive plan called for Falco to sink to a few feet from the bottom, trim to neutral buoyancy, and move short distances to test power and controls in a forty-five-minute submersion.

Everyone aboard watched the buoy. Toward the end of the dive it wobbled a little, which I attributed to wind or current. When forty-five minutes had elapsed, the submarine did not appear. Men began pulling on fins and clamping pressure gauges on Aqua-Lungs. Minutes passed. The buoy stopped bobbing. I looked over my people, picking an emergency diving team. As I was about to put them in the water, a watcher at the fantail yelled, "She's coming up!"

A swimmer jumped in and made fast the lifting tackle. We swung the DS-2 up to her deck cradle and gathered around, curious and elated, as the hatch handle turned. Falco came out shouting, "*Ça c'est de la bagnole!*" which might be translated as, "What a hot rod!" He said, "She spins. The controls are responsive." He handed me the tape recorder. I threaded the voiced log of the first Diving Saucer cruise onto the ship's public address system so that Calypsonians anywhere in the ship could hear the story.

Against a low background of soughing pumps and whirring motors the men started talking. The laconic Mollard turned into a chatterbox. He cried out in marvel at sights commonplace to Falco. The pilot explained things to him and from time to time broke in with log entries, which were the real purpose of the tape recorder. "Pumping mercury forward," he said. "She goes down by the bow. Pumping mercury aft."

Mollard's voice broke in, "*Zut alors!* What are those fish?"

Falco said, "She's now level. Quick response on mercury trim. Those fish are just jacks."

"Now cruising at one knot, three feet off the bottom," continued the pilot. "Sonar okay. There is a tall coral coming up. I am suppressing the starboard jet to turn away from the obstacle."

Mollard said, "Well dodged!"

Falco said, "Touching down on a patch of sand. Light as a feather. I'm spinning her about. Facing aft. Pumping mercury forward. The bow goes down. Sand bottom about eighteen inches from our eyes."

"Look at that!" cried Mollard.

"Small head pops out of the sand," said Falco. "It's a little silver fish that comes out of the sand and stands on its tail. It is looking at us. Hey, it's digging in by its tail. It's gone back underground. Here it comes out again." Falco reflected, "We're going to see fish behavior from this thing that a diver could never see."

Falco started cruising again. "What's that giant fish?" demanded Mollard.

"A grouper," said the pilot. "Let's follow him. He's stemming the current. And we're able to do the same."

Mollard said, "Say, you turn right with the fish."

Falco replied, "Isn't that what you built into her? But the steering mechanism seems a little stiff."

The engineer said, "I know what's wrong. We'll fix it tonight."

"We're not moving," said Falco.

Mollard retorted, "The jets are flowing. The motor is running all right." During a moment without conversation the tape clearly relayed the hum of the motor.

Falco said, "I know what it is. That line we've got trailing behind has fouled on something." The Diving Saucer was tied down by her own "security" cable. Although Falco knew that we would send divers if he became overdue and that he had only to sit and wait, he turned back along the line and successsfully disengaged it from a coral snag. He said, "We've got to get rid of cables forever." I agreed. We had made a mistake. Safety lay in freedom from lines.

Dissatisfied with these turbid waters, I scanned the charts of the Antilles looking for a shelter from the trades that were roiling the underwater climate in the Puerto Rican grounds. I found a neck between Guadeloupe and an islet called Pigeon that looked as if it were protected from the wind and had appropriate depths varying from seventy to three hundred feet. We sailed for Guadeloupe, and the water was perfect, depth transparency 130 feet.

We anchored on a seventy-foot-deep plateau, and everyone dug out a mask to have a look down. The life forms on the Caribbean floor were quite different from those we had seen before, but the biotope was almost as profuse in species as in the Red Sea. Tall gorgonians and many kinds of sponges grew on the white sand floor at Pigeon Island.

We programed eight test dives—all within Aqua-Lung reach in case anything went wrong. We would let Falco master his machine before going deeper. Guadeloupe became at once the test bench of a prototype vehicle and the driving school of its first pilot. He made two free cruises on the plateau beneath a school of attentive menfish. We watched him demonstrate his quickly developing proficiency as a continental shelf navigator. Breasting a slight current, he climbed the *DS-2* and landed right on top of a basket sponge six feet high. Falco rested her there, as though on the deck cradle, for two minutes, then kicked up the jets and sailed away.

We wondered if motor sounds would repel fish from the *DS-2*. Divers know how easily fish are frightened by a noise and how they retreat from even the low-frequency pressure wave set up by a brisk finstroke. But the residents came right up to the humming and whistling saucer. Schools of jacks and creole fish circled her a few feet away. Rarely will they come that close to a diver. They understand that man is probably a harmful animal, but this big yellow thing, notwithstanding its noises, seemed to strike the fish as she struck us—a creature of the sea with big intelligent eyes and nothing but friendly intentions. When a new noise started, the fish shuddered but continued circling the saucer.

To the north, our nursery depth sloped away at thirty degrees to a lower plain 250 feet down. We moved there for the remaining shallow trials. I curbed a gnawing temptation to place myself at Falco's side; should anything happen to the *DS-2*, it was my responsibility to remain on the surface to make the decisions. I intended to make the terminal thousand-foot trial with Falco, but until then, I belonged on deck.

The third man to go down was André Laban, head of the laboratory that built her. Then I said to Dr. Edgerton, "Like to make a dive?"

He said, "You mean it? Boy, would I!" I felt that he deserved the first saucer dive by a scientist, just as he had merited the first such descent in the bathyscaph *F.N.R.S.-3*.

Edgerton's dive log read: "Now we are slowly sinking, free of the cable. Above us, through the optical ports, we can see *Calypso* at anchor in the exceptionally clear water. Falco turns on the jets. We begin to move. Like an airplane we descend to where the reef drops off into deeper water. We are getting good clean oxygen. Being in the saucer is no different from being in an automobile, except that we are more comfortable and loll on our mattresses like Romans at a banquet.

"Falco spots a squadron of squids, swimming on the bottom in perfect formation, but out of camera range. He cuts the jets and the submarine settles slowly into an undersea garden with a slight crunch of coral. A host of fishes of many colors circles us. One special beauty, a large blue-and-yellow queen angelfish, passes closely in front of the camera. I want her further away for a better shot, but she insists on a close-up. This nonchalant behavior is common among the fish."

The essence of the *DS-2*'s agility was absolute neutral buoyancy. Before a dive we conducted a picturesque weighing-in ceremony, entering the results on a blackboard. On a bathroom scale we put Falco, his companion, and their racks of CO_2 absorbent, tape recorder, cameras, and bottles of wine. When this total was added to the DS-2's gross weight, we knew how much water ballast was needed and added it to the stainless steel tank in the saucer. On the outside, two streamlined 55-pound blocks of pig iron were held mechanically to the belly of the submarine. One was the descent weight, which gave the saucer negative buoyancy to sink. When Falco released it, the saucer was in equilibrium. The other pig was the ascent weight, which he dropped to lighten ship for the return to *Calypso*.

The diving operation began on deck with the saucer crew closing themselves in by turning the hatch tight from the inside. Riggers shackled a tricornered lifting tackle to cleats on top of the hull. Through a telephone line jacked into the saucer the pilot announced when he was ready, and we began the launch. The little submarine's comings and goings were handled by a ten-ton hydraulic crane, the Yumbo, on the port stern quarter of *Calypso*. Conventional cargo cranes that suspend their burden from long cables could not have been used for the work. Swaying on a wire, the DS-2 would have battered the afterquarters of the mothership. Searching widely for a suitable crane, we had come across the Yumbo, which was designed to clear heavy wrecks from highways. We modified the type for its first use on shipboard. The Yumbo could bend its joints and extend its proboscis into the afterhold to pick up the saucer without an intervening length of cable. It could thrust the saucer into the water, holding her all the while in a tight grip.

Yumbo's mahout, Maurice Léandri, swung the DS-2 into the sea, and a masked man, "the topman," went into the water to detach the lifting tackle, leaving two lines to the ship—the phone and a nylon retaining rope. I phoned Falco, "Everything checked?" When the reply came, *"Oui, Commandant,"* the topman removed the two last lines and stood on the submarine, lending his weight to sink her. As is always the case with depth vehicular travel, the most obstinate phase was passing through the boundary of air and water. The topman walked on water for a spell while pockets of air rumbled out of the Fiberglas fairings. Falco helped him by squirting the jets to expel air from the pipes. Gradually the topman sank until he was afloat, looking down at the Diving Saucer shrinking into the blue.

On these trials Falco did not make power dives; he merely sank by the descent weight. When his eyes and the sonar told him he was fifteen feet from the floor, he dropped the weight. Momentum carried the submarine on down until it sat softly on the bottom. There Falco adjusted to neutral buoyancy. If the boat was light, he worked a lever back and forth, admitting a sip of water to the central trimming tank on each swing. If she was heavy, he switched on the electric ejection pump, which expelled a liter in twenty seconds. These minutes of adjustment were well spent. They assured the *DS-2* of perfect three-dimensional maneuver.

Falco then switched on the jets, turned the nozzles down, and took off. The *DS-2* had a top cruising speed of one-and-a-half knots, but we rarely needed or used it. Speed is the enemy of observation. The joy of traveling by automobile was lost when speed began to blur terrain and congeal leagues of landscape into a postcard. The Diving Saucer was a scrutinizer, a loiterer, a deliberator, a taster of little scenes as well as big. She gave us six-hour periods in which to study accurately the things below.

Once she was down, I joined half of *Calypso*'s crew to sprawl with a mask on the roof of the test bed and watch Falco break her in. We could clearly distinguish between the whirr of the propulsion motor and the clatter of the oil pump as it started automatically when the hydraulic pressure had dropped to thirty atmospheres. We could also hear the pump stop when the pressure was up to eighty atmospheres. We heard the whistle of the electronic flash converter and the drone of the movie camera. We were thrilled when Falco confidently slalomed down, hugging a thirty-degree slope. At a depth of a hundred feet we could see the movie flood lamp spar thrust out five feet and suffuse the bottom with light. As she faded from sight at a depth of 130 feet, the noises, still audible, conveyed the progress of the dive. And a visual reminder of the hidden machine came with each flash of the electronic camera.

When the *DS-2* was swallowed in the dark, it was an emotional moment for me. She was going out of sight of *Calypso* like a baby whale on its first independent ventures from its mother. Falco neglected nothing in his investigation of how a Diving Saucer worked. It was as though we had really had nothing to do with making the machine, but had found it on the beach and were learning its characteristics. Sometimes, while out of sight, Falco cut his motors to make a quiet observation and remained so long that I called for divers. But always, before they got down, we would hear power coming on in the submarine.

On the last two dives of the shallow test series, Falco roamed so far from the ship that we lost his sounds. I sent lookouts aloft, expecting him to surface at a distance. However, no matter how far he went, his sense of underwater orientation, developed on thousands of free dives, would bring him back, often over stretches of unfamiliar land, to pop up near the ship. He announced the return by jetting twenty-five-foot pillars of white water. "Thar she blows!" the lookouts would yell at the two-spouted whale. Thanks to this trick, we were confident that we could locate a saucer if she should surface far away.

The ninth dive was designed to obtain motion pictures of DS-2 maneuvers. With Jacques Ertaud as my assistant, I dived fifty feet with a movie camera, a white dinner plate, and a grease pencil. I wrote instructions on the plate for each stunt and held it in front of Falco's window. The saucer obeyed promptly like a veteran actor. We were having so much fun that I ran out of air and had to surface quickly for another lung. I rejoined the DS-2 at a depth of seventy-five feet to take the last film sequence—the dropping of the ascent weight.

I was close to the bow when there came a loud, hollow explosion from the saucer. I darted to Falco's port and looked in. His face was gone from the window. So was Mollard's. It was completely dark inside. I felt a poignant fear. Perhaps the auxiliary silver-zinc battery had exploded inside.

Falco's face appeared in the left eye. He made a thumbs-up gesture. The men were okay. Falco grimaced, conveying that he did not know what was wrong. When the blast came (he told me later), he and Mollard had pulled back from the windows to look at the voltmeter. As Falco and I continued our dumb show, I saw streams of gaseous bubbles coming through the outside fairings. That could only mean a burning short circuit in the external nickel-cadmium batteries. The pilot needed no writing on my dinner plate to grasp the fact. He jettisoned the ascent weight, and I swam up ahead of the saucer, glancing below at her expanding volume of bubbles. I scrambled aboard and took over the Yumbo crane as the topman quickly made fast the lifting tackle. As I put the DS-2 on the deck cradle, she was pouring off furious billows of smoke. Seamen squirted carbon-dioxide snow on the batteries. "Wait!" I yelled. "We've got to get them out first." Falco and Mollard bailed out of the saucer. The pilot immediately got back on her hot plates in his bare feet and began ripping off the fairings. The CO_2 foam was unequal to the fire. "Stand clear," I said. "I'm putting her back in the water." I plunged the DS-2 into the sea and extinguished the blaze.

We stood around the saucer with grim faces as Papa Flash removed the ruins of the short-circuited battery. It looked like a calamitous setback. The extremely expensive, revolutionary batteries had been an essential part of the design. Lighter than lead batteries, they were supposed to be very durable, and we had been assured they could not be damaged by a clean short circuit. We had enclosed them in Fiberglas boxes filled with oil. Now it seemed that the boxes were poor temperature conductors and that the oil had reached the boiling point from battery heat.

The future was perplexing. Right after the *DS-2* tests Professor Jacques Forest was scheduled to take over *Calypso* for a biological program in the Cape Verde Islands, so the ship could not immediately return the submarine to France. I decided to fly the plastic boxes to Marseilles. Simone, Mollard, and I took off from Guadeloupe, leaving the crippled submarine crouched useless in the hold. In three weeks the O.F.R.S. made brass battery boxes with gas exhausts, and we flew them to the Cape Verdes. The lights went on in *Calypso*'s afterhold, and the four invincible engineers toiled in smothering heat to install the new boxes.

We picked Baïa Do Inferno, a bay of Santiago Island, for the design test to a thousand feet. It was a familiar diving ground for me. I had first gone down at Inferno Bay soon after the war and had nominated it to Professor Piccard as the proving ground for the first bathyscaph in 1948. Falco and Mollard took the Diving Saucer on a very successful shallow dive. Then we lowered her empty to 1500 feet. When she came back without incident, I said to Falco, "Now, we're ready to take her to a thousand feet." He smiled in anticipation. I did, too. I was going with him on my first Diving Saucer ride.

I had lived saucer-diving so long in my imagination that preparing for my first take-off was routine. I opened the oxygen inlets and turned on the fan. Falco uncovered two racks of CO_2 absorbent and started the hydraulic plant. "Okay, we're set," said he. I phoned the word to Laban, who had taken my place as divemaster. He placed us neatly into the water. Falco's face was tinted with the blue ocean light rippling around the walls of the saucer.

To conserve power, the pilot sank by gravity, dropped the descent weight, and landed softly on a slope of dark gray sand a hundred feet down. He expelled a small surplus of water ballast, turned on the jets, and levered mercury ballast into the foretank, pitching the boat to the angle of the slope below. We started down tangent to it. The ground seemed to be sterile volcanic dust. Hardly a fish was in sight.

Two hundred and sixty feet down, the *DS-2* came to a halt of its own volition and remained in place as though caught in aspic. "Don't take in any water," I requested. "We're lying on a thermocline on top of a dense cold layer. Let's let her cool off, then we'll be in sinking trim again." We pulled on sweaters. "From now on," I said to the pilot, "we're on our own. The divers can't help us if anything goes wrong." Falco looked at me with a calm expression. He was not in the least perturbed over our isolation. The DS-2 settled, and we went on down.

At a depth of 360 feet the saucer touched the slope. Falco had not put her there; she had lost positive buoyancy and scraped the volcanic ash. He turned off the motor. We listened for clues to what was wrong. We heard hiccups outside. Then came a teakettle boil of bubbles.

Falco said, "The batteries again!"

I said, "Back to the surface." He dropped the ascent weight.

The saucer took off reluctantly amidst an increasing production of fiery bubbles. The voltmeter jerked, confirming a major battery short circuit. Gas was being generated in the brass battery boxes, and the pressure had exploded them. Falco said, "Look, we're sinking again!" Through the port I saw plankton moving up. The DS-2 was in a critical situation.

But our design had anticipated such a moment. I slashed the safety tape on an emergency lever and heaved it, dropping the 450-pound emergency weight under the saucer. We heard no noise of impact, but it had certainly fallen clear. The saucer tilted up her stern to thirty-five or forty degrees and headed for the surface. We ate a chicken sandwich and drank some wine.

It was clear that our advanced batteries were too dangerous. Calypso sailed home to Marseilles to tackle the problem of replacing them. The saucer was at home underwater, but we were having a hard time keeping her there.

SPACE

chapter   WITHOUT
sixteen
SUN

We replaced the Diving Saucer's advanced bat-
teries with more conventional ones and improved the electrical circuits. On
February 2, 1960, in the Bay of Ajaccio, Corsica, Falco and I undertook
the thousand-foot dive to design depth. Our sonar charts revealed that the
continental shelf and slope on the bay were adorned with many high rock
pillars, giving Falco an ideal test track.

We ran over the preflight checklist, shut ourselves into the DS-2 and
phoned the divemaster, Commandant Jean Alinat, to hoist away. We sank
rapidly, for some reason markedly overweighted. We found ourselves seventy
feet down amongst violent surges that swung the DS-2 to and fro, banging
her on the rocks. Her encircling rubber bumper preserved the outside power
plant from disablement while Falco switched into high gear to get out of
there. Although she was still heavy, he revved up and vaulted out of the
boulders. He descended toward a sandy patch at a depth of a hundred

291

feet, where we would be beneath the surge, and landed to trim water ballast. This was my second *DS-2* dive, and I felt completely at home with Falco. Outside, several Calypsonians were swimming around us. I thought, *We are about to leave you far behind. We are going to lands you will never reach in the lung. You will soon have to go up, perhaps to decompress, while we plunge on down, breathing at normal pressure.* Falco switched on the motor and took off. As the last diver waved and turned toward the surface, the Diving Saucer pilot sighed and said, "At last!"

We had not yet installed a gyrocompass in the *DS-2*. The critical test flight depended entirely on Falco's sense of orientation. We had descended from the north shore of the bay; the edge of the continental shelf lay south. During the first phase we could guess south from dancing sunrays on the bottom. After that we looked for a pattern on the bottom in the rows of dead posidonie leaves and roots that were roughly aligned with the coast. By crossing them at right angles, we would be headed for the drop-off line of the shelf. Deeper in the thick gloom the course led us into a sand valley that looked to be at right angles to the north shore. On both sides of the pale bottom were the rock pillars we had detected on sonar, lifting darkly in the haze like church spires at vespertime.

At three hundred feet the bottom changed to mud and the cathedrals were hard to see in the fog. A half-hour had passed. Daylight was nearly filtered away. We switched on the running lights. Falco was contour flying close to the bottom, which was smooth with a very light incline. I wondered how far we had ventured from *Calypso*. The pilot drove on.

After fifteen more minutes in the featureless gradient we approached a sharp black horizon line. "The end of the shelf," I said; "the beginning of the continental slope. Depth 400 feet. Let's stop close to the edge." Falco landed two feet from the brink. The bottom was sharply creased like folded paper. We looked at the drop-off line with awe and a feeling of vertigo. I had been far deeper in a bathyscaph, but that was like ballooning at night. Falco had never been this low before and was living on a bottom far beyond his accustomed range. We were stirred by the intimacy of the Diving Saucer with these deeplands.

Before we leaped off the shelf, we relaxed and checked our equipment, attaching proper importance to the first crossing of the unbelievable edge. I asked Falco, "Everything okay?"

He said, *"Oui, Commandant."*

I said, "All right, let's go."

Falco eased up on the jets and glided over the brink. He shoved the mercury ballast lever forward, and the saucer went down the slope, tilted to thirty-five degrees, very near the ground. In the total darkness the running light picked out a school of pink boarfish, which fell behind like June bugs encountered by an automobile after dark.

Along the barren mud we passed rows of red-and-white worms that stood up from the ground like cactus. Falco was nudging his jets to keep us flying about a foot above the continental slope. The saucer brushed the ground, and a few mud clods rolled down the decline, stirring up expanding gray puffs. The deep bank was very soft. To maintain our sharp visibility, we would have to be careful not to touch it or stir it up with our jets. As we were discussing this, a long dogfish swiftly crossed our bows an inch or two from the mud and left no disturbance whatsoever. What did this stupid shark have that we didn't? Its tail design probably did the trick. A dogfish tail has practically no lower part, but the top rises like that of a jet liner, thereby propelling the animal without agitating the mud.

Off to the right at the boundary of vision I saw a pronounced squarish shape. Angular objects are alien to the sea. This must be some man-made thing. "Steer fifteen points to starboard," I requested. We came up to the thing. Lying in the mud was an almost perfect three-by-five-foot rectangle of white pebbles. An enclosure like that had to have an owner. Soon I spied him. Dug into the bottom in one of the corners with only two large eyes showing was a pink-and-gray octopus. As Falco set off again, I thought about the octopus ranch. There were no pebbles within hundreds of yards of the stockade. Why such a heavy transportation job just to fence in a barren yard?

We had now been planing down for a long time. Although our couches were comfortable, I was beginning to feel like an amateur yogi who had been standing on his head too long. It was a relief to hear Falco say, "We will soon reach a thousand feet." As the needle of the depth gauge touched design depth, Falco stopped the motors, and the *DS-2* sat on the emergency weight aft. The cabin settled level. We turned off all mechanisms and lay in deep silence. We could distinctly hear our heartbeats.

The saucer trembled from two jolts. *"Merde!"* said Falco. "There go the batteries again."

"No, no," said I, "that was only some gas bubbles escaping from the vents in the new battery boxes. That jolt is a good one. It means the batteries are okay."

It was 1530 hours—two hours from take-off. We checked all systems again. "Everything normal. We've got plenty of amps left," said Falco. He opened two fresh racks of carbon dioxide absorbent. I uncorked the wine, and we toasted the successful dive.

We extinguished all lights inside and out and were embalmed in unending night. After a while we both saw through the ports a faint pale light twenty-five feet away. It did not move. It was not an animal, it was a presence. When we turned up the headlight, there was nothing there.

I said, "Let's start back and try to see as many things as we can." Falco pumped mercury aft, wheeled about, and started uphill on zigzag sweeps. Three hundred feet higher, I sighted several rectangular octopus gardens —a crossroads hamlet of these artful beings.

On the five-hundred-foot level we came to the church spires again. Falco, in high spirits, decided to show off his skill as a Diving Saucer pilot. He put on maximum thrust and bore straight at a rock tower, simultaneously working the jet nozzles and the mercury pump. He jumped the pinnacle and planed down the other side into a narrow canyon. He said, "You noticed the way she skids several meters after you make a turn? Well, I've found a way to turn sharp." He headed for a rock. Almost on top of it he spun 180 degrees. The stern fender touched the rock and bounced us smartly into a reverse course. He began working this billiard effect for turns at narrower angles. I was thrilled by such a stock-car-racing demonstration five hundred feet under the waves.

My eyes were feeding on the sights. It was my first time in these lower rocks, twice as deep as an Aqua-Lunger could go. I turned on the three-thousand-watt movie flood lamp, and we saw an entirely new gamut of color. The deepest Aqua-Lung dives with lights had led us through green, blue, and yellow in the first hundred feet and then into deep orange, red, and brown, extending to the emergency three-hundred-foot limit of compressed-air diving. Now the Diving Saucer had placed us among the most elegant chromatics of them all. About us the living forms were tinted suave pink, mauve, and white, with touches of lemon yellow. The hundred-fathom land was in very good taste. On top of almost every boulder I saw a melon-size sea urchin with purple spikes, many of them surrounded by wedding-white bouquets of hydroids. My Red Sea dream of seeing what was the second reef had come true. The Diving Saucer was going to reveal colorful new associations of animals almost as easily as free diving had opened the sunlit layers.

We were in no hurry to finish the big dive. The saucer was not only the key to the continental shelf but the bestower of observation time. As we toured along the base of a cliff, we were brought back with an ugly jolt to the world above: lost grapnels, broken fishing lines, and old lobster pots reminded us there was no fairyland left. Between two rocks an octopus had collected a junkyard of broken dishes, scraps of metal, and brickbats— far less romantic than the neat country homesteads of its cousins below.

From octopus home to church spire, from spire to mountain, from mountain to canyon, we were slowly making our way back to the surface. We no longer glanced at the depth gauge; we could determine our altitude from the sunlight and the biotope outside. Two hundred feet from the surface, Falco parked the *DS-2* at the foot of a rock tower, and we looked out at familiar lobster terraces and branches of red coral. After what we had seen below, jeweler's coral looked vulgar.

We ate our lunch, chattering about these new sensations, forgetting time. Falco complained of a headache. I got out the CO_2 meter. No wonder he felt bad. We were breathing two-percent carbon dioxide. Time to go. Anyway Simone, Alinat, and the rest would be getting worried. A little after 1800 hours Falco surfaced very near the mothership after his long three-dimensional cruise without a compass. *Calypso*'s champagne party cured his headache.

The trials were over. The Diving Saucer had proved herself. Her scientific career could now begin. Falco started taking down biologists and geologists with programs suited to saucer exploration. As I write, the *DS-2* has made sixty scientific missions in the Mediterranean at Corsica, Cassis, Villefranche, and Banyuls. Her hydraulic claw has brought back supermarket-basket loads of treasures. She has discovered dozens of species for science. Her mud and rock samples have confirmed and destroyed hypotheses on the formation and make-up of submarine canyons. Except for two dives with André Laban at the controls, Albert Falco has conducted them all. His tape-recorded logs have yielded a mass of fresh information on life in the sea.

On Dive No. 26 off Villefranche, the California marine geologist Robert F. Dill embarked on the *DS-2* as observer. Falco put the submarine on a 350-foot floor to collect mud samples for Dill. In the arena of the searchlight they saw a six-inch-high cone with two little eyes looking out of a hole in the top. A tiny white fish, a goby, was taking in its first view of a Diving Saucer. Into the light darted a small cuttlefish, taking advantage of the goby's fixation upon the saucer. The cuttlefish shot out its two longest arms to snatch the prey off the peak. The goby ducked underground. The pigmentation of the cuttlefish drained white with anger. It swiftly undulated the veils over its eyes and dug into the mud to hide in ambush by the goby's hole. Behind the marauder, the little one popped out of another of its entries. The cuttlefish backlashed its tentacles, but the goby went underground again and thrust its head from a third hole. Falco and Dill lay on their mattresses, shaking the saucer with their laughter and shouting to the goby, "Watch out! He's lying by that hole. Pick out another one!" The goby didn't hear their advice or need it. It unerringly came out of a hatch that the cephalopod was not watching. The little one toyed with the predator for five minutes. At last the cuttlefish flushed red, went into reverse, and left the scene of its ignominy.

In his travels through the hundred-fathom layer of the shelf, Falco often saw fish retreat into the mud tail first. He saw many octopuses buried to eye level. Subterranean spider crabs, at the approach of the *DS-2*, showed only their claws, which they brandished in a menacing manner. Gliding into a canyon floor, Falco saw two huge uplifted arms ahead. It was a dead olive tree fallen from the land above. Along its branches, scattered like cherry blossoms, hung snipe fish and boarfish.

On DS Dive 40, Falco took Dr. Jacques Laborel, a biologist from the Endôume marine station, to collect fixed fauna from the rocks at the head of the Cassis Canyon four hundred feet down. Most of the specimens the passenger wanted were pasted on the wall behind a screen of gorgonians. When Falco reached in with the claw, the slight contact with the gorgonian would brush the saucer away. He would drive off and come back again. He felt like a small boy at Coney Island trying to manipulate the bucket-claw machine to catch the wristwatch instead of the jelly beans. In two hours of patient attack the pilot plucked a basketful of exotic sponges and yellow corals. Then the scientist desired a six-foot antipater gorgonian. Falco clawed it and reversed his jets, but the saucer could not uproot the bush. The saucerman went away along the cliff, turned, and drove at the gorgonian with full jets. The ram attack knocked the trophy loose. The claw picked it out of the water and clasped it to the bow. Falco surfaced, flaunting the bush, and framing it with spouts like a fountain display at Versailles.

As we discovered more capabilities of the little jet submarine, we conceived an experiment in physical oceanography that had not been tried before: the measurement of horizontal light transmission at considerable distances under the sea. Dr. George L. Clarke lent us his photomultiplier for "Operation Lumen," as the experiment was called.

On a moonless night off Corsica we prepared the saucer for her unusual mission. Inside we hung a blackout curtain between the crewmen. Falco was to work entirely in the dark, while the technician on the other mattress needed light to read his data. Clarke's light senser was placed at the second porthole, shrouded from the interior lamp. Thus we had two eyes to look into the absolute darkness—Falco's and the instrument's.

We overweighted the saucer by fifty pounds and hung her eighty feet under a launch on a light line paid out by hand. We lowered from *Calypso* to that level a 500-watt GE bulb with a vertical filament. Above the lamp there was an empty compressed-air cylinder to serve as a sonar target for the Diving Saucer. Falco's technician could determine from the horizontal recording sonar the exact distance to the light dangling from *Calypso*.

With this apparatus in position, *Calypso* drew away from the launch at her slowest pace—one-twentieth of a knot. Falco regularly reported being able to see the light to the man on the other side, who entered his calls, the sonar distance, and the reading of Clarke's photomultiplier until the light disappeared from view. On the first trial at a depth of eighty feet the light disappeared at exactly the same moment for Falco and the electronic device —750 feet away.

We repeated the run at a depth of 165 feet. Here dense plankton, come up from the deep, snuffed out the light at a distance of five hundred feet. We lowered the *DS-2* and the light to 330 feet, then by stages on down to 825 feet. At the greatest depth the light was visible to both Falco and the instrument at a distance of 1320 feet. To the pilot it looked like a blue star until it was 800 feet away, then it suddenly turned into a white halo.

The measurements confirmed the theory that plankton accumulated at night in the upper layers. The deeper one went, the more transparent was the water. I imagined a future fleet of exploration submarines exchanging reconnaissance signals with blinker lights as surface vessels do.

Falco conducted a series of dives with scientists under the supervision of Professor Georges Petit in a narrow submarine canyon, the Rech Lacaze-Duthiers, off Port Vendres near the Spanish border. This *rech*—the geological name for the characteristic canyons splitting the continental shelf of Spain and France almost as far east as Marseilles—was named after a famous oceanographer who founded the Arago marine station at Banyuls near

Port Vendres. Professor Lacaze-Duthiers and five succeeding generations of scientists have made his canyon one of the best-studied submarine features on earth.

As he was filling his basket with red-and-yellow corals on dive No. 43 Falco saw a creature as big as a boulder swimming up the slope toward the *DS-2*. When it came into the light, Falco recognized a grouper weighing more than a hundred pounds. The big fish, perhaps blinded by the headlight, banged its nose on the bow, tilting the boat. The grouper hovered in front, nearly covering the ports, its dorsal spines bristling. It remained there, shouldering the saucer, for some time before going back down the hill. Falco's log said, "We were sorry he didn't stay with us a little longer."

On dive No. 46, also at Port Vendres, Falco took Jean-Pierre Reyss to a depth of 995 feet. Three-quarters of the way down they came upon an unknown species of fish. It was charcoal gray with a white belly, somewhat resembling a conger eel. It had long spiky teeth and a small round tail. Falco steered toward it through a crowd of smaller fish that seemed hypnotized by the headlight. The big one kept a uniform distance of about thirty feet from the saucer. Falco stopped. The mysterious one streaked into the school and snapped up a little fish. It struck again and again until surfeited, then wandered away. At her maximum depth the saucer brushed through white coral bushes adorned with big red shrimps that leaped and cavorted in the light.

Dive No. 47 was one that Falco vividly recalls. He took Lucien Laubier 1080 feet down into the Rech Lacaze-Duthiers on a wild ride. The saucer pilot had previously dived there through poor visibility and strong currents in the top layer, but nothing like the turmoil he met this day. In the murk the *DS-2* was carried off course, her power unequal to the current. Falco deemed it best to surrender and wait for the stream to spill him into calmer water. He stopped the jets. He said nothing to alarm Laubier, who had no idea of the danger they were in. The current bore the submarine at three knots toward a canyon wall, visible only to sonar. Falco knew that the precipice had many overhangs. The *DS-2* would be in real trouble if she was swept up under a ledge. Through the mist directly ahead the pilot saw exactly what he feared—a deep vault in the cliff. He went full jet to dodge it, but the saucer was carried on in. As she was about to crash, the *DS-2* bounced softly and was tossed out of the cave by a countercurrent. Falco said to Laubier and the tape recorder, "This makes diving in canyons safer than you might think." Later he experimented with the recoil effect to assist navigation in canyons.

Seven hundred and fifty feet down, the opacity and current disappeared, and the *DS-2* entered a land of magnificent white corals extending from the canyon walls. Undulating in midwater were transparent worms; their only tangible organs were two red horns on the head. The region was alive with phosphorescent squids and juicy plankton. Through the top ports, the saucer-men saw a circle of red shrimps forming a halo over the submarine.

Pierre Drach, our companion in the Red Sea when we were first struck by the need for this deeper diving apparatus, was Falco's passenger on dive No. 57 in the Lacaze-Duthiers canyon. No longer did we need to guard his legs against sharks, and the saucer put the professor's nose very close to the fixed fauna. The preflight weigh-in had been especially accurate that day, and the *DS-2* was weightless and highly responsive. Nearly a thousand feet down, Drach got excited about a hanging garden. Falco obligingly moved up under the coral shrubbery and hooked the mechanical hand on a bush to anchor the saucer. He relaxed on his stomach to share the scientist's pleasure. They saw something beyond imagining.

Silvery ribbon fish, ten inches long and as flat as paper, swam into the light and began rippling up and down, hypnotized. They impaled themselves on coral horns and writhed themselves to shreds, turning into a glittering cloud that sank into the dark.

Drach finished his notes, and Falco went deeper to a new station on the cliff. Two conger eels that must have weighed a hundred pounds each came into the light and passed back and forth close to the saucer. For fun, Falco clamped the mechanical hand on a conger's tail. The next instant, the *DS-2* was spinning giddily. The conger ripped its tail loose, flinging the saucer off the wall. She revolved several times under eel power.

When Professor Petit, who had planned the Port Vendres dives, saw the report of his men, he said, "We will have to do the Rech Lacaze-Duthiers all over again. Most of what we thought about it has been overthrown." Direct human observation and controlled photography and sampling by the Diving Saucer had upset masses of data secured by instruments dangling from ships.

TEMPLE OF THE SEA

chapter seventeen

I parked my car in a broad plaza on the rock of Monaco and paused in front of a stately white limestone building. Its lavishly carved façade was a hundred feet high and three hundred and thirty feet long. On the high architrave I read the names of oceanographic vessels of the past: *Albatross, Pola, Blake, Buccaneer, Siroga, Challenger, Hirondelle, Princess Alice, Vitiaz, Belgica, Talisman, Valdivia, Washington, Vega, Fram* and *Investigator*—valiant ships of many countries. Above the main portal the stone words read, *Institut Océanographique, Musée.*

Throngs passed in and out of the great door. On the plaza were tourist buses from a dozen nations that had brought folk to the oldest and largest institution of its kind. It was March, 1957. I was about to report for duty as director of this oceanographic museum, having been elected by its international *Comité de Perfectionnement,* or Improvement Committee.

I went in and met my predecessor, Commandant Jules Rouch, a former

French Navy captain, a man of letters, and a captivating gentleman, who was retiring at seventy-two. He received me in the spacious office that would be mine. It was furnished in yellow oak on the scale of the room, not a piece of it changed since 1910. In effect it was a memorial to the founder, Albert the First of Monaco, and his first director, Dr. Jules Richard, who had served for forty-six years. Rouch, who was Richard's successor, showed the third director the cherished mementoes of this museum within a museum: personal letters of the founder, logs of his pioneer oceanographic cruises, a wall safe containing his medals and decorations, his personal reference library on the sea, and his eight-foot shelf of published scientific results. From behind a cabinet Rouch tenderly drew a gold-handled umbrella left by the founder one rainy day in 1921. The silk was in dusty shreds. "Dr. Richard found it behind the cabinet after it had been there for many years," said Rouch. He handed me the umbrella as though it were my mace of office. The golden crest bore the initial *A*.

I held a belonging of *Son Altesse Sérénissime*, Albert the First of Monaco, a founder of modern oceanography and the builder of the museum which he called "The Temple of the Sea." Rouch gave me the keys to the place and jauntily bade me good luck and adieu. I looked around the big room, which I might well occupy for the rest of my life. I touched the enormous desk and, walking around it to take my august seat, stopped short. On the director's chair lay a trouser-polished *rond-de-cuir*, a mellowed leather cushion shaped like a doughnut, which in France is the symbol of clerkly passion and endless quill pushing. It brought me back to reality. If I sat on it, I felt I would be betraying my life and the confidence of my companions. I took my first executive decision by buzzing for a guard. I pointed to the *rond-de-cuir* and told him, "Please take that thing away." I did not intend to give up the sea or abandon diving. For that decision I drew encouragement from the active life of Prince Albert.

Albert Charles Honoré Grimaldi (1848-1922) was an extraordinary man by the standards of any age, although his status as the ruler of a wealthy principality and his own modesty have obscured the fact for historians of science. He was known as the "Prince Savant" and was at once an openhanded patron of learning and a vigorous field explorer. He reigned over a pleasure dome and received lavish profits from the Monte Carlo Casino. Yet he put aside luxury for a rough life at sea and the company of the scientific and cultural leaders of his time.

Albert's love of the sea was formed in the Spanish Navy, in which he became a professional navigational officer. In 1889, when he succeeded his blind father to the ancient Grimaldi throne in Monaco, he bought his first yacht, the *Hirondelle*—not to plod from harbor to harbor but to sail the big seas on distant voyages. Among the early guests on the *Hirondelle* was a marine scientist, Professor Alphonse Milne-Edwards of the University of Paris, who turned the prince toward his lifelong pursuit: investigation of life in the deep. Before long, Albert was dredging specimens ten thousand feet down with a hand winch on a boat without a motor.

Albert built a succession of bigger steam yachts designed for oceanography —*Princess Alice, Princess Alice II,* and *Hirondelle II*—which deserve to be cited with the immortal *H.M.S. Challenger,* the Russian *Vitiaz,* the American *Blake* and Fridtjof Nansen's noble *Fram.* As the prince's marine collections increased, he decided to house them in a new museum with laboratories, a library, and meeting halls. He selected a most romantic and imposing site on the prow of the great rock, with buttresses and lower floors extending seven stories down the cliffside. Albert laid the cornerstone in 1899; and during the eleven years that the rocks were being hung on the steel girders, he enlarged his vision to the idea of a temple of the sea for the whole world. To assure the permanence and supranationality of his museum, he chartered a controlling Institut Océanographique in Paris under a self-perpetuating international committee of scientists. To endow permanent operation, Albert provided a fortune in bonds of the Third French Republic—then the most secure investment known.

The Prince Savant's interests extended beyond the sea. In 1906 he sponsored an early helicopter flight in the unfinished lecture hall. Albert built Monaco's harbor, drilled a tunnel under the rock, and established schools and a museum of prehistoric anthropology. He traveled between Monaco and Paris on a motorbike. He was a friend of both Kaiser Wilhelm II of Germany and Jean Jaurès, the French social revolutionary.

To this disparate group of friends, as well as to all, Albert lifted the lamp of peace among men. He held that the human condition would be improved by turning combative and competitive drives toward exploration and learning. His personal example consisted of directing more than four thousand scientific stations at sea—more than any oceanographer has made before or since.

At the time the Oceanographic Museum was dedicated, Albert's royal cronies were making threats of war. He founded an international peace institute, a forerunner of the League of Nations and the United Nations, and journeyed to the capitals to plead with his sailing companions to keep the peace. When Wilhelm II made the first war declaration and the others joined him in the sacrifice of millions of lives, Albert was prostrated. He lingered on in bitterness until 1922.

Upon the passing of this just and noble heart and the accession of Prince Louis, who cared little about the sea, Albert's museum fell stagnant. Postwar inflation ruined the value of the endowment, and Dr. Richard was left without means to continue research and exploration. The place became a pious monument to the founder instead of the active center of oceanography that it was intended to be. The workers left the laboratories, and the *Hirondelle II* was sold to a motion picture studio, which blew her up as a dramatic effect. Commandant Rouch could do little more during his administration because the franc had again been devalued during the Second World War. Indeed, when he took over the museum in 1945, it seemed that his first duty would be to board it up.

Then came the miracle of tourism. Europeans who had been pinned down by the war erupted in buses and trains. They thronged to Monaco and paid to see the museum and its aquarium. They saved Prince Albert's temple. Rouch, a careful administrator, handed me a tight but sound economy. It was the only scientific institution in the world entirely supported by public admissions.

Thus I took charge of an establishment unaltered, in effect, for forty years. There was not a secretary or a typewriter in the place, and the instruments in the silent labs were themselves museum items. I was convinced that if Prince Albert were alive, he would fill the museum with computers, radioactivity analyzers, and all the latest gadgetry. He would be using free divers, depth vehicles, and electronics in marine research. It was my duty not to mark time but to go ahead and re-equip, take on staff, expand and revive the builder's spirit. Looking over the deserted rooms, I found a dozen ancient *pince nez* in desk drawers and pinned them on my wall as reminders of the sedentary perils that surrounded a museum director.

The Board of Directors gave me a fine house-warming gift in a brand-new, smartly-equipped research vessel, the *Winaretta Singer,* provided by the Singer Foundation. Now I was looking after an oceanographic flotilla of the *Winaretta, Calypso, Espadon,* and the saucy aquarium catch boat *Physalie.*

The Navy detached my old comrade Jean Alinat to be my alternate at the museum. He and I drew up a ten-year plan. We would modernize and improve the aquarium to attract more visitors, shake out the administration,

and activate the wretchedly catalogued library, one of the largest archives
on the sea. While working on these aspects, our main drive would be to
rebuild the research plant. The Délégation Générale à la Recherche Scientifique of the French government gave a substantial grant to bring it back
to life. With our scientific advisors we outlined four main fields of research:
nuclear techniques applied to oceanography, physiology and ecology of
deep-sea animals (Albert's own field), continuous recording of physical and
chemical data on sea water, and marine geophysics. We also made houseroom
for Prince Rainier's applied radioactivity laboratory. The young ruler had
inherited his great-grandfather's love of the sea. As honorary chairman of
the Institut Océanographique, he was friendly and encouraging.

Divers Kientzy, Jacques Boissy, and Claude Wesly collected live fishes
for the aquarium. They transformed the display tanks with living gorgonians
and anemones and replaced short-lived fixed growths with fresh ones. The
inmates seemed to like the natural surroundings. The colors of tropical
fish ceased to fade as they usually do in aquaria.

We sent air expeditions to the Red Sea to bring back live specimens.
Falco led one with Georges Alépée and Pierre Goupil. The lonely beach
was too hot to stand on barefooted, and each afternoon a dense, burning
sandstorm passed over, dropping dozens of dead swallows that had been
smothered by the dust. When Goupil imprisoned his hands in a charging
bag to load his camera, flies ravaged his face. To submerge was a benison.

Falco had several systems for trapping fish without hurting them. He took
down nylon gill nets with cork floats and draped them around well-populated
coral heads while the fish hid from him. When he departed to place another net, the fish came out and became stuck in the meshes. Falco would
circle back over his trapline and gently collect the captives. He placed
them in transparent plastic bags of sea water. Going to the surface with a
cluster of bags inhabited by many-colored fish, he looked like a balloon-
seller at a submarine fair. On the beach his heat-blistered confederates
injected the water bags with oxygen, packed them in padded cartons, and
shipped them by plane to Nice. We lost very few fish in transit. From the
wild to the aquarium they never left the water.

Falco also used rigid Plexiglas traps. His most artful device, however,
was capturing them by hand. The triggerfish were too cunning to leave their
caves and be fouled in a net. The species has a high, hinged, mastlike
dorsal ray that it normally carries retracted along the spine. When the
hunt is on, the triggerfish rushes home, erects its mast to brace itself inside,

and locks the prop upright with a bony latch. The system frustrates most triggerfish predators, but not Falco. He reached in and pressed the latch. The mast collapsed, and a surprised triggerfish found itself moving through the sea in an invisible cell. When Falco captured another triggerfish species that we called "Fernandel," it gave a despairing cry that the diver likened to the grunt of a pig.

After three years in the museum our team had progressed with the ten-year plan, and we projected two ambitious leaps forward in popular and scientific oceanography, the odd twain that worked successfully in Monaco. We planned to build underneath the monolith on the cliff wall, fifty feet above the Mediterranean, a big outdoor "marinarium," inspired by the prosperous marinelands in the United States, plus some ideas of our own. This plant would enlarge our tourist income and underwrite increased research.

I also discussed with Prince Rainier, an experienced free diver, the idea of creating in the sea off the museum an inviolable area of six square miles as an experimental farming area called the Marine Biotron. There we could manipulate the submarine environment, establish artificial housing, plastic kelp, machine-made currents, unnatural photosynthesis, and chemical nutrition, to check against neighboring control areas of undisturbed nature. All fishing and sport diving would be fenced out.

We built a concrete prototype for the fish house and designed the control network for the Marine Biotron, which would be tended by Aqua-Lungers, depth vehicles, and robot instruments, including television, all reporting to the museum above. Under the museum the depth was fifty feet, gradually sloping to a thousand feet at the outer boundaries of the park. A rift opened near shore and split the downgrade into an interesting submarine canyon.

The very year we started the idea, however, disaster came for the Biotron. On both sides of the preserve, at Fontvieille and Monaco Beach, the principality was expanding its territory with land-fills. Queues of dump trucks poured down the wreckage of old houses, quarried rocks, gravel, and sand, whose dust swelled into the site and settled. The water was suffused with mineral particles that killed most of the delicate marine organisms. The fish went to greener pastures. Under my office window the territorial expansion went on, staining a pretty plateau called St. Nicolas, where we dived periodically to look at the changing environment. Most of the algae and clinging animals were smothered and replaced by disgusting brown seaweed.

There were land-fills all along the booming Côte d'Azur. On helicopter trips I saw construction dirt discoloring the sea several miles out. Beyond that, there was often a black, iridescent belt where ships had shamelessly pumped tons of oily filth from their bilges, scattering death over miles of the continental shelf. I postponed building the Marine Biotron until the land-fills stopped and the floor could be stabilized with new sediments. And I hoped for some kind of efficient protection against pollution of the sea. Then in 1959 there came a new and ominous threat.

We were trying to renew Prince Albert's hospitality to free world scientific meetings and therefore invited the International Atomic Energy Agency in Vienna to hold a congress at the museum on the controversial question of disposal of nuclear wastes. At the opening session I welcomed 450 delegates from all the nations that had atomic energy programs or that wished to have them. I knew little about nuclear rubbish but, as host, was obliged to sit politely through the morning before going back to work.

I found myself taking notes, as official delegates outlined long-range plans for expansion of civil atomics and gave estimates on the amount of medium- and low-level radioactive wastes they would produce in the expanding years ahead. They talked glibly of curies of poison in six and seven figures. From the rostrum I saw the oceanographers passing notes and whispering to each other.

After the session the physicists and the biologists did not mingle. The oceanographers were talking to each other about the consequences of all this manufactured poison. When I left the room, I picked up a radio headset, used for simultaneous interpretations in four languages, with which I could listen to the afternoon session in my office. I eavesdropped on an increasingly tense atmosphere upstairs and decided to attend the next day's meeting dealing with methods of atomic waste disposal.

In the morning a scientist gave a paper advocating burying irradiated material in deserts. Another wanted to parachute it onto the Greenland icecap. Others destined it to guarded caves and abandoned salt mines. However, the most popular refuse dump with the atomists was the ocean. Several delegates spoke matter-of-factly of how their countries were already sinking the stuff in the sea.

The differences between the physicists and biologists were now pronounced. After the meeting adjourned, dignified gentlemen exchanged impassioned dialogues. I heard one biologist say, "Strontium 90 will contaminate fish."

A nuclear physicist replied, "Strontium 90 concentrates only in the bones. Who eats the bones?"

"Chickens eat them," the oceanographer said. "Bone-meal is a by-product of fish canning. Our children's eggs will become radioactive."

I said to a group of distressed oceanographers, "Don't worry. Professor A is coming to chair tomorrow's meeting." I named a world-famous marine scientist. "I'm sure he'll defend the sea."

Professor A arrived five minutes before the meeting and had no chance to note the agitation among his colleagues. In his genial introductory remarks the professor said, "The sea, being obviously the natural receptacle of atomic wastes . . ." There were low groans. I couldn't believe what I heard. I invited him to my house for dinner with two biologists. I told him that I was astonished to hear him say the oceans were a natural receptacle for long-lasting virulent wastes.

Professor A is a calm, reflective person. He said gently, "Jacques, this is not the problem. There is only one problem for the future of mankind, and that is the population explosion. Soon we will have ten billion people, later twenty. Perhaps it will reach a hundred billion. We will have to feed all these people. The natural resources of the sea and land put together will fall far short. But, thank God, there is an equivalence between food and energy. We will have to develop nuclear energy without limit to run factories that will produce the protein to feed the whole of mankind, no matter how many.

"*That is why we must go full ahead with atomic energy, even at the cost of closing the sea to all human use, including navigation.*"

A complete silence followed his remarks. I had a vision of the masses giving up the port cities—New York, London, Marseilles, Shanghai—and retreating inland to geodesic concentration camps to receive their daily balanced ration of ersatz food from atomic factories. I saw crowds standing in the Alpes-Maritimes looking down at the blue, poisoned sea, the crumbling blond cities, and the ships that would never sail again.

It was another round in the struggle of technocrats against humanists. In our time the technocrats have the upper hand. Almost everywhere, they have power alignments with the politicians. It is obvious, however, that this trend will be reversed. Biological sciences will in the end take the lead, for without life, there is no science.

As the congress resumed, national delegations split: a Russian and an English biologist would dispute with an English and an American atomic scientist. I thought that while these men were together, it was time to organize the defenders of the sea. The appalling thing was that none of us knew what would be the effect of large-scale distribution of radioactivity.

The physicists had cited some local studies of radioactive effects on fish that were pitifully inconclusive. While time and reason were left, we had to unite physicists and biologists to make comprehensive, objective measurements of the consequences. Before the scientists disbanded, we had reached a tentative agreement to establish in the museum an international center for studying radioactivity in the sea. Prince Rainier put life in the plan by suggesting a treaty between his government, the Oceanographic Museum, and the International Atomic Energy Agency, the latter to operate the laboratories. Soon the establishment was in full swing under the leadership of the Finnish scientist, Professor Ilmo Hela, with specialists from Sweden, the United States, Israel, Russia, Japan, and other countries.

Some months after the congress I received a phone call from Paris. An old acquaintance working for the French Atomic Energy Commission asked me to drop by on my next trip to Paris.

"Costeau," he said when I arrived, "what is your opinion about disposal of atomic wastes in the ocean?"

"It's dangerously premature," I said. "We know so little about biological effects!"

He said, "What would you do if we got rid of our wastes in the Mediterranean?"

I was momentarily stunned. "I'm sure you won't do it," I said. "Why do you ask?"

"Just to know your attitude," he said.

I thought it over before replying, "I would protest as loudly as I could."

"I guessed as much," he said. "I just wanted to warn you beforehand. I am aware of your connections with the press—but I don't believe they will publish what you have to say."

I got up and left. A sea-dumping was imminent. The decision had already been taken. A few days later, October 6, 1960, newspapers said that the nuclear station at Marcoule near Avignon was dispatching 6500 barrels of radioactive waste to be "experimentally" deposited in the Mediterranean. The scheme was approved by Euratom, the council of European nuclear nations.

A leading paper also carried a "background" story by a science reporter that made me flush with fury. "The experiment will be made in a trench eight thousand feet deep between Antibes and Calvi, Corsica," he wrote. It was "chosen after studies made by such oceanographers as V. Romanovsky and Cdt. Cousteau." This may have been planted by the atomic commission man to compromise me. I began writing a statement to the press but thought better of it. If my ex-friend had actually been able to close prominent papers to my views, my protest would be carried only in left-wing journals, and I would start the contest with a nice big "Communist" tag around my neck. I tore up the draft.

My secretary was holding urgent phone calls from mayors and deputies along the Côte d'Azur, but I told her, "I'll take no calls until further notice." I needed to think about the coming menace to the sea—and think to some purpose. Probably the quantity of refuse—two thousand tons with four to five hundred curies—would not appreciably damage the Mediterranean, but the "experiment" was actually industrial and would set a precedent for bigger loads. I needed to get advice and to sound out support before I acted.

Next morning I took the first Caravelle to Paris and visited my master, Professor Louis Fage, the doyen of French oceanographers. He was deeply disturbed about the nuclear intent and encouraged me to resist it. I called on Dr. Vsevolod Romanovsky, whose name had been falsely linked with mine as having surveyed the dump site. He wrote two statements: a declaration that none of his work on *Calypso* had been connected with the disposal plan and a protest letter to the atomic commission, pointing out that he had expressly warned them that the operation was premature, to say the least.

Two days later the nuclear commission announced that the dumping would take place on October 20th. Now we had a timetable: we were on D (for Dump) Day Minus 12. I called on the Minister of State of Monaco and gave him a memorandum on the affair for Prince Rainier, in case the ruler wished to oppose the waste disposal. Still without showing my hand to the gentleman who tried to shut me up, I told my secretary to return the calls from the coastal authorities. The mayors of Nice and Menton and senators and deputies in Marseilles, Toulon, and Nice were decidedly against disposal at sea and wanted to know my opinion. It agreed with theirs.

D-Day Minus 11 was Sunday. I spent the morning in my office drawing up a statement and figuring out how, despite the warning, I might break into the same prominent Paris daily that had published the report implicating me with the dumping. Normally, when we have news at the museum, I talk to reporters from the regional papers and the Agence France-Presse (A.F.-P.), the national news bureau. I was certain that the A.F.-P. would put my story

on the wire, but the atomic commission man might have actually influenced nationally important editors so that whatever I said would be
ignored. If, however, I could get into the paper that had run the erroneous
story, it would surely lift the lid off all the rest. I thought there might be a
chance if I had patience enough to wait until the right minute of D-Day
Minus 11.

On Sunday the newspaper's staff would be thinned out, and senior
editors might be gone before Monday's first mail edition went to press. I
wore out my office rug during the afternoon, then at six o'clock phoned the
paper and asked for the managing editor.

"*Il n'est pas là, Commandant,*" said the operator.

"Then give me the assistant managing editor," I said. He too was absent.
"Then give me whoever is in charge. I have an important story." I got a
subeditor and said, "One of your science reporters has given you wrong
information about my work. In view of the good relations I have had with
you, I don't want to demand a printed retraction but will just give you a
short article explaining the facts."

The desk man said, "We appreciate your consideration. We're on top of
a deadline. Could you read it to my secretary?'"

My statement said that, first of all, there was no trench at all between
Antibes and Calvi but only a flat bottom eight thousand feet deep. Further,
none of my ships or organizations had ever made studies for atomic waste
disposal. Finally, the area was just about the worst that could be selected
because of its measurable scattering currents.

On the morning of D-Day Minus 10 the paper ran the whole statement,
and I found twenty reporters representing all shades of publishing politics
in the administrative foyer of the museum. I threw my doors open and
welcomed them in. During our animated discussion my secretary put through
a call from the atomic commission man. "How dare you!" said he. "My
minister is very angry. I am warning you on his behalf to keep quiet from
now on."

I said, "I don't believe that a minister of France would single out anyone
for the sort of treatment you gave me." I hung up and went on with the
press conference.

Friends of the sea came to the museum and set up round-the-clock information headquarters, manning the phones, rolling out mimeographed statements, and dispatching speakers to organizations wanting to know what it
was all about. We sent oceanic propaganda not only to the press and the

municipalities but to everybody with a stake in what was coming: chambers of commerce, real estate men, hotel owners, trade unions, restaurateurs, tourist agencies, and fishermen's syndicates on the Côte d'Azur and Corsica. The vital tourist and fishing industries could be ruined by the mere rumor that the sea was tainted by radioactivity.

On D-Day Minus 8 the newspapers announced that Prince Rainier had appealed to President Charles de Gaulle to cancel the dumping. The next day the City Council of Toulon in a tumultuous public meeting called on the government to stop it.

We had no news from the opposition except an announcement that they had sunk some radioactive wastes five years before in the Seine and Rhône rivers. I think this must have aroused the anglers because we now heard outcries from many parts of France.

On D-Day Minus 3 our old friend of Port Calypso days, the lighthouse tender *Léonor Fresnel,* arrived in Nice carrying a monstrous buoy. The shamefaced crew said it was to be placed over the atomic dumping ground.

The city council of Nice voted a stinging protest, and the mayor spoke of an administrative strike. Corsican officials sounded off against sea disposal. Hardly had the mayor of Antibes forbidden importation of nuclear wastes when the police turned up ten barrels of it in a local lab. The mayor called on the army to seize it. The mayor of Marseilles urged the atomic commission to store wastes in the ground instead of sinking them at sea.

On D-Day Minus 1, the mayor of Toulon, from whence the dump ship would presumably sail, assured his alarmed constituents that the waste train would not be allowed to come into the city. That evening a front-page, banner-headline story reported that the people of Nîmes had gathered on the railway tracks to stop the waste train. I do not know whether that was accurate or not, but in the prevailing popular temper it was conceivable.

Dump-Day arrived—October 20, 1960.

The *Léonor Fresnel* remained in Nice with the big nuclear buoy. No sailing order came. The waste was not dropped that day.

On D-Day Plus 1 the mayors of the south coast converged on St. Cyr to plan concerted action to defend the sea. The next day they passed a unanimous resolution denying passage of any kind of radioactive material through their towns. "Committees of Action" were being formed, calling on the government to renounce the plan permanently.

On D-Day Plus 9 I was invited to a meeting of senators and deputies in Paris, where I spoke about the dangers inherent in placing poison in the sea without knowing what the effect would be. A debate opened in the Senate. A week later the atomic commission quietly called off the dumping operation.

The immediate danger was over. In the wake of the campaign I caught my breath and thought about what had happened and what was to come. Obviously the sea had only a temporary respite. The vigorous rally of its friends might never be repeated.

A month afterward at the museum Prince Rainier presided over the annual general meeting of the International Commission for Scientific Exploration of the Mediterranean, which discussed nuclear waste disposal in the oceans. At the closing session the secretary general of the French Atomic Energy Commission took the rostrum and pledged that it would never attempt massive dumping in the Mediterranean and would consult oceanographers before disposing of wastes in other seas.

Noting the qualifications "massive" and "consult," the assembly passed a unanimous resolution. It saluted the intent of the French commissioner and called on nuclear bureaus in all countries to refrain from dumping atomic wastes in any ocean. It insisted that experiments be made with burial of the poison underground—the only way to isolate it from the living world. It asked that official oceanographic committees be included in any waste disposal experiments and asserted that this question, involving the destiny of the race, must be carried out internationally.

How long could the *détente* be held?

We had to use the truce for a concerted drive to find out something about artificial radioactivity in the sea—a drive in which I believed most nuclear experts would sincerely join. All scientists—and laymen like myself—who are concerned about the problem must help the nuclear physicists to control the plague they have created. The only remedy is knowledge, which has pulled man through so far. The workers in the Oceanographic Museum and the labs of the International Atomic Energy Agency are devotedly toiling to contribute data on marine radioactivity.

Since 1960 a laboratory in the museum has been taking daily readings of radioactivity in the atmosphere and in rainfall. When the major powers resumed atomic bomb testing, our measurement of the radiocative content of rain at Monaco jumped to more than a thousand times that of the previous level. At least two-thirds of atmospheric fallout goes directly into the oceans, and more follows in land drain-off.

Recently I attended another world oceanographic meeting, at which a delegate offered a resolution that the oceans should be protected from all pollution whether from chemicals, oil, sewage, or radioactive material. An official scientist of an international organization offered an amendment to strike "protection of the sea" and substitute "protection of the resources of the sea." This was a casuistry that would condone poison-dumping as long as nobody could prove that it was ruining marine resources.

Why do we think of the ocean as a mere storehouse of food, oil, and minerals? The sea is not a bargain basement. We are blinded by our gloating over the wealth below. The greatest resource of the ocean is not material but the boundless spring of inspiration and well-being we gain from her. Yet we risk poisoning the sea forever just when we are learning her science, art, and philosophy and how to live in her embrace.

chapter
eighteen

CONSHELF

ONE

Again the *Calypso* team was working at a bald white limestone island off Marseilles, this one called Pomègues, which was near the Château d'Îf where the legendary Man in the Iron Mask was imprisoned. In a narrow, unfrequented cove *Calypso* and the *Espadon* were standing on either side of a *mahonne*—a big pontoon barge—burdened with busy men and gear. The vessels were surrounded by spherical buoys, rubber liaison boats, mooring wires, and a helicopter sweeping low. Ashore in a ruined, windowless stone house draped with ganglia of temporary power and communications lines, I was sitting behind blackout curtains watching an invisible front on television. The scene was like an amphibious beach head in some preposterous military game. But war was far from our ambition here. We were attempting to accommodate men to living on the sea floor.

Beneath the vessels was Continental Shelf Station Number One, in which we hoped Albert Falco and Claude Wesly would be able to stay under the sea continuously for seven days, while working five hours a day in the open water. They would be the first men to occupy the continental shelf without surfacing for a significant period of time. It was a logistical experiment more than a physiological one. Our confidence rested in Jean Alinat's special computations for a week's submersion with Aqua-Lungs, using an air chamber as a refuge. "Conshelf One" was centered around a cylindrical dwelling and workshop seventeen feet long and eight feet high, anchored with eight chains seven feet above a floor forty feet deep. It was a halfway house that permitted the divers to work in the open water eighty feet down. Falco called the installation *Diogenes* after the truth-seeking Greek philosopher who lived in a tub.

On the bottom of the chamber there was a hatch always open to the sea, which was kept down by internal air pressure. The continental shelf men lived in constant air and water pressures of two-plus atmospheres. Through their liquid door they passed in and out to perform labors that anticipated those of workers and technicians in the industrial continental-shelf stations of tomorrow.

The idea was ancient. In the seventeenth century Bishop John Wilkins foresaw it. In the nineteenth century Simon Lake operated wheeled submarines with hatches open to the water. In this century Sir Robert H. Davis made designs for dwellings on the floor, for which Commander George F. Bond of the United States Navy worked up further plans that inspired us. Edwin A. Link was testing a liaison vehicle for deep continental shelf stations. It was the privilege of our research group, the O.F.R.S., to run the pilot establishment at Pomègues.

Falco and Wesly themselves had looked after construction of the chamber they were using below. The electrical engineer, Henri Chignard, and the men of O.F.R.S. had labored to the collapsing point to assure that the station was safe. Every system was backed by at least one duplicate: the air compressors that pumped doubled atmosphere to Conshelf One, two television monitors by which we kept the men under twenty-four-hour surveillance, a stand-by generator, phone lines, and a pair of one-man recompression chambers inside the undersea billet. All of the power and air lines fed into *Diogenes* from the shore station in case a storm should drive the tenders away.

Falco and Wesly entered Conshelf One at 1220 hours, September 14, 1962. As they went down the diving ladder, Falco, a bachelor, bade adieu to his mother and sister and Wesly embraced his wife and young daughter. In the blacked-out TV room we watched them settling into their quarters. We knew everything about them as soon as it occurred. We heard every word and noise. They were to be visited twice daily by the O.F.R.S. physicians, Xavier Fructus and Jacques Chouteau, who would give them complete examinations, including electrocardiograms and blood tests.

During the first afternoon I swam down to Conshelf One and found the men in lofty form. They were excited by the water encompassing them, by the easy way into it, by the long periods they could spend outside with no worry over diving tables, and by the comforts of their billet. They had a television set bringing in the national network, a radio, a library, and even an abstract painting by Laban. They had a hot fresh-water shower piped through a plastic tube from the *Espadon*. Their meals were sent down in pressure cookers by Michel Guilbert, the cook of the *Espadon,* who pledged any dish their hearts desired. There was an electric stove in the billet to rewarm food or to cook it should meal delivery be interrupted. Above, there were sixty men to look after them. The stand-by continental shelf diver, Raymond Kientzy, was in charge of fifteen *plongeurs* who served the pair below.

Their euphoria was evident on television: Falco and Wesly were self-conscious and eager to please. They grinned into the camera and played harmonica duets. At the first medical check-up the doctors found them in tiptop shape. The two-and-a-half-hour examination twice a day cut into diving time; the men couldn't get enough of the freedom of spending hours outside. The first night they slept dreamlessly and awoke with a burst of energy, rushing through wash-ups and breakfast before the physicians arrived.

Wesly, aged thirty, was five years younger than Falco and had begun diving later in life, having been converted from an instructor in skiing and sailing. He admired Falco above anyone in our outfit and was proud of having been selected to accompany him in Conshelf One. Wesly, who was sure nothing could happen to him while he was with Falco, had a highly competitive nature. He entered the test with a high sense of mission.

Falco was a contrasting personality, with as much courage as anyone I have known but not one hint of bravado in his make-up. In physical endeavors Falco met the Olympian ideal: he put all his heart and skill into the test, but he was not upset if he came in last. I placed him in tacit leadership because he would do things well, calmly, and wisely. If living conditions became unbearable, Falco would not let pride interfere with a decision to break off the trial.

There was no medical precedent for what life would be like in a continental shelf station. The reactions of submarine boat crews had been studied extensively but were not pertinent to this. The submariner was not adapting to the sea but holding it back with blind steel plates. His morale was constructed partially of nostalgic reminders and promises of land—pin-up girls, jukeboxes, movies. The submariner was an in-patient, forbidden to look at his world except through a periscope, while our men were living in the open water in abnormal pressure twice that of a submarine. *Diogenes* was an enormous Aqua-Lung into which Falco and Wesly retreated for warmth and food, sleep and hygiene. It was like the air bubble that a water spider takes down to sustain itself in its activities beneath the surface. For our men, the five daily hours outside were more important than the nineteen hours within.

On the second night Pierre Goupil, our motion picture cameraman, went down with ten assistants to film a nocturne of the men on the continental shelf. From *Calypso* I looked through the clear water at the big yellow chamber bathed in floodlight. The exhaust bubbles boiling out of *Diogenes* splintered the undersea light. Around the Conshelf area flood lamps held by Goupil's assistants came on and signal torches blinked as he positioned them to film Falco and Wesly. There appeared a new dazzle of lights in a parallel row leading from *Diogenes* under the stern of *Calypso* and down a slope toward the mouth of the cove. I decided to descend and have a look.

I pulled on a black isothermic suit with yellow tapes on the seams and a black hood that makes a diver look like the Grand Inquisitor. I adjusted the webbing on a four-tank Aqua-Lung block to ride firmly and not impede movement, checked the regulator for an easy flow of air, picked a pair of snug fins, and attached belt weights for a good neutral trim. I became aware of a gray-haired man silently lending a hand with my gear. Henri Plé was tactfully reminding me that we were the same age. I felt a tremor. Of course, my friends called me "the Pasha" (the Old Man), but never before on this deck had I asked or been given aid before a dive.

The water had an extra shiver to it. I stood on the ladder rinsing my mask and shaping it on my face. Below, spelt in cabalistic lights, was the first occupation of the continental shelf, for which I had yearned for years.

I plunged. In the illumined acres of Conshelf, Goupil's men hovered as shadows, concentrating lights on Falco and Wesly, who were swimming side-by-side down the radiant boulevard. They had placed its lights today and named it the Holothurian Way. The pair was moving in a relaxed, fluent tread that concealed disciplined muscular power, economical breathing, and trained responses bred in thousands of forays on the sea bed. They stroked their rubber fins as if they were natural prolongations of the feet. They were wearing pale blue gloves in order to be distinguished from the other divers. Falco was the best of us, the master manfish. Watching the rhythm and authority of his advance, I felt gauche.

They did not look like men condemned to this place, although if they ventured above the invisible stratum of two atmospheres, they could be attacked by massive, perhaps fatal, bends. They could not rise above their billet but could, as they were doing now, safely descend to eighty feet. They cleaved to the bottom as the giver of life.

They swam down the Holothurian Way, across sand, posidonies, and somnolent sea cucumbers, toward the open sea beyond the lights. Goupil signaled his link-boys, and all the lights went out. The film sequence was finished; the earthlings had to return. I consumed less compressed air than most divers and so was able to linger awhile after the film team had surfaced. In the darkness all that I could see was two wands of light as Falco and Wesly moved along, hypnotizing fish with their stiletto lights and caressing them with blue gloves. They stopped and petted a cuttlefish, unaware that anyone was watching. Then I revealed myself by swimming into a torch ray. The light moved away from me, and they continued on down as though I was not there.

I hung forsaken in the night, full of thoughts. The gist of my life's work had been to free man from the bondage of the surface, permit him to escape beyond natural boundaries, breathe in an irrespirable medium, and resist pressures of ever-increasing intensities. And not only to put man there but to help him adapt, explore, subsist, survive, and learn. Now he was beginning to live in the ocean, of the ocean, and for the ocean in the person of those two possessed men who calmly ignored me. I had a pang of envy for them. Men of a new kind were beginning to evolve, and I was not one of them. Sadly, I returned to the barge.

On the third morning the two men awoke simultaneously and, without a word to each other, took their breakfast. It was a half-hour before they spoke, then spontaneously they sang. The physicians returned from the morning call to report a marked reduction in the over-inflated spirits of the first two days. Falco and Wesly came in from their morning chores with gloomy faces, moving listlessly, no longer glancing at the camera. Liaison divers arrived with lunch and announced, "It's raining." The Conshelf men ignored the news, although they knew that rain would inevitably be followed by the mistral, perhaps forcing the hovering boats to leave. Above we were reinforcing the moorings. The rain lifted and the wind came tearing in. Outside the cove white caps were seething. However, our protected spot could be held, although the vessels were rocking and banging fenders. In this agitation the undersea chamber did not move. We noticed an odd thing about the dutiful and terse replies of Falco and Wesly to phone calls: for the first time neither inquired about his family. Not until the end of the experiment did we learn the inner history of that day. Falco's log read:

"I feel small. I have to go slowly, otherwise I'll never make it. I'm afraid I can't hold out. The work in the water becomes terribly hard. Everything is getting too difficult." Wesly's diary for the same day mentioned no problems and read like the confident reports of a Soviet cosmonaut. Yet the doctors found Wesly's physical stress greater than Falco's.

For them the afternoon was harrowing, and I thought they might be cheered by a visit from Falco's old friend, Paul Brémond, who was going to *Diogenes* for dinner. The expansive Brémond sat through a glum, mumbling meal, unable to start a lively conversation. Over coffee Wesly had a flash of his usual sly humor. With an expressionless face he said, "We should go on strike. Let's overthrow those people above. They couldn't do anything without us." The TV watchers laughed. Wesly knew we were listening. But we were not certain this was a joke. He said, "But we'll never win the strike. Our employers up there will cut off our air."

The night watchmen saw them go to bed at 2300 and fall asleep. Two hours later Falco threw off his blankets and tossed about. In the middle of the night he got up and looked down at the pool of sea. He checked the internal air pressure and the hygrometer, which measured humidity. He tested the safety lamp, drank a glass of water, and returned to bed. Falco wrote in his log what he was going through on the third night:

"I have not had a dream for years, but I am making up for lost time with a nightmare I shan't forget. Oppression, suffocation, anguish, and panic. A hand is strangling me. I must get out. I must go back to the surface. I wake up and look at the hole. Everything is normal. Claude sleeps quietly. I go back to bed, but cannot sleep. I feel completely alone, isolated and trapped. We are sentenced to remain underwater for a week. We are not free to surface. We can only get rid of nitrogen with the help of those above. I am afraid, unreasonably afraid. To calm myself, I think of my comrades up there. They have taken every precaution. At this moment they are watching me. But I can't calm down. I am obsessed with a ridiculous idea: what if the air pressure falls and the water comes in? At what rate? Of course, there will always be enough air compressed at the top of the chamber, and we will have time to put on Aqua-Lungs and get out. But then? We cannot go directly to the surface. We must stay down until they find some way to decompress us.

"The noise of air escaping at the water level is infernal, much more noticeable than during the day. It is a ceaseless bursting of bubbles as in a giant cauldron. Or like the noise of pebbles thrown on the shingle by the surf in bad weather. I don't manage to get back to sleep. Claude is completely out, oblivious to my troubles."

Was this Albert Falco, the imperturbable, the whacker of sharks, the depth pilot? There was something radically different between living in this undersea chamber at two atmospheres and cruising at atmospheric pressure in the sealed Diving Saucer—here the water was close, real, and omnipresent. The fact that for the first time in his life Falco was prey to anxiety, to nightmares, to delusions of danger, and never hinted of them to us, was the measure of the courage of these men, facing a hundred more hours in the sea.

As the fourth day began, Falco was near the edge. When the attendant delivered breakfast, Falco grumbled for the first time in the years we had known him. "The biscuits are broken!" he cried. We couldn't have been more astonished if he had socked the liaison diver on the jaw. Guilbert, conscience-stricken, dived to Diogenes and apologized to Falco. There was a flicker of a smile on Falco's drawn face as he in turn asked the cook to forgive his nasty temper.

This morning the medicos gave the divers various psychotechnical tests. Falco and Wesly sat at a metal table in front of Diogenes and assembled patterned cubes to copy a design held by Chouteau. The physicians reported they did quite well. I went down for a brief call and told the men we were cutting out the evening visit of the medical examiners. Falco and Wesly were quite relieved. I returned to the barge, feeling that their morale was improving.

No longer did we hear popular music from the radio in Conshelf One. The library of detective stories was untouched. During the first days they had watched commercial TV. Now they yawned through a chorus girl show and clicked the set off for good in the middle of the news. Wesly phoned, "Could you send us a phonograph with some classical records?" After it was delivered, we heard nothing but symphonies and chamber music for the rest of their stay. No longer could the devoted Guilbert tempt them with regal sauces and pastries; they were asking for steaks, fruits, and green vegetables—low calorie meals.

The caloric drain of swimming was offset by the amenities of the living quarters. We maintained a temperature of seventy-one to seventy-nine degrees Fahrenheit with infrared heaters and avoided moisture with foam rubber padding inside the cylinder. The deck on the workshop end of the chamber was bare metal, which collected condensation. The men did not feel cold. Indoors they wore fleece-lined boots, wool pullovers, and red knit tassel caps—the traditional bonnet of helmet divers.

There were too many visitors from the surface. Before the experiment started, we had ruled that no one who was not directly serving Falco and Wesly would be allowed underwater. We had cordoned off the cove from outside divers and boats and confined photography to Goupil's movie team and to Jean Lattès as still photographer. Otherwise only physicians and delivery men went down. Yet Falco's diary read, "We are in an electronic house. You have only to push a button to get an immediate reply. We have sixty arms and sixty legs. All wonderful, but too many of them. People come into the chamber with a hubbub of words that tires us. You cannot talk for long. You must take it easy. I know these people are doing everything for our welfare, and in their place, I would do the same, but the entrances and exits—what a painful performance. Sometimes I have to take a real grip on myself to keep from exploding. But, if they let me lie down for ten minutes—only ten minutes—I feel better. In the next undersea house we build there will have to be at least two rooms—one in which to isolate yourself. Also there has got to be telephone discipline. They ring us up from the island and the boats, often on unimportant matters. This first experiment is too mechanized. I see the next one differently. They should give us huge tanks of compressed air and say: 'There are fish all around you. Get on with it. If you need anything, call us up. Otherwise we'll ring you only on vital business.'"

Kientzy reduced liaison descents to a minimum. Falco wrote, "It's more peaceful now. The Pasha has taken steps to give us decent rest. I now believe that life under the sea for a long period in greater depths is possible. But, what if one should completely forget the earth? When I think about that, I realize I simply don't care what's going on up there. Claude feels the same. We are running on the same clock as them. I know because they tell us the time of day, but I couldn't care less. Down here, everything passes so quickly, time is no longer useful. If they told me we only came down yesterday and still had six days to go, it wouldn't bother me a bit.

"A phone call from the Pasha. He heard about a scare we had yesterday. Somebody sent Claude a four-bottle lung that was half empty. We were several hundred feet from the chamber in the sixty-foot zone in a big cloud of shrimps, knocking them down into the tentacles of the *Cerianthus* anemones, which closed over the shrimps. Suddenly Claude made a sign he needed air. I handed him my mouthpiece. He took a lungful and started for the house. I went along with him, sharing my mouthpiece. He made the last sixty feet in one breath, faster than I could keep up with him. There was no panic, but the Pasha thinks we need an emergency system if something like this happens again. He is sending us a lot of empty barrels with anchors. We'll lay these out upside down in the working area, then take a pipe from the surface and fill them with compressed air. If we run out of air again, we can put our heads in a barrel and move from barrel to barrel back to the chamber. In future continental shelf stations, when we get rid of most of the surface operation, such barrels will be reassuring.

"The water is beginning to come into our grasp. I feel happy when I am alone with Claude. The surface people with their photographic gear stir up the silt and make a real mud bath. I never like to leave a trace. They spoil the scenery for me. It is the first time in twenty years of diving that I really have *time to see*. For example, the posidonies shelter an intense life, especially at night when they swarm with sea horses, expanded anemones, shrimps, and fish laying eggs. We have actually witnessed the birth of hundreds of fish. And there are fish that escort us, always the same ones."

The next morning the men were out in the water building a fish corral of bolted angle irons, over which they stretched netting. The medicos found them in good shape, but Wesly complained that he had a painful toothache. Such was the prevalence of diving in Marseilles that, within two hours, we had a dripping dentist at his side.

Concepts of "inside" and "outside" were fading away. Falco and Wesly passed from air to water and water to air with insouciance, as if the antagonism of the elements had been abolished. They were bearers of marvelous news, that a species of man would come—men-of-the-water, creatures of inner space—who, bypassing the more exact sciences, would bring to life old Neptunian dreams and the myth of Glaucus.

They took their shower baths before the TV camera, no longer ducking out of its field like modest schoolgirls. In the blackout room Laban watched a television view of Falco soaping himself and said, "They know we are watching them, but they don't give a damn."

I said, "They are slipping away from us. They are becoming strangers."

The fifth day in Conshelf One began with physical examinations showing the two men to be at the peak of perception and calm robustness. They went outside and constructed cement-block fish houses, rearing a hamlet of the sort that would turn future continental shelf stations into ichthyological ranches. With the flow of visitors curtailed, the undersea men were in high good humor when their comrade, Antonio Lopez, arrived in the evening with a waterproof bag of tools and cut their hair.

On the sixth day they surrendered more blood samples to the physicians —a nuisance below as it was above—and worked on the fish ranches. They visited the grave of an ancient ship nearby, which they had accidentally discovered after *Diogenes* was placed on the floor. Falco had scouted for the site of Conshelf One in many places within logistical range of Marseilles and had picked this cove without knowing an old ship was there. But, in their busy schedules, there was no time to dig it.

They invited me to lunch. I took along caviar, and when I tried to open the wine, pressure forced the cork into the bottle. I remarked on the odd, muffled sounds in the chamber. Falco said, "Commandant, whistle a tune for us." I tried, but no sound came out. My friends pursed their lips and blew a jaunty duet.

"It took a lot of practice to learn how to do it," said Wesly.

I saw a small ship model that I had not noticed on my previous visits to Conshelf One, and Falco said, "We made it for you in our spare time."

Wesly said, "If somebody phoned me to go out to work without an Aqua-Lung, I would have to think twice about it. When I am out there, I forget I am wearing compressed air on my back."

Falco added, "This is not like any dive before. We have new reflexes. Space works in a different way. Dimensions are somehow wider. Time has changed."

Falco's log said of the lunch: "The Pasha is thinking of deeper stations, several buildings constructed in stages—a Himalaya in reverse with Base Camp One, Camp Two, and so forth on down; where we would stay weeks,

even months, to work. In the deeper ones we would breathe mixtures of
gases lighter than air. To stay on the sea bed—that's tempting!

"At Grand Congloué we worked several years at a hundred and forty
feet, but after a quarter of an hour, shots on the surface forced us to ascend.
If only we'd had a house on the floor for that job!

"The Pasha is eloquent, full of ideas—the wine or the pressure? He talks
about colonizing the continental shelf. We would all live underwater with
wives and children. We would have schools and cafés. A real Wild West!
I can see Claude as Sheriff of the Deep."

The last day began with Fructus preparing them for the return to the
old world. The two lay on their parallel cots with rubber respirators on
their faces, breathing a mixture of eighty percent oxygen and twenty percent nitrogen—almost exactly the reverse proportion of these gases in
normal air. Originally we had believed that the men would require extended
decompression in a big air tank at Marseilles, but Alinat firmly maintained
that the oxygen-nitrogen formula would desaturate the nitrogen Falco and
Wesly had absorbed in their bodies during the week below. Fructus fed
them the special mixture for two hours, more than Alinat thought necessary.

It was a beautiful calm day above Conshelf One. On the tenders a
hundred people awaited the return. Out of the boil came Dr. Fructus and
after him the cameramen. Now there was no one below but Falco and Wesly.
Through the placid surface I saw them coming slowly, close together. They
halted just beneath the surface, within reach of the ladder. They were
gesticulating. Kientzy, leaning over the barge next to me, said, "It's the
debate of Alphonse and Gaston, each insisting that the other come out first."

Wesly broke water at 1328 hours and pulled the black hood off his yellow
hair. Falco emerged behind.

"*Hou Hop!*" the Calypsonians howled. "*Hou Hop!*"

The undersea men stayed on the ladder, gripping it tightly. They had
wide, fixed grins, but their eyes wavered as if they were afraid they would
fall. The sun or too much oxygen was impeding re-entry. I suppressed an
impulse to give Wesly a hand. In a few seconds the dizzy spell was over and
Wesly stepped nimbly on the *mahonne,* Falco close behind.

Wesly said, "I'm ready to start again, Commandant—this time longer
and deeper."

Falco said, "The sun is good. The land is beautiful."

I asked him, "What would you like?"

Falco replied, "To walk."

Calypso untied and put back to Marseilles while they bathed and dressed and walked around the ship, greeting one and all undemonstratively. As a precaution against the slightest occurrence of bends from nitrogen that might be lingering in their joints, I sent them to a hotel with Fructus, who would look in at them periodically for two days while the big recompression chamber was kept manned and ready nearby.

After a day of this, Falco and Wesly begged to be allowed to walk around the streets. Fructus agreed, if they did not wander too far. The undersea men strolled through the clamorous city at loose ends, estranged from these familiar surroundings as if they, and they alone in the world, shared a tremendous secret.

Fructus released them two nights after they had left the sea, and I dined with them at a noisy restaurant in the Vieux Port.

Falco told me, "I don't know exactly what has happened. I am the same person, yet I am no longer the same. Under the sea everything is—" He paused to be sure of what he wanted to say. "Under the sea, everything is moral."

ABOUT THE AUTHORS

Ten years ago JACQUES-YVES COUSTEAU published *The Silent World,* a book immediately recognized as a classic of exploration and adventure. It has been published in twenty-two languages and has sold more than three million copies in the English language alone. Captain Cousteau's film of the same title won the grand prize of the 1956 Cannes International Film Festival and a 1957 Motion Picture Academy Award.

Writing and movie-making are merely by-products of Cousteau's main activity—scientific exploration of the undersea world with new devices and techniques his group has developed. With Émile Gagnan he invented the Aqua-Lung, the independent diving apparatus used by the U.S. Navy and hundreds of thousands of sportsmen and explorers the world over. *The Living Sea* describes more advanced Cousteau equipment and methods to realize man's occupation of the sea.

Born in 1910 in St.-André-de-Cubzac, schooled in New York, and graduated from the Brest Naval Academy as a gunnery officer, Cousteau founded his famous civilian Calypso Oceanographic Expeditions in 1951 and retired from the French Navy in 1957 to assume direction of the Oceanographic Museum at Monaco. His work at sea is supported by the French Ministry of National Education and the National Geographic Society and technically backed by the O.F.R.S., an undersea research and development center in Marseilles. He is president of the World Underwater Federation, representing free divers in thirty countries.

JAMES DUGAN comes from Altoona, Pennsylvania, and has been associated with Captain Cousteau since 1944. He has accompanied Cousteau's research vessel, *Calypso,* in the Mediterranean, Red Sea, Persian Gulf and Indian Ocean. Mr. Dugan is the author of *The Great Iron Ship, Ploesti* (with Carroll Stewart), *American Viking* and *Man Under the Sea,* the standard history of underwater exploration. He lives in Philadelphia.

Format by Katharine Sitterly
Set in Linotype Baskerville
Composed, printed and bound by The Haddon Craftsmen, Inc.
HARPER & ROW, PUBLISHERS, INCORPORATED